OBSTRUCTION
DANGER

OBSTRUCTION DANGER

Significant British railway accidents, 1890-1986

ADRIAN VAUGHAN

GUILD PUBLISHING
LONDON · NEW YORK · SYDNEY · TORONTO

Dedication

To the injured parties — passengers and railwaymen alike

©Adrian Vaughan 1989

This edition published in 1989 by Guild Publishing by arrangement
with Patrick Stephens Limited.

CN 9460

First published in 1989

British Library Cataloguing in Publication Data

Vaughan, Adrian, *1941—*
Obstruction danger; significant British
railway accidents, 1890-1986.
1. Great Britain. Railways. Accidents, to
1986
I. Title
363.1'22'0941

ISBN 1-85260-055-1

Patrick Stephens Limited is part of the Thorson's Publishing Group,
Wellingborough, Northamptonshire NN8 2RQ, England.

Typeset by MJL Typesetting, Hitchin, Herts
Printed by The Bath Press, Bath, Avon

1   3   5   7   9   10   8   6   4   2

Contents

THIS IS A RAILWAYMAN'S BOOK OF RAILWAY ACCIDENT STORIES. Accidents are not entertaining subjects, but the events leading up to them are interesting and even educational; if I knew in 1960, when I became a signalman, what I now know after writing this book, I think I would have been scared away from the job. As it was, no training was given and no warnings were issued as to the sort of disasters which were constantly lurking in wait for all railwaymen and their precious cargo of passengers. Even a message not passed on to the correct department (as at Ince Moss in 1958) can open the way for a crash. I have written this book partly for those volunteer drivers and signalmen who work so hard on the preserved lines of Britain to make them aware — as I was not made aware — of just exactly what they are dealing with.

I have tried to avoid the well-known accidents and take a look instead at those which, whilst not spectacular in terms of numbers of casualties, are interesting for the way they were caused. Some of my stories contain no incidents of fatality at all and cannot be regarded as 'railway disasters', but I disapprove of making death a qualification for an incident to be written about. Hence for my title I have chosen the phrase, immortalized by generations of railwaymen for 100 years, drawn direct from the Book of Regulations for Train Signalling — 'Obstruction Danger'. This was the code of six beats on the signalling bell which a signalman sent when he wished to prevent the approach of a train due to an accident or other exceptional cause.

Acknowledgements

I WOULD NOT HAVE BEEN ABLE TO COMPLETE THIS BOOK WITHOUT THE willing co-operation of many friends and relations. I want to thank Ian Coulson of British Rail records warehouse for his help in locating the Ministry of Transport accident reports on which all but two of the stories in this book are based, and also for his general sympathy and support.

I must thank the Signalling Record Society in the persons of Mike Christensen, Larry Crosier, David Collins, Richard Foster, Reg Instone and John Morris for their help in supplying signalling layouts where these were lacking from the official report, and also for general advice regarding signalling. Jerry Plane, also of the Society, provided photographs of the remotely located signal boxes around Singleton, Lancashire.

The staff of the Associated Press and the BBC Hulton picture libraries were very helpful and friendly, as were the staff of the many libraries up and down the country whom I contacted in my search for photographs, in particular the staff at Aberystwyth (University of Wales), Birmingham, Carlisle and Lichfield. Doctor Jack Hollick, a life-long railway enthusiast, put the Hixon report into my hands and put me in touch with another great enthusiast and railway historian, Driver Mike Bentley of Buxton shed who supplied rare views of the Chapel-en-le-Frith crash. I am indebted to Mr E. Russell of Castletown for his kind assistance with pictures of Lichfield Trent Valley. Whilst having my hair cut in a Fakenham barbers, the barber, Austin Gill, put a set of photographs showing the Fakenham crash into my hands. Mr Stuart Sellar sent me prints and negatives and put me in touch with Douglas Hume and Jack Kernahan so that I was able to cover the Arkleston crash when I had almost given up hope of doing so. Mr John Smith — Lens of Sutton — was most kind and helpful in the supply of prints. I would also like to record my appreciation of the patient and efficient help given to me by staff of the Public Record Office, Kew.

Last but by no means least I must thank my good friends Ron and Jo Price and my sister Frances for accommodating me on my frequent research trips to London and, perhaps most of all, my thanks to my wife, Susan, for her loyal support for me in my somewhat unremunerative pursuit of my second love — railways.

Introduction

ONE HUNDRED YEARS AGO THIS YEAR, 1989, THE 'REGULATION OF RAILways' Act became law. There had been earlier attempts to make the railway companies live up to a certain standard of safety — the 1871 'Regulation of Railways' Act, for instance — but this was the great and all-embracing safety ruling, perhaps the greatest piece of railway legislation from the foundation of railways until the Act forcing the amalgamation of the railway companies in 1921. For many years prior to 1889, the Government, through its Board of Trade, had urged the railway companies to run their trains under the 'block' system of signalling (only one train to occupy a block section at any one time), to install 'frames' of mechanically interlocked levers to operate points and signals and to fit some kind of power brake, vacuum or compressed air, to all their passenger vehicles. The passing of the 1889 Act was a classic example of the old saying 'it's an ill wind that blows nobody any good'. The Great British Public had been outraged, in 1888, by the carnage of the Armagh crash, one in a long sequence of appalling railway disasters, when a passenger train without any proper brake ran away backwards down a steep incline to collide with one allowed to move forward because a sufficient time had elapsed since the first train had passed — the simple-minded, 'time-interval' system of signalling. Armagh generated the heat which had raised the steam to work the great safety regulations Act through Parliament. Triumphantly, the Board of Trade gave the railway companies one year in which to install electrical systems of block signalling and 18 months to install interlocking frames.

The companies were appalled. Safety cost money which could be better spent in dividends. It was all very well for the Government to give orders — the Government was not footing the bill for the new equipment. The major railways in 1889, the GWR, LNWR, Midland and LBSCR for instance, already had more than 90 per cent of their points and signals worked from interlocking frames, but more than 40 other companies were below that figure: the North British had 78 per cent locked, the South Eastern 70 per cent, the Cambrian 45 per cent and the Great Northern of Ireland only 26 per cent of its points and signals locked (see Appendix I). The majority of these unmodernized lines were those with the least profitability and therefore the outlay on signalling and brakes was seen as the way to bankruptcy. The great English Midland Railway reckoned that to complete their signalling installations to the standards of the Act would cost £100,000, and they could not afford that kind of outlay over such a short period. Another objection was that the equipment to make the improvements was not forthcoming; for instance, the Great North of Scotland Railway was gradually pursuing a policy of equipping its single lines with the electric tablet system of block signalling but, that company protested, their contractors could not provide 110 tablet instruments in one year. Moreover, to carry out the installation work in such a short space of time as a year to 18 months would require a large intake of skilled technicians, but such men were not available in large numbers; they would have to be recruited and trained, and when the work was complete they would then have to be laid off. Yet another objection was that, if the work was to be carried out, to all practical purposes, immediately, then stations which were due for rebuilding in the next five to ten years would have to be 'locked' at once then re-locked at additional expense in five to ten years time.

All these were valid objections put to the Board of Trade then cracking its lawful whip over the heads of the railway managers, but behind all was an unspoken prejudice against any form of government control over the free and independent railway companies. In a mild form it can be read in the words of George Findlay, General Manager of that legendarily mean company, the LNWR, when he said: 'I think that the Board of Trade, having once approved the signalling system, ought not to step in now and order such improvements or additions as they think necessary'. In extreme form, the companies' attitude was well expressed by the General Manager who said: 'I would prefer the occasional Penistone [24 dead] to being compelled by the Government to put on something I did not want'. The physical impossibility of complying with the Act in the time laid down by the Board of Trade enabled individual companies to ask for and be granted time extensions, a godsend to those impoverished concerns where a lack of money rather than a lack of equipment prevented the improvements from being made. Some railways, especially those in Ireland, were still working on this sufferance as late as 1900.

All the major railway companies of mainland Britain, with the lofty exception of the Great Western, took part in the brake systems trials at Newark in 1875. The result of this was that the Westinghouse air brake was found to be the most powerful and the fastest acting, although it was expensive and somewhat complicated, while the automatic vacuum brake was proved simpler and cheaper but slightly less effective. It was also discovered that the so-called 'simple' vacuum brake was very cheap and quite effective from a purely operational viewpoint. The Great Western was then pursuing its own version of the automatic vacuum brake and by 1880 it had taken the cheapest way out by installing the best possible system from the outset — the GWR version of the Sanders-Bolitho vacuum brake. This fail-safe system, with a very few modifications made over the years in the light of experience, is still in use today. The London & North Western on the other hand took the most expensive way out by doing nothing after the Newark trials except to cling with all the obstinacy of a miser to the utterly out-dated chain brake. This, I suppose, is hardly surprising given the parsimony of the Chairman of the Company, Sir Richard Moon, and the fact that the chain brake was of a design drawn up by his Chief Mechanical Engineer, Francis Webb. Even the great Mr Webb did not really approve of this modicum of mechanization and as late as 1882 he still thought that the best way to bring a train to a stand was to put its engine into reverse. This was years after the truly excellent Westinghouse air brake had become available and was indeed in use on the LBSCR and other railways. The 'Westinghouse' was an American invention, and when the Locomotive Superintendent of the London & North Western Railway was asked why he had not adopted it he replied (doubt-less with great dignity and drawing himself up to his full height): 'I am an English-man, Sir'.

Pressure from the public press and from the Inspecting Officers of the Board of Trade, and the difficulties other companies faced when they had to convey unbraked LNWR carriages in their vacuum or air braked trains, eventually forced miserly Crewe to adopt a power brake. Webb did not consider the need for inter-railway running, and in his reluctance he turned to the cheapest solution, the 'simple' vacuum brake. By this arrangement, the train's brakes were applied by the creation of a vacuum in the brake pipe and on the upper side of each brake piston. It was not a fail-safe system, and it would not stop both parts of a train should a coupling break and, say, the rear part run away downhill. Fur-thermore, only the driver could create the vacuum to apply the brake — neither the guard nor the passengers had any control over it. The simple vacuum brake saved steam in that it did not require an 'ejector' to be running all the time to maintain the vacuum as was the case with the automatic vacuum brake (unless you were on the Great Western with a cross-head-driven pump) so it was a cheap system — cheap and nasty. It worked in exactly the opposite way to the ideal and was so utterly *wrong* as a brake that it left the way open to all kinds of unpleasant malfunctions. The worst of these was that condensation from the steam ejector, used to create the vacuum, could run back into the piping and would then collect in the bight between the engine and tender brake hoses. In sub-zero temperatures it froze there, to create a complete or almost complete blockage which then prevented or very seriously delayed the extraction of air from the brake pipe which prevented the brake from coming on when required. It is true that the automatic vacuum brake is also subject to this type of block-age, as indeed is the Westinghouse, but in both these cases the brake can be applied by the guard from the other side of the blockage.

After only four years of the simple vacuum brake, the LNWR management had to spend £45,000 to convert it to automatic whereby the brake became a fail-safe device capable of being operated by driver, guard or passengers and

Carlisle Citadel station in about 1905, admittedly some 15 years after the crash but nevertheless looking very much the same as at that time. The silk-top hat and gleaming shoes in the foreground could well belong to the Station Master. It was into such an orderly scene that disaster erupted when the locomotive Niagra *with its train ran through the station, out of control, ice in the brake pipes rendering the brake inoperative.* (Cumbria County Library)

capable of running in other companies' trains without any problems. But of course the conversion took time, and before it was complete the 'simple' system had claimed at least four lives. On 3 March 1890, an overnight express from Euston ran into Carlisle Citadel station behind one of Mr Webb's dreadful 'Dreadnought' Class 2-2-2-0 compounds, No 515, *Niagra*. It ran past the platform at about 40 mph, its wheels churning round backwards in a desperate effort to stop, and, being unable so to do, crashed into a Caledonian Railway engine, killing four people. The driver had been unable to apply his simple vacuum brake because a block of ice had formed in the manner I have just described. At the Inquest into the deaths, a jury heard the evidence and found that the driver was blameless while the LNWR 'incurred great responsibility in using a brake of such an uncertain and unreliable character'. This did not cheer the cold hearts of the LNWR management, but their spirits were raised when Captain Rich RE made public his report into the crash, having been commissioned to do so by the Board of Trade. His verdict was that the crash was the fault of the driver who 'mismanaged the brake'. The national press in general and the railway press in particular were outraged at this, and wrote stern articles on the subject, but all to no avail, for the Captain's verdict, reached by him alone in the very teeth of all the evidence, was never overturned. The hypocrisy of Rich and the LNWR becomes all the more disgusting when one learns that, on the same day as the Carlisle crash, three other LNWR passenger trains had passed signals at danger. These instances were reported to the Board of Trade as the law required, but as no one was hurt in the incidents, the occurrences were never made public. In each case the cause of the 'run past' was attributed, by the LNWR, to 'ice in brake pipe'. The Carlisle crash, a real *cause célèbre* at the time, may well have been the genesis of that famous railway saying, 'when in doubt, blame the driver'.

CHAPTER 1

Manor House

1892

THE FEAR THAT MANY MEN HAVE OF BEING SEEN TO CRY OR TO SHOW their fear has a large part to play in this story. This, together with a total lack of sensitivity on the part of the secondary players in the drama, a fear of the Company and a fear of causing delay to trains, brought about the Manor House crash.

James Holmes was 33 years old and had worked for the North Eastern Railway as a signalman since he joined the service in 1881. Since June 1891 he had been working Manor House signal box on the York-Darlington main line, three miles north of Thirsk and five miles south of Northallerton. It was a small, brick-built cabin on the up side of the line with seven levers to work distant, home and starting signals on the up and down main lines and a point lever for a short siding on the down side. The next signal box to the north was Otterington, the next south was Avenue Junction, each roughly 1¼ miles away. He lived 2½ miles from the box with his wife and several children in a small house at the village of Thornton le Moor. Every day, twice a day, he walked through the lanes to work, come snow, rain or sun, on 12-hour shifts; he was happy enough, for the hours were no longer than in any other job and, after the walk, he was in the warm and dry and his pay of 20 shillings a week was above average for that area and it was regular.

Sunday 30 October 1892 was his day off and he rested so well that he spent all Monday working in his orchard picking apples for market before walking to the signal box for the 12-hour night shift. Between 6 pm and 6 am, James Holmes signalled about 95 trains including several very important expresses such as the Up Scotsman with Pullman cars. At 6 am he was relieved by his mate, but he waited until the signalman from Avenue Junction arrived at Manor House so that they could both walk home to Thornton together. He arrived home at 7.15 am, put his bag in the kitchen and began to clear the ashes from the fire to relight it, and while he was doing this his wife came in to say that their youngest daughter, Rosy, who had been unwell for several days, was decidedly unwell and was breathing heavily. James said: 'I'll go to bed now, put her in with me. You get Teddy off to school, see to the other children and when you've done bring me some tea and a bite to eat.' Two hours later, Mrs Holmes brought James his bit of breakfast; he ate and fell asleep at 9.30. Two and half hours later he was shocked out of a deep sleep by his wife, shaking him and shouting: 'Jim, Jim, Rosy's in a fit!'

Jim tumbled out of bed and told his wife to fetch a neighbour, an older woman. This worthy took one look at the child and said that she needed a doctor. The doctor lived in Northallerton, five miles away. Jim Holmes walked and ran the mile to Otterington station, got a lift on a down goods train and hurried to the doctor's house only to be told that he had gone out on his rounds — including calls in Thornton le Moor. Jim went to a pub, had a 'half' and a sandwich, and then set out on the long walk home, hoping to meet the doctor on the way. He did not see him. He arrived home to find his wife in tears and their daughter Rosy dead.

Mrs Holmes was devastated and could not be left alone; Jim was shocked and physically exhausted. He had had 2½ hours sleep in the previous 29 hours, he had walked nine miles since 6 am that morning and that on very little food. He now set out to walk the mile to Otterington station to send a telegram to his mother in York, to ask her to come to Thornton. He also intended to ask his Inspector, based in Northallerton, to relieve him of duty on the approaching night shift. He sent his telegram to York and asked his Station Master, Mr Kirby, to arrange relief for him that night 'as I have just had a child die very sudden and I'm in bad fettle for work'. There must be times when the English 'stiff upper lip' is a bad thing. This was just such an occasion. Mr Kirby was unimpressed by James' child dying and said that he would do what he could with the Northallerton Inspector but that he, James, must go home, prepare for work and return to the station later to see if he had been relieved or not. James Holmes walked another mile home.

He returned to Otterington station at 7.30 pm, having slept for 2½ hours in the preceding 35. Station Master Kirby may not have known this, but he knew that James was tired and distressed, 'in bad fettle for work'. When he told him that he could not be relieved, Jim said: 'It's a bad job. I shouldn't care so much for myself, I am most bothered about my wife.' Jim would reveal his true feelings no more than that, while Kirby, scared of having delay to trains set at his door, did not suggest the obvious solution, that of switching Manor House box out of circuit. Before James set out to walk along the track to work, he spoke to the signalman in Otterington box, saying: 'Harry, I am about done up for work. I have never been off my legs since 12 o'clock. I have had to walk from Northallerton and twice to Otterington and back. Never did he utter the precise words 'I am unfit for work', and this was later used against him. He gave out all kinds of warnings — his very appearance should have been enough — but neither he nor anyone else wanted to stand firm and refuse to work.

He worked well for the first part of the shift and by 3.40 am on 2 November was actually priding himself on how well he was bearing up. By that time he had been awake and working hard for 48 hours with only 2½ hours sleep. The night was cold with patchy fog and the trains were running seven or eight an hour, one passing the box every 8½ or 9 minutes. The up Scotsman that night was running in two parts with a goods train between them. The first part of the express ran by at 3.38 am; James gave it 'On Line' to his mate in Avenue Junction, sent 'Line Clear' (corresponding to 'Train out of Section' in more modern times) to Otterington and put his signals to danger behind the express. It was at that moment that James Holmes' stamina ran out. He sat down in his chair and was instantly asleep. Not ordinary sleep, but the deep sleep of an exhausted signalman. I have experienced it myself, a strange sleep where the bells still have power to command reflex actions from a man. Harry Eden in Otterington box rang 'Call Attention' for the goods train, Jim got out of his chair, gave the road and went back to sleep. He probably never woke while he was working his instruments.

The goods train driver found Manor House signals against him and came to a stand at the up home signal at about 3.51. He did not blow his whistle and James Holmes slept on. Harry Eden was reading by his fire when he received 'Train on Line' for the second part of the Scotch express at 4 am. Only then did he see that the instrument for the section to Manor House was still showing 'Train on Line' for the goods train. The North Eastern Railway block signalling regulation allowed Harry to send the 'Be Ready' signal to Jim Holmes even though the instrument showed the line was occupied ('Be Ready' was the equivalent of 'Is Line Clear?'). The bell code woke Jim Holmes who, hearing the express passenger code and seeing that he still had 'Train on Line' showing on the instrument, came to the instant conclusion that he had omitted to clear the instrument after the passing of the first part of the Scotch express. He had not entered the goods train in his register and had no recollection of it in his confused and exhausted state.

Jim at once gave 'Line Clear' from Avenue Junction and lowered his up line signals. After a minute or so, the goods train, which had been waiting in silence at the home signal for ten minutes, started off with a gentle chuff and a creaking of couplings. Meanwhile, the second part of the Scotch express, 13 coaches hauled by 2-4-0 No 178, went through Otterington at 55-60 mph on the dead straight, slightly falling grade. Jim Holmes was now doubly confused. He heard the goods train starting and telephoned Harry Eden. 'Is this the express passenger you have asked?' he said, and put the phone down. Eden was puzzled and went to his window, looking up the line towards Manor House. The sound of the crash came dully through the intervening mile and a quarter in spite of the fog.

The driver and fireman of No 178 were Roland Ewart and Edward Head. The train was a heavy one, and both locomotive and fireman were taking a pounding as the driver did his best to keep time. At times, the fog was so thick that he was unable to see a signal until he was 'on top of it'; at other times, such as when approaching Manor House distant signal, he saw it at a range of 50 yards. The fireman, stoking continuously on the small, overloaded engine, took no part in the signal sighting business, placing his trust, indeed his life, in the steel nerves of Driver Ewart who took the train into a wall of fog at 60 mph, trusting in the signalling. All this just to adhere to the timetable.

Driver Ewart saw the red triangle of lights on the rear of the goods train brake van at a range of 50 yards. He had no time to brake and the next thing he knew he was waking up, in mortal pain, on his back on the frost-covered grass of a field 60 feet from the lineside. One thigh was smashed, his ribs broken. The conductor from the Pullman car 'India' found him and gave him some brandy, and together they watched as the first small, flickering flame grew to engulf the wreckage of their train. Fireman Head woke in the same field, utterly at a loss to know how he got there. Physically uninjured, he staggered to his feet and set off to protect the rear of his train, but woke again in a farmhouse kitchen. He was taken to Northallerton hospital. Signalman James Holmes was so utterly devastated by what he had done that uninjured passengers coming to the signal box to see if there was space there for the wounded had to console him. One eye-witness said that it had it not been for the 'sweet kindness' of one lady, he, the witness, believed Holmes would have lost his mind that night.

Ten people were killed, including George Petch, the guard of the goods train, and 39 were injured, trapped in the burning wreck. Eight passenger carriages were destroyed, including the Pullman sleeping car 'India', and eight wagons of the goods train were lost. An inquest was held on the deceased and the jury's verdict was 'culpable negligence' on Holmes' part, 'but we are convinced that if Holmes had been relieved when he so urgently appealed this would not have happened and the persons really responsible for the deaths are the Directors of the North Eastern Railway'. This verdict must be a classic case of 'running with the hare and hunting with the hounds' and although the 'persons really responsible for the deaths were the Directors of the North Eastern Railway', it was James Holmes who stood trial for the manslaughter of George Petch.

There was a great deal of public sympathy for James, and while letters to *The Times* castigated the North Eastern Railway Directors, James and his family were recovering somewhat from the shocks they had suffered in the Sussex home of Henry Farmer-Atkinson, MP for Boston, who had invited them with their children. The trial was set for 2 December 1892 at York Assizes. The judge was on the side of Jim Holmes — as far as he could make that plain — and warned the jury that 'manslaughter' is a very difficult thing to prove and every case had to be judged on its merits, but the essence was 'causing the death of another by gross or culpable negligence, and Holmes had a great sorrow on him at the time and was not himself, he was distressed and tired'. Many searching questions were put to Station Master Kirby and to District Inspector Pick by the defence counsel. 'Why did you not give Holmes a companion in the box — a porter, say, from Otterington?' 'Why did you not switch the box out?' 'Why did you not realise the seriousness of Holmes' condition after his protests at having to work?' 'Why were there no relief signalmen to take his place in the box? In reply to the last it was revealed that the North Eastern Railway considered that 17 relief men for over 300 signalmen was a reasonable provision. The verdict of the jury was that James Holmes was guilty of the manslaughter of George Petch but added a very strong plea for mercy. The learned judge, in passing sentence, said that this was the only verdict that could have been brought. However, he evidently felt the mood of the time because he then said to Holmes. 'I do not want to add to your troubles — you have suffered a great deal already. I bind you over for 12 months in the sum of £50'.

CHAPTER 2

Douglas Park

1949

THE CIRCUMSTANCES OF THE MANOR HOUSE CRASH HAD EVERY possible extenuating circumstance for the signalman and, indeed, his grief over the incident did him great credit. At the other end of the spectrum of signalmen-induced crashes are those very rare incidents where the extreme youth and folly of the signalman caused a deliberate derailment, and where the man concerned did not have the grace, publicly at least, to express regret.

On 25 April 1949, a 23-year-old signalman was in charge of Douglas Park signal box on the main line from Glasgow to the south near Motherwell. He had been on the railway nine months with two months as a signalman. The signal box had 16 levers to work the up and down line signals and a goods loop in the up side. That night the 10.10 pm Glasgow to Euston sleeping car train, ten 'sleepers' and four other vehicles weighing 497 tons, was hauled by the splendid 'Pacific' No 46230 *Duchess of Buccleuch*, just out of Crewe Works and in first class order.

The engine driver, Thomas Quinn, had been a driver for 37 years and had worked over that stretch of line for 50 years. He brought his train up the 1 in 135 gradient at 35 mph and passed Douglas Park distant signal at 'All Right', a fact corroborated by the signalman in Bothwell Junction box whose starting signal was placed above Douglas Park distant signal on the same post. The fact that the distant arm was raised when the train passed it proved that all signals through Douglas Park section were cleared and the points set for the main line at that moment. Driver Quinn therefore expected to see green lights ahead, but even so he kept a sharp look-out because he knew that an emergency might arise when the signalman would have to throw the signals back to 'danger'. Normally he caught sight of the home signal at a range of 400 yards, but owing to smoke from the engine he was only 100 yards from Douglas Park's home when he saw it at 'danger'. He braked at once, but it was too late to be effective. The engine ran past the danger signal, lurched to the left and derailed as the engine tried to negotiate the 10 mph curve into the goods loop at 35 mph. The engine, tender and leading bogie of the first coach had been derailed, the leading driving wheels of the huge engine had dropped, straddling the left-hand rail of the main line and the diverging right-hand rail of the goods loop and had, as the engine went forwards, drawn the two routes together, neatly fitting sleepers in between sleepers as if they were a giant zip-fastener.

Subsequent examination showed that the main to loop facing points were shut tight for the main line direction with the facing point bolt partially inserted in its port. There was no sign that the engine had mounted the rails, but broken chairs and marks on the sleepers between the switchblade and the stock rail showed that the points had been partially open when the engine reached them. On the facing edge of the switch rail, the first two inches had been burred over to the right, proving that it had been open about the thickness of the wheel's flange when the bogie wheel reached it. The fouling bar had marks on it to prove that a wheel had struck it as it was falling towards the approaching train, ie as it was being moved towards the 'unbolted' position as the train approached. Indeed, it was found to be jammed at the top of its travel, where it had no right to be, proving that it had been moved while the train was within inches of moving on to it.

There was no doubt at all that the points were unbolted and opened as the train approached, and closed after the derailment. This movement required six levers to be moved and Colonel Walker, the Ministry of Transport's inspecting officer, was left with no other conclusion but that the signalman or someone else with his permission had moved the facing points. The signalman was cross-examined for two whole days but he could not be moved from his denial of any knowledge of how the derailment occurred. Colonel Walker rapped British Railways over their corporate knuckles for employing men in responsible positions without first obtaining character references, and there was an end of the matter.

CHAPTER 3

Conington South

1967

T HE DOUGLAS PARK INCIDENT REMAINED UNIQUE UNTIL MARCH 1967. Conington South signal box was a lonely place to work in very flat country between Peterborough and Huntingdon, 67⅜ miles from King's Cross. The line here ran north-south on a low embankment dead straight across the Fens, going away on the dead level, northwards to Peterborough and rising at 1 in 200 towards Abbott's Ripton and Huntingdon.

The 'Welwyn' block controls were in use on the signalling instruments so that the signalman could not give 'Line Clear' for a down train to approach unless the home signal, lever 14, was at 'Danger' and the berth track circuit 'TC G' was unoccupied. The berth track circuit commenced 200 yards on the approach side of signal 14 and extended 58 feet beyond that signal. From that point, track circuit 'TC A' extended along the down main line through the facing points to the down goods loop. When 'TC A' was occupied, the lever operating the facing point bolt, No 26, could not be moved as it became electrically locked in the reversed position and also, by the mechanical interlocking between levers, the facing points, 27, could not be moved. Conversely, a train could be 57 ft 11¾ in past the down home signal, moving towards the facing points, and, providing signal 14 was at 'Danger', the facing point bolt lever was free to be moved.

On the night of 5 March 1967, the signalman in charge was twenty-year-old A.J. Frost. He had been a signalman for less than a year but was described by the Divisional Movements Manager at King's Cross as 'an intelligent young man with a good knowledge of the rules and regulations'. The 22.30 King's Cross to Edinburgh express left the terminus on time in charge of Guard J. Wright, a Grantham man. There were 11 vehicles including three GPO sorting vans, a sleeping car, four carriages and two brake vans. With 147 passengers on board, the train was hauled by 'Deltic' No 9004 *Queen's Own Highlander* with driver Oakton and second man Wheaton, both of King's Cross.

They had a good run down. Guard Wright had to put his head out of the window once, when they were checked by signals through Huntingdon down to 15 mph. Thereafter acceleration was rapid and by Abbot's Ripton the wheels were singing happily over the rails down the bank towards Peterborough at 80 mph. At Abbott's Ripton, driver Oakton shut off power to see if the 1 in 200 downgrade would maintain his speed. Very gradually the velocity decreased. He and his second man saw Conington South's down main distant signal at green and watched the double green signal of Conington South's home over Conington North's distant signal until both were behind them. Passing Conington South box, Oakton checked his speedometer, it was reading '75' and a few moments later the train's brakes were applied, bringing the train to a stand roughly half-way between the two signal boxes Mystified, the two locomen got down on the track.

Back in his cubby hole in the eleventh and last coach of the train, guard Wright was thrown to the floor. One moment he was sitting peacefully on his seat, under electric light, the next he was rolling about the floor like a pea in a pitch-dark drum to the accompaniment of a terrifying cacophony of rending crashes and rattling ballast. The vehicle came to a stand at last, leaning over at an acute angle. Bruised and stunned, guard Wright groped in the dark for his hand lamp but could not find it after a few moments, so, with great difficulty, he managed to find a door, open it and climb down on to the track. In the darkness he could see the looming shapes of the tumbled coaches and hear the cries of the injured. Seeing the lights of the signal box about 200 yards away, he ran towards them and as he drew near he called out: 'Are you there, Bobby?' Signalman Frost came to the window and Wright shouted, as he ran towards him, to call for doctors, ambulances and the fire brigade. By then he was running up the steps of the signal box just in time the hear Frost ring out the 'Obstruction Danger' signal to Abbott's Ripton and Conington North. As Wright entered the box, Frost was commencing to speak to the Controller by telephone; the guard took the 'phone, advised Control of what had occurred and what assistance was required and then at once returned to render what help he could to his passengers.

Signalman Thaxter at Conington North box had received 'Train Entering Section' from Frost at 22.38 hours and almost at once heard a suspicious noise and saw his down line signal repeaters fall to 'wrong'. He at once telephoned Frost to ask him what was wrong with the Conington North signals, which were visible to the signalman in the South box. Frost had replied that the signals were in order but the train appeared to be coming to a stand. Only as guard Wright rushed into the box to raise the alarm, several minutes after the crash, did Frost send 'Obstruction Danger' and commence to call for assistance. Four carriages had, at 75 mph, become derailed about 200 yards north of his post, but Frost maintained, at the time and at the railway internal inquiry, that he had been unaware of the crash until advised of the circumstances by guard Wright. At the later inquiry, conducted by Lt Colonel McNaughton for the Ministry of Transport, Frost said that he had both seen and heard the crash but that he was so horrified by what had taken place that he had been unable for several minutes to take any action.

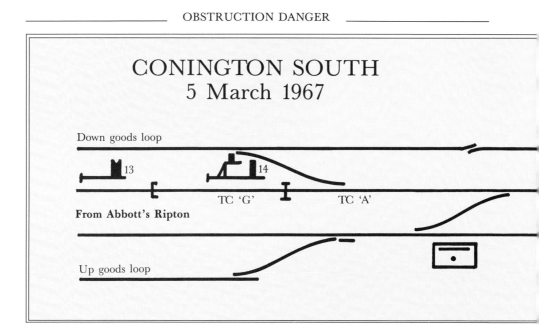

CONINGTON SOUTH
5 March 1967

Down goods loop

13

14

TC 'G'   TC 'A'

From Abbott's Ripton

Up goods loop

The train had broken into two parts. The first seven coaches and the engine were intact and had come to a stand with the engine 832 yards north of Conington South box. The rearmost coach in this portion of the train was derailed all-wheels and was leaning over somewhere about 670 yards north of the signal box. Twenty-two yards south of the seventh coach, the leading bogie of the eighth coach was lying between the up and down main lines and 110 yards south of this the eight to eleventh coaches were derailed and de-wheeled. The eighth and ninth were lying on their sides along the down goods loop while the tenth and eleventh were leaning sharply over, also along the goods loop. The impression given was that the facing points (signal box lever 27) had been switched under the speeding train so as to divert the rear portion into the loop.

This would appear to be an impossible event. The facing points were found in good order with their bolt (lever 26) driven fully home through its port in the stretcher bar, and they would have been thus locked mechanically and also electrically in this position while the train was approaching and passing over them. While the home signal was cleared for the train to proceed — lever 14 reversed — the mechanical interlocking held levers 26 and 27 solidly in position, while from the moment the leading wheels of the locomotive occupied track circuit 'A', the electric circuit feeding the electric locks on levers 26 and 27 was broken so that the locks could not be lifted when their respective plungers were depressed. There was an emergency release for these locks, but this had a glass cover which was intact. All this locking equipment was found to be in perfect order, and both driver Oakton and his second man were certain that they had seen Conington South's home signal showing a green light even as they flashed past it at 75 mph. Signalman Frost professed complete ignorance as to the cause of the crash, and the Chief Signal & Telecommunications Inspector, Mr A.D.

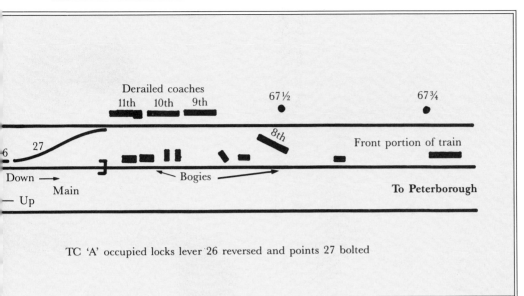

Derailed coaches
11th   10th   9th   67½   67¾

                                    8th

                         Front portion of train

6   27

Down →   ← Bogies →

       Main   **To Peterborough**

— Up

TC 'A' occupied locks lever 26 reversed and points 27 bolted

The wreckage of the ninth, tenth and eleventh coaches resulting from the facing points over which they were passing apparently being moved deliberately. The points involved can be seen in the distance, just below the jib of the crane. (Associated Press)

Roulstone, found himself quite unable to explain how the train had become derailed. Five passengers were killed and 18 were injured, two of them seriously.

Even more mysterious was the presence beneath the left-hand switchblade of the facing point (left-hand looking in the direction of travel) of a tiny piece of cast iron which had been broken from a 'chair'. This fragment caused the switchblade to twist and stand away from the stock rail at the top edge by about 3/16 in while fitting tight against the stock rail at the foot. There was also a slight bruise in the nose or facing tip of the left-hand switch blade as if it had taken a heavy blow, but at that particular spot the wheels of trains ran with their flanges hard against the right-hand rail and passed well clear of the bruised blade. Owing to the twist in the left-hand switchblade, the detector blade had been moved beyond its normal travel by about ⅜ in, and had it been in that condition before the derailment, the signalman would not have been able to reverse lever 14 to clear his down home signal. Furthermore, if this damage had occurred after the signal was cleared, then that signal would not have returned to 'Danger' when lever 14 was put back in the frame or, if it had returned to 'Danger', there would have been distinct score marks on the detector slides as they were dragged through the 'out-of-register' notches of the detector device. Signal 14 was at 'Danger' and the detectors were unmarked, so the signal had been replaced to 'Danger' before the derailment took place.

Mr Roulstone still could not account for the derailment because the electric locks were in perfect order and would have held the facing point bolt lever for the main line direction. The bolt was a tight fit in its port; if the switchblades had been open by as little as $1/32$ in, the signalman would not have been able to get it into its port and it seemed a certainty that those facing points were closed and bolted for the main line when the train passed over them. Yet, on the planed or left-hand side of the left-hand switchblade there could be quite clearly seen the cycloidal marks of several wheels which had obviously passed between the open blade and the stock rail as the rear of the train was diverted into the goods loop.

Mr J.D. Swindale of British Railways' Research Department at Derby examined the points and the bogies of the derailed coaches and came to the conclusion that the trailing bogie of the seventh and the leading bogie of the eighth coach had been derailed and passed between the left-hand switchblade and the stock rail. He also discovered that the wheels on the leading bogie of the eighth coach were of unequal diameter, which would have led to 'hunting' — a rapid lateral movement under the coach — but this would not have been sufficient to derail the bogie, much less derail the bogie just ahead, under the seventh coach. At that stage, then, the investigators had only a vague theory that somehow the trailing bogie of the seventh coach had ridden up on the facing point and the flanges had forced open the — admittedly — very flexible switchblade, thus permitting the eighth coach's bogies to pass through the gap and become derailed, dragging the rest of the train 'off the road'.

It was this very unsatisfactory and inconclusive evidence which was given to the full Ministry of Transport inquiry on 14 March 1967. Although signalman

Frost had contradicted himself on some matters, and although he denied having replaced the home signal prematurely when the evidence made it quite plain that he had done so, he denied any knowledge of the cause of the crash and at that time there was nothing in the evidence to suggest that he had caused it. However, cause had to be found and extremely meticulous investigations were undertaken, including searching the track for hidden defects which, combined with defects in the bogies and/or wheels might have thrown the train off the rails. Absolutely nothing was found and so the inquiry had to turn to the impossible — that perhaps the mechanical and electrical locking had been circumvented in order to open the points underneath the train and that, if this could be done, the resulting derailment would have caused the marks and distortions which had been observed.

If signalman Frost had opened the points under the train, he would have had to place the down main home signal (lever 14) to 'Danger' without the driver being aware of it and then to have thrown the facing point bolt lever (No 26) back into the frame and then lifted the latch of the facing point lever (No 27) so that when track circuit 'A' became occupied by the train, the electrically operated lock would not be able to locate its port in the locking slide attached to the lever. The signalman would then have the facing point lever in his hands, free to be pulled whenever he wished. The question was — would signalman Frost have had time to carry out these movements in front of a train travelling at 75 mph? On examination, the speedometer of No 9004 was found to be reading 2 mph fast, so in fact the train was running at 73 mph, 108 ft per second, as it passed the facing points. A test was made to see when driver Oakton lost sight of the down home signal, and this was found to be when the leading wheels of his locomotive were 36 ft 10 in from the signal post. Travelling at 108 ft per second, the leading wheels would take .88 seconds to pass from that point to the commencement of track circuit 'A' (58 ft beyond the home signal) which, when occupied, would interrupt the electric currents passing through the solenoids holding up the locks on lever 26 and 27, thus causing the locks to drop into place and hold the levers. To this .88 seconds was added .95 seconds as the estimated time it would take for the relay to switch off the current and for the locks to drop. There was thus a total time for beating the interlocking of 1.83 seconds.

A trial was run in Conington South box using a 'Teledeltos' timer. A signalman stood with lever 14 reversed and its latch, or catch-handle, raised. The work was timed precisely from the moment that he moved the lever. He flung it into the frame, side-stepped to lever 26, slammed that into the frame and then snatched up the latch of the facing point lever, No 27. At first the man could not carry out the sequence within the allotted time but — after some practice — he was able to complete it in 1.5 seconds. The timing was extreme and could not, even with practice, be achieved at every attempt — however, once was obviously enough.

Further examination of the locking equipment revealed that the electric lock on No 27 lever had been broken in so far as the spring, which held down the lock after it had been released by the solenoid, was broken. Without this spring, it would have been very easy to slide in a table knife blade to hold the lock up and prevent it falling, and if the lock had been tampered with in this way, the job of beating the purely mechanical interlocking between levers would have been much easier. The Inspecting Officer, Lt Colonel McNaughton, was at pains to emphasize that there were no marks to show that such abuse had taken place; he merely recorded the fact of the broken spring and the possibilities it opened up.

However, it was proved conclusively that it was possible to beat the mechanical and electrical interlocking by 'extremely rapid and premeditated movements' and ' if the signalman did succeed in circumventing the locking in this manner, he must then have stood holding the point lever a short distance from the full normal position to prevent the re-engagement of the electric lock, for a further 7 seconds before the trailing bogie of the seventh vehicle reached the facing points and the derailment commenced . . .there was thus still ample time for thought during which time safety could have been assured at any moment by pushing the lever back to the full normal position whereupon the electric lock would have re-engaged. If the derailment was caused in this manner, I cannot accept that it was an accident'. Thus wrote Lt Colonel McNaughton in his report to the Minister of Transport.

Having demonstrated that it was possible for the signalman to unlock and alter the points as the train approached and passed over them, the Colonel had also to show that such an action would have caused the derailment to occur in the manner that it did and with the damage which was caused. The cycloidal marks which had been noted on the wheels of the trailing bogie of the seventh and on both bogies of the eighth coach, and a minute study of the marks on the foot of the switchblade rail, showed that five wheels had passed between the stock rail and the switchblade. The conclusion drawn from this was that only the trailing bogie of the seventh and both bogies of the eighth coach had taken the wrong line at the facing points; the rest of the train had been routed along the main line and was dragged into derailment by these two coaches. This was consistent with the theory that the points were opened and shut under the train. Using a 'Teledeltos' timer, it was found that for a facing point to be moved from the main line to the loop direction would take .6 seconds. For the points to be opened wide enough to permit the left-hand flanges to pass on the wrong side of the switchblade took only .25 seconds. In this, partly open, position, with the switchblade 1½ inches from the stock rail, the blade had only to move ½ in, in .05 seconds, for the left-hand flange to pass on the correct side of the blade.

A set of points similar to those at Conington South was built in Hitchin yard, and slow-speed tests were carried out with a passenger coach similar to those involved in the crash, to determine how far a wheel, running along the correct side of the switchblade, must be from the facing tip before the signalman, using his usual lever, could begin to move that blade — and, secondly, to see if the switchblade was sufficiently flexible as to permit the closure and re-bolting of the points while a wheel was running on the stock rail with the planed side of the switchblade bearing against it.

The long, planed and slender switchblade was found to be very flexible indeed. The points could be moved their full, 4 in, throw when a wheel was only 8 ft 6 in from the tip of the blade, and an opening of 2 in was possible with the wheel 4 ft 6 in from the tip. In the second test, it was found possible to close the points but not to be able to re-bolt them when a wheel was 10 ft 6 in from the tip of the switch blade with that wheel running on the stock rail and the switchblade therefore closing against the wheel. It was proved possible, therefore, to replace the points under the trailing bogie of the eighth coach before it became derailed at the 'wide to gauge' point and before the leading bogie of the ninth coach arrived. That coach and the other two were thus directed along the down main and left plenty of time for the signalman to replace the bolt in its port in the stretcher bar, their wheels forcing the somewhat twisted blade tight against the stock rail. In the slow-speed tests, it was seen that after the left-hand switch-blade had been forced closed by the lever while there was a coach wheel between it and the stock rail, the rail took on a permanent twist just as had been observed in the points at Conington South after the crash.

The result of Lt Colonel McNaughton's inquiries was that signalman Frost was committed for trial and duly appeared at Nottingham Assizes on 26 November 1968 where he pleaded 'Not Guilty' to the 'unlawful killing' of three men and two women passengers, and 'Not Guilty' to the charge of 'Endangering the safety of railway passengers by the unlawful operation of signal and points mechanisms and by the wilful neglect of his duties as a signalman'. If my readers are still with me, they will have observed that the evidence supplied by the prosecution was technical and complicated so that, perhaps, the jury could not grasp the meaning of what was being said. On 6 December, a three-lever frame was brought into the court, arranged as at Conington South, and with the levers weighted to simulate the drag of the signal wire and the point rodding. A demonstration was given of moving the levers in 1.5 seconds, and the members of the jury were invited to try their hands at working the frame, with a view to showing the impossibility of causing the crash accidently. Mr Roulston, Chief Signal & Telecommunications Inspector, testified under oath that 'the actions must have been premeditated and very carefully worked out by a person having a good understanding of the system', but the jury remained unconvinced of the 'wilfulness' of the deed. The court was then cleared and for no less than 2½ days legal arguments were made to the learned judge, Mr Justice Fisher, by the defence counsel, Mr Nial McDermott, and the prosecution, Mr A.W. Michael Davies QC.

On 10 December, the jury was re-called and the trial proceeded with Frost now pleading guilty to the lesser of the two charges, that of 'endangering the safety of the passengers'. Mr Justice Fisher directed that the jury ought to hear police evidence from an interview which Mr Lockie, Mid-Anglia CID, had had with Frost. Lockie said that he told Frost that expert evidence showed that the points had been moved and that he (Frost) must have made the movements. Mr Lockie stated that Frost replied: 'I might as well jump in with both feet I have told a pack of lies from the start'. Frost went on to explain that he had replaced the home signal as soon as the train passed it instead of waiting until it had gone over the points. He then accidentally unlocked the points by swinging on lever 26, and realizing his mistake, panicked, made a grab at the lever but moved 27 instead, which opened the points. He then closed them again. The policeman then suggested that it could not have been done in that way and Frost replied, according to Lockie: 'You know damn well it didn't. I knew I was doing it but I didn't intend to de-rail the train. It was sort of force of habit. I went down the frame as I often used to — wham, wham, wham, three levers (over) when I should have done two'. In the court, Mr McDermott spoke for Frost and said that his client was unable to say with certainty how he had caused the accident, but accepted that it must have been by his act. Learned counsel went on to suggest that it happened because Frost developed the bad habits of (a) replacing the home signal lever too soon and (b) replacing the facing point bolt lever when a train was not standing on the track circuit.

Mr Frost had come to the railway from the Royal Marines, where he had been a bandsman from 1961 to 1964, bearing a reference of good character which gave no inkling of the real reasons for his discharge, saying merely that he was below their standards of physical fitness. In fact, he had twice made suicide attempts and had been discharged from the service suffering from 'hysteria and immature personality'. After the crash he was taken back into the Army as a bandsman, and at the time of his trial he had been characterized as 'a brilliant musician'. At the end of the eleven-day trial, Mr Justice Fisher said that Frost had 'developed bad habits which caused him to open points while an express was passing them...As a result of what you did in the signal box that night, five people lost their lives...as a signalman you had the lives of all those people in your hands and that means that your degree of responsibility was very high'. The learned judge instructed the jury to acquit Frost on the manslaughter charge, but sentenced him to two years imprisonment for 'unlawfully operating the signal and points mechanism of the Conington South signal box so as to endanger persons being conveyed on the railway'. Mr Frost said to journalists, before he was taken away: 'I tried to get myself to believe that I was not to blame. The thought of those five people has been with me since that night. Despite my uncalculated action I did not intend at any time to cause the death of those people, the wrecking of the train or any other damage'.

CHAPTER 4

Curry Rivel

Junction

1923

T HIS IS A STORY THAT ALL STEAM AGE LOCOMOTIVEMEN AND SIGNAL-
men will recognize, and after the preceding pages it might qualify
as 'light relief'. On 15 April 1923, a 'Special' goods train left Swindon
yard at 2.45 pm for Plymouth carrying traffic which the regular train had been
forced to leave behind due to the engine being overloaded. The Special's load
consisted of 32 loaded coal wagons and 20 trucks of general merchandise weighing
in all 712 tons, including the 20 ton brake van, and was hauled — surprisingly
perhaps — by a 'Star' Class 4-6-0 No 4048 *Princess Victoria*. The railway then
was choked with traffic as it had been for some years due to a shortage of motive
power. Swindon Works had fallen behind in its repair work due to the work it
had done on munitions during the war, while at the same time everything that
had to be moved around the country had to go by rail. Every siding was full
of delayed traffic and the railway was hard pushed to cope.

Averaging 12 mph, the 2.45 pm Swindon made its way through the Wiltshire
and Somerset countryside under fine blue skies until it arrived at Frome North
box at 5.30 pm. Here it backed into a siding to pick up another 16 loaded coal
wagons detached from an earlier train; the siding points were closed and there
sat the train and its crew, awaiting a 'path' westwards. It was a beautiful spring
evening and, had there been anyone around to admire it, No 4048 would have
made a fine sight — even if she was only at the head of a coal train. Her driver,
George Steer, and his mate Fireman Purdie were glad the weather was fine, otherwise they would have been cold, if not wet, from the time they had spent twid-
dling their thumbs in refuge sidings. After 50 minutes watching other trains going
by, George sent his mate to the North box to arrange with Westbury Control
that they be relieved at Taunton because, the way things were working out, by
the time they reached that place they would have completed their 8-hour shift.
Purdie came back to say that the Controller had agreed to let them go and had

arranged a priority run for them and for relief to be ready at Taunton.

The Frome North signalman let them out of the siding ahead of the 4.5 pm Swindon to Plymouth goods and with nearly 900 tons behind the tender, Purdie got down to some serious shovel work. There were 68 wagons behind, most of them with primitive, grease lubricated axle bearings, and the line ahead to Brewham summit was 'in the collar' for seven miles, much of it rising at around 1 in 116. After Brewham, the line fell at 1 in 50 for several miles and was gently falling from Castle Cary on the 'New Line' towards Taunton. They left Frome at 6.50 and had a clear road until they spotted Curry Rivel's down distant at 'Caution' against them one hour later.

They had *averaged* 30 mph with their massive load so, in railway parlance and not putting too fine a point on matters, 'they had not been hanging about'. Indeed, Inspector Meticulous might have thought their performance rather racy given the enormous weight of their totally unbraked train, but he was not around to complain. George Steer, having driven all through the Great War, knew all about very long hours on the footplate and was anxious to avoid them; he had made an agreement to run well in exchange for a good run, yet here was a distant signal against him. There is no doubt that he was displeased.

Curry Rivel Junction was where the line to Yeovil Town turned south-eastwards off the Taunton-Westbury line, the junction points facing trains from Taunton. The signal box was manned by Fred Adams on that fine spring evening, and

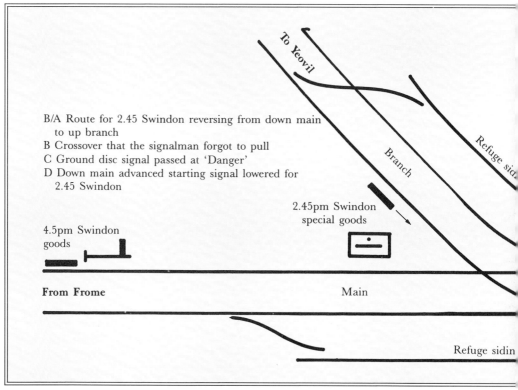

B/A Route for 2.45 Swindon reversing from down main
    to up branch
B Crossover that the signalman forgot to pull
C Ground disc signal passed at 'Danger'
D Down main advanced starting signal lowered for
    2.45 Swindon

4.5pm Swindon goods

2.45pm Swindon special goods

From Frome

Main

To Yeovil

Branch

Refuge sid

Refuge sidin

he had been told by Exeter Control to stand the 2.45 pm Swindon Special to one side and allow the following 4.5 pm Swindon regular train to pass. Exeter Control did not know about the need for relief for the men on the 2.45, and they did not care that that train was 'running like a stag'. It was to be put aside and that was that. George Steer managed to bring his massive train under control and coasted very gently past the signal box as the signalman shouted out: 'Back on the branch!'

The train was far too long to fit in either of the refuge sidings and it could not reverse on to the down branch because the signalman was expecting a passenger train on that line, so he routed it to the up branch line. The long train snaked carefully around the reverse curves until the engine was alongside the box and clear of the main line. Adams gave 'Train out of Section' for it to Long Sutton & Pitney at 7.55 pm. As soon as his train was at a stand, George Steer went to the signal box and demanded to know why he had been side-tracked. Adams contacted Exeter Control, told him the arrangements that had been made earlier with Westbury Control and asked which of the two trains he should allow to go first. Exeter told him to hang on while enquiries were made.

At 8.6 pm, the 4.5 pm Swindon goods was 'asked' to Curry Rivel from Long Sutton & Pitney, and Adams 'gave the road' for it. At 8.7 pm, Athelney 'asked the road' for the 7.50 pm Taunton to Castle Cary 'auto train', a small tank engine with one coach. Adams 'refused' this as he was hoping to let Steer's train leave

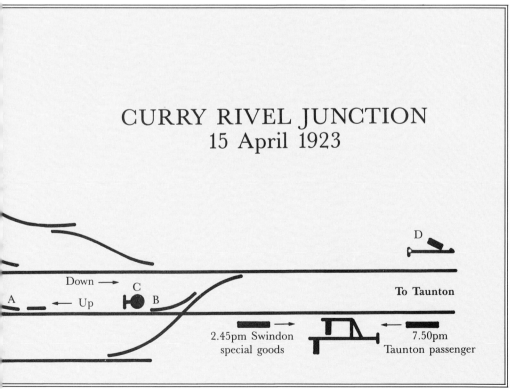

CURRY RIVEL JUNCTION
15 April 1923

D

Down →

C

To Taunton

A ← Up B

2.45pm Swindon
special goods

7.50pm
Taunton passenger

the branch and he could not do that if he had given 'Line Clear' for a passenger train on the up main line. At 8.10, Athelney again offered the 7.50 pm Taunton, and as Exeter Control had not yet rung back with instructions about the goods trains, Adams gave 'Line Clear' for this train, obtained a 'Line Clear' for it from Long Sutton but did not lower his signals. No sooner had he finished with his bell signals than Exeter Control rang to say that the 2.45 pm Swindon was to leave in front of the 4.5 goods.

Keen to help his colleagues on 4048, Adams dashed to his levers and set the road from the branch to the up main, asked 'Is Line Clear?' to Athelney and lowered his down starting signal. He then strode to the back window of the box to call 'Right Away' to George Steer. Steer actually called back: 'Is it all right?' Adams assured him that it was and urged him to get a move on. At 8.14, as the 4.5 Swindon was drawing to a stand at the down main home signal, the 2.45 Swindon was steaming off the up branch and heading westwards, couplings tight with 11 miles to go to Taunton and relief. George Steer did not look for the ground signal at the crossover from up to down main, and Purdie was busy with the fire. George had 4048 in full gear and was writing in his notebook. Having finished with his writing he put the book in his pocket, wound the reverser back several turns — and then realized he was driving down the up main. He leaped for the brake with one hand and hauled down on the brake whistle chain with the other. Fred Adams heard the racket, looked out and to his horror saw the train on the wrong road with the steam of the 7.50 Taunton in the not too far distance. He had forgotten to pull the crossover lever.

The auto train was hauled by the 0-4-2T No 215, and the coach was a 70 ft trailer, No 79. The driver, Edward Timms, had no chance of avoiding a collision. When he first saw the smoke of the goods train he naturally assumed it was on the opposite line, and only when he was much closer and had come through a bridge and around a bend did he realize his danger. He shut off steam, braked to a stand and was trying to make his engine reverse when the big 'Star' Class engine hit his little 'tanky' at about 10 mph. The men on the tank engine baled out right and left a moment before the impact, and afterwards Edward Timms expressed his disappointment at not being able to avoid the collision. He had actually got the engine into reverse gear but when he gave the engine steam it would not start. 'She must've stopped on a bad angle,' he said ruefully. The engine and coach went backwards after the impact — a full 200 yards, in fact, with nine passengers injured by the sudden acceleration. Adams, who had had nine years as a signalman and two years at Curry Rivel Junction, sent the 'Obstruction Danger' bell to Athelney even before the collision, and at the Inquiry afterwards honestly and bravely made no attempt to cover his mistakes; not only had he forgotten to pull the crossover lever but he had also forgotten, in his haste to help out a mate, that he had given 'Line Clear' for the passenger and accepted the 'Train entering Section' bell for that train as well. He was as puzzled as the rest at his lapse.

CHAPTER 5.

Hixon

1968

THE VIRTUOUS VICTORIANS TOOK THE VIEW THAT THE RAILWAY COM-
panies had to protect the public from their trains. In 1839, and again
in 1845, Parliament imposed strict rules on the companies regarding the
fencing-in of the line and the provision of 'good and sufficient gates' at all level
crossings, which gates were always to be manned and always to be closed against
the road. In America, meanwhile, trains roared down the middle of the High
Street in towns, cities and villages between the lines of shops and with children
playing on and around the rails. At the 'grade crossings' the only protection
was a sign 'Look out for the locomotive', and if any man, woman or child did
not look out — well, that was his or her own fault. After 100 years, we in England
have now reached this happy state — and happy it is, because, curiously enough,
there are fewer fatalities on modern level crossings employing the Yankee principle than there were on those handsome, virtuous, gated and manned level
crossings.

The closed gates of a level crossing soon became a source of irritation to the
road user, as when a shunting engine at work kept them closed for 20 minutes
at a stretch, or during what felt like an interminably long wait for an express
train to pass. In 1919 the regulations were amended so that the gates could be
kept closed across the railway line, as a matter of routine, at any crossing where
the signals were interlocked with the gates. This resulted in a lot of level crossing gates being carried away on the buffer beams of locomotives. As the twen-
tieth century wore on and road traffic became denser, while road users became
more aggressive, even those crossings whose signals were not interlocked with
the gates were permitted to keep their gates closed across the tracks so that the
road vehicle and its impatient driver should be paramount. But still when the
gates were closed for rail traffic, delays could mount up. At Radstock there were
two sets of gates on a 100 yard stretch of road, while at Lincoln there was a simi-

lar situation, and as an ever-rising tide of cars and lorries pressed against those gates, the delays and frustrations became enormous. Demands were heard for a relaxation of the strict 1845 rules, the road lobby was desperate that nothing should impede the headlong rush of juggernaut and Jaguar — such as can be seen on any weekday on the A515 over Sudbury crossing north of Lichfield — and the British Transport Commission was desperate to reduce costs. For once, road and rail interests had a common ground.

Late in September 1956, a group of Ministry of Transport and British Railways officials went to Europe to look at automated, unmanned level crossing control systems. The SNCF had installed 700 of these crossings during the preceding 18 months, where half-barriers came down across the road when they were triggered by the train passing over a treadle back along the line. In the time that these crossings had been in use, the French officials proudly announced, there had been only 18 deaths on them — 11 road users and 7 railway passengers. Given French standards of driving, I suppose this was an excellent record. The French said that the secret of the crossings' success was the principle of 'brisk operation'. There were only 25 seconds between the barriers falling and the train passing, thus the road user realized that it would be dangerous to attempt to 'beat the barrier' or to 'zigzag' around them. Those 18 deaths would provide a salutary lesson to the rest, and the installations would become safer through the years because of their inherent dangers and because people became sadder and wiser from bitter experience. That was the correct, official reasoning which the joint study group brought back with them from *la belle France* — which was in any case working to the Yankee principle. The safety of the public was to be left to the public and safe working depended on fear — and 'the fear of the Lord is the fount of all wisdom', after all.

But these principles were concerned with people in vehicles using the crossings. What about adult and juvenile pedestrians? The official report of the Ministry of Transport stated that 'the dangers to which pedestrians are exposed on the roads are at least as great and certainly more frequent than those at level crossings'. So the frequent perils of the all-conquering road were to be extended to pedestrians using railway crossings; children could walk under the barriers, but the hope was that the danger would be so obvious as to deter them.

The early Victorian legislation on level crossings was superseded in 1957 by an Act permitting unmanned, automatic half-barriers (AHBs), and the first one was installed at Spath, in Staffordshire, not so far from Hixon, in February 1961. By 1965 there were 56 AHB crossings in Britain. As a signalman at Uffington, Berkshire, I had two such crossings in my section from 1965 to 1968, since when both have been replaced by bridges. I was given no instructions as to the action to take should the barriers fail or should there be an emergency on one or both of them. I had no indication in my signal box — unlike at other places — as to whether the barriers were working correctly, and they were not interlocked with the signals. I and my colleagues raised the obvious question. What if a tractor hauling a load of hay should pass over a crossing with a line of three or four cars behind it? From the time that the barriers dropped to the time the train passed was less than 20 seconds, so what would happen if the cars were to be trapped on the crossing? There was no answer to such questions and we were brushed aside as mere irritants standing in the way of the twin gods of 'progress' and 'cost cutting'. The AHB crossings were a godsend to the economy-mad management, and awkward questions about safety were undoubtedly unwelcome.

There was also the other side of the coin — the thoroughly stupid motorist who seemed impelled to attempt suicide while he was using the crossing. In April 1967, an AHB crossing was installed at Nantwich and twice in the next eight months a motorist deliberately drove off the crossing and proceeded along the rails. At Pooley Green, two cars were waiting at lowered barriers when the second driver, having become suicidally impatient within 15 seconds, started past the man in front, zigzagged around the barrier and was promptly crushed by an electric unit. His two friends died with him.

The name of Robert Wynn & Sons Ltd is synonymous with the heaviest road haulage. On 8 November 1966, one of their Scamell low-loader transporters, carrying a 15 ton crane, drove over the recently installed AHB crossing near Leominster. The road surface was in the process of being relaid and there was a drop of 4 inches on the far side of the crossing. The Scamell's driver, Mr Horton, went across with great caution and his low-loader grounded when the front part of the vehicle dropped off the 4 inch ramp. The signalman, seeing the stationary lorry, called out: 'Oi! You can't park there', to which Mr Horton replied (polite approximation): 'Park indeed! I'm grounded on the crossing'. The low-loader with its heavy load was athwart the tracks, and in considerable agitation the signalman replied that a train was very close and that once the lights began to flash the train would be into the lorry in a matter of seconds. To which the Knight of the Road replied: 'You had better stop it then, because I am going to be here for an hour jacking this lot up'. At that moment the sound of the warning bells of the crossing galvanized him into action and with great courage he leapt into his cab and, by dint of a great deal of throttle and heavy use of the clutch, managed to drag the loader over the tarmac and off the crossing a fraction of a second before the train whizzed past. Mr Horton reported the incident to his employers and they wrote to the Chief Civil Engineer of Western Region a very concerned, polite letter, describing what had happened and ending with these words.

'If our information is correct — and it is this that causes us concern — the trains themselves actuate the warning lights and barriers and, with regard to express trains, there is only ten seconds before they are on the crossing. In addition, there is no way of warning the driver or of stopping the train. There is no need for us to enlarge on the disaster which could have occurred at Leominster on 8 November had not our driver, with what we consider to be considerable bravery, succeeded in removing his vehicle.'

The reply to this was written by the Assistant General Manager of Western Region, who stated:

'I am as concerned as you are about this incident which might have had much more serious consequences. Automatic crossings have been installed at a number of points on British Railways and Leominster is no different to any other. The design is approved by the Ministry of Transport and the contingency of a road vehicle stalling on the level crossing and becoming immobile was one that was considered and *found too remote to be taken seriously. . . in brief, road vehicles must not become immobile on these crossings.* [author's italics] If they do, they become not only a hazard to themselves but also to the trains and whoever is travelling in them . . . nothing which has been said above detracts from the action of your driver. We are obviously grateful that he removed the hazard at risk to himself. I must emphasize that the hazard was of your making.

This peculiar letter, thoroughly arrogant and lecturing Wynn's management as if they were naughty schoolboys, gives a fine example of the response the signalmen at Uffington got when they pointed out the dangers of slow-moving or stranded vehicles on AHB crossings. In giving Wynn's the 'brush-off', the Assistant General Manager lost a golden opportunity to educate a company that might have benefited from the lesson — the country's leading heavy haulage contractor.

It would appear that Robert Wynn & Son, having received the letter, did not follow up their protest. Furthermore, the experts at the Ministry of Transport never, prior to the Hixon crash, specifically focused their attention upon the hazard of the slow-moving vehicle, and over the years from February 1961 never once was anyone instructed to investigate what was, to an ordinary railwayman, an obvious problem. Not until *after* Hixon, that is.

The signalman-operated level crossing gates at Hixon, on the electrified Euston-Manchester line, were replaced by an AHB crossing in April 1967. The road approach to the crossing is straight and roughly level with the A51 road to the west and Hixon airfield, disused as such, very close on the east. In snowy weather one day in February 1968, a traffic census showed that, excluding bicycles, 870 road vehicles and 26 trains used the crossing in 24 hours. For trains, the approach to the crossing was over a long, gentle curve, so that drivers could not see the crossing until they were about 400 yards way. On that section, expresses were running at 75 mph and would require 1,520 yards in which to stop with the usual 400 ton train. The train-depressed treadles were placed 1,000 yards before the crossing in order to set, first, the warning bells and flashing red lights to work and then to lower the barriers, there being a period of 24 seconds between the warnings commencing and the train passing.

The lane over the crossing seemed like any other rural lane, but it led to a depot where the English Electric Company of Stafford stored huge transformers, so it was frequently used for the conveyance of these ungainly loads on the famous red 32-wheeled transporters of Robert Wynn & Sons Ltd, or the dark blue equivalents operated by Pickfords Ltd. Besides transformers, there were also being carried over the crossing heavy loads of long steel pipes for a gas pipeline project. Both British Railways and English Electric were aware of the loads which used the crossing because EE had requested BR to widen the roadway to permit wider loads to pass and this request was refused. However, when the crossing was auto-mated, BR took the opportunity to widen the road specifically to permit the heaviest road-borne loads to pass. No one in authority gave the slightest con-sideration to the dangers inherent in an obstruction like a Wynn's transporter being placed across the rails for a longer period of time than the 24 seconds between the red warning lights flashing and the passage of an express. When the crossing was inspected for safety by the Ministry of Transport, no attention was paid to anything but the equipment and the immediate geography of the crossing. The Inspector did not take into account what might come over the crossing to or from the airfield depot which he could see from where he was standing on the crossing. This is paradoxical because the Ministry of Transport expected mere lorry drivers to recognize dangerous situations simply by look-ing at the road ahead. Had the Inspector given consideration to these heavy loads — had he known about them — then he might well have decided that an unmanned AHB was not a safe proposition at Hixon. But his mission was only to ensure that the equipment specified by the Act of Parliament was in work-ing order and safe as such. His superior, Colonel Reed, defended this very nar-row view in these words:

'If we are going to think on those lines, then any level crossing in relation to any built-up area would have to be specially considered in relation to the industrial use generally throughout the area.'

This seems to be deliberately blinding oneself to the danger of the slow-moving vehicle simply so that an AHB crossing could be installed, and up until the Hixon crash they were being installed rapidly with a consequential saving of wages and other costs. The author of the Ministry of Transport's report into the Hixon crash wrote that he was 'sorry' to hear Colonel Reed defending, at the Inquiry, his narrow view of safety at AHB crossings.

Two and a half years after the installation of Spath AHB crossing, the Home Office managed to deliver to the Chief Constable of Staffordshire a full expla-nation of the way in which this type of crossing worked. A cursory glance was enough to indicate that this missive was of no interest to him and thus he failed to read paragraph 18 which dealt with the need for drivers of heavy goods vehi-cles to telephone the signalman, before crossing the line, to make sure there was time to make the crossing in front of a train. Police constables would, of course, be called upon to escort such loads and therefore they would have to be made aware of this need, but if their Chief was unaware of the dangers and the counter-measures to adopt, then the constables could hardly be expected to know.

Yet there ought to have been a general awareness throughout the Stafford-shire police force of the perils of the AHB crossing. By July 1967 there were six such crossings in North Staffordshire besides Hixon, and on numerous occa-sions they had failed and the police had been called to supervise traffic over them, so one would have expected that a general knowledge about their working would have grown up. Scattered around the country there were, undoubtedly, concerned laymen who realized the problems, members of parish councils for instance and, of course, the signalmen who monitored the crossings, many of them voicing their fears and one and all pacified or squashed by the experts because it was Government policy to install the crossings as quickly as possible and the public would just have to learn to live with them (See Appendix 2).

At approximately 12.20 pm on 6 January 1968, a 32-wheeled transporter carrying a 120 ton transformer, pulled and pushed by tractors front and rear, turned off the A51 and proceeded along the Hixon lane towards the railway level crossing at 4 mph. This road train was owned by Robert Wynn & Sons Ltd. It was 148 ft long, 16 ft 9 in wide and, with the transformer, 16 ft 9 in tall although the low-loader could be lowered by 6 inches if required. The weight of the entire equipage was 162 tons. As it turned into the lane, the 11.30 am express from Manchester to Euston, hauled by E3009 with 12 coaches at 491 tons, was about to pass Meaford box, approximately 7½ miles to the north.

The road train had a crew of five with Mr Groves the leading driver, a man with 20 years' experience in heavy haulage. Ahead of him was a single police car acting as escort and containing two constables to stop oncoming traffic, clear the road and generally keep law and order. Neither the constables, who had only five days before been placed on road traffic duties, nor any of the five-man crew of the transporter had more that the haziest notion of the workings of the AHB ahead; the simple instructions in the Highway Code which, if observed, would have prevented the accident, were forgotten. No one gave that old-fashioned nuisance — the railway — much thought at all.

The only concern which was mildly felt regarded a sufficient clearance below the 25,000 volt electric traction wires. The police had pointed out to Mr Groves the laneside headroom sign warning of a 16 ft 6 in restriction ahead, but the experienced lorry driver was not inclined to lower his load at once because from previous experience he knew there was usually a couple of feet more headroom than that which was posted. He was prepared to take the lorry on to the crossing and check its clearance then. Asked at the Inquiry what he would have done if, having got on to the crossing, he had discovered that his load was too high, he said: 'I would have had to reduce height.'

'While you were reducing height there would have been several expresses going to or coming from London, would there not, while your vehicle was immobilized on the crossing? That seems to be the difficulty you have if you ignore the notice' [referring to the notice telling drivers of exceptional loads to telephone the signalman before using the crossing].

Mr Grove agreed that this was a difficulty. When he was asked if he had not considered this, he replied: 'I thought everything was in order.'

At another stage of the Inquiry, Mr Groves was asked: 'Did you stop to think for one moment "Oh, the police will have enquired whether the railroad is clear", or did you not think of it at all?'

'I am afraid I did not think of it at all'.

This was a very different attitude to that of another Robert Wynn driver, Mr Cromwell, who, before he took his lorry out of the depot, telephoned his head office to ensure that he had clearance below the 25Kv wires and, on the day, asked his police escort to telephone the signalman to ask if there was time to cross before venturing on to the crossing.

Movements of such vast loads along the highway can only be carried out with a special authorization from the Ministry of Transport, and the driver of the load, being authorized, is given his route and with that any 'cautions' he must observe along the way. Mr Groves was 'cautioned' about some bridges but he was not warned about the need to contact the signalman before using the crossing, nor about the very restricted clearance beneath the power cables. In excusing itself for this, the Ministry of Transport stated that it did not, as a matter of policy warn drivers in respect of hazards which were 'visible and capable of being appreciated by the driver of the vehicle'.

So, the 148 ft long transporter approached the level crossing at 4 mph with the police car 50-75 yards ahead. The latter passed over the crossing and stopped on the far side. The 11.30 am Manchester was about 3 minutes away. Neither the two policemen nor the five-man team on the transporter saw the 14½ in by 30½ in white sign with black lettering which instructed:

IN EMERGENCY or before crossing with exceptional
or heavy loads or cattle PHONE SIGNALMAN

This notice did not directly face oncoming traffic but was at an angle of about 26° to the road because the man who had fixed it had been unsure of his instructions and had made a compromise between having the plate parallel to the road and at right-angles to it. But even if the police or the transporter crew had seen and read the notice, would they have stopped? The Colwich signalman who monitored the crossing said that he could not recall anyone phoning to ask for permission to take an abnormal load across, yet there must have been several occasions when heavy loads used the crossing. In making this statement, the signalman had forgotten the solitary example of Mr Cromwell.

As the road train's leading tractor reached the crossing, Mr Groves reduced speed so that three crew members could walk alongside to check clearances under the wires and above the road. The time was about 12.25 pm, the warning bells were silent, the warning red lights were not flashing and the barriers were vertical. The 11.30 am Manchester express was about one minute away.

The lead tractor had cleared both tracks and the 120 ton transformer was squarely across them while the rear 16-wheel bogie was still creeping towards the crossing when the express 'struck in' on the treadles 1,000 yards to the north. Immediately the barriers' warning bells began the jangle and the red lights to flash. After 8 seconds, the half barriers began to drop, that on the far side of the crossing fouling the top of the transformer. From that moment to the time the train arrived was 16 seconds. The crossing was 30 feet wide. For the 148 ft long vehicle to clear it within the 24 seconds between the warning sounding and the train passing it would have had to have been moving at 6 mph. Its speed had been reduced to 2 mph for the reasons stated.

Mr Groves did not see or hear the warnings, but he did see the express slipping swiftly and silently through the flat green fields towards him. The driver of the train, Mr Stanley Turner, had no such visibility and came on at full speed. Groves shouted to his mates on the ground to get clear and accelerated the transformer. The rear driver, Mr Illsley, saw the warning lights and heard the bells and he too 'put his foot down' so as to remove the vast solid bulk of the transformer from the path of the train. By so doing he was bringing himself closer to the danger so his was an act of calculated bravery, sticking to his post in order to mitigate the effects of the inevitable impact. Rounding the long, gentle curve, driver Turner saw the huge obstruction across his path from a range of not more than 400 yards. He was travelling at 75 mph so, given the time lag for his reflexes and the braking mechanisms to work, the brakes were not applied until the train was 300 yards from disaster. At 12.26 pm, with a noise like an explosion which was heard half a mile away, Class '81' electric locomotive E3009 cut through the transporter at its weakest point — the 'swan-neck' connection between the low-loader and the rear bogie. The engine was destroyed, killing driver Turner, his second man James Toghill and a third driver simply riding down to London with them prior to working a train back to Manchester. The front six coaches were scattered about the tracks, wrecked; eight passengers were killed, one restaurant car attendant and 44 passengers were injured, six of them seriously. The

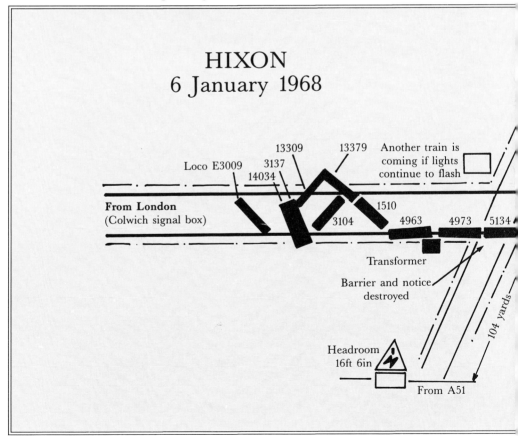

overhead wires were brought down and both tracks wrecked for a distance of 120 yards. The 120 ton transformer was thrown off its platform and turned through 90° to land beside the up line, 30 feet south of the crossing, the still moving carriages scraping past it as they tumbled off the line. Considering the circumstances, the fatalities were relatively light. This was due in part to the determination of the transporter drivers and due also to the fact of it being Saturday — the leading six coaches were all 'firsts' and were almost empty in the absence of commuting businessmen.

The signalman at Meaford noticed that the track circuits on his diagram had not cleared, suggesting that the train had stopped. He telephoned Colwich but found that the line was dead and therefore telephoned his fearful suspicions to Stoke power box at 12.27. The crossing keeper at Pasturefields heard what sounded like an explosion at 12.26 and had telephoned the news to the Colwich signalman by 12.27. The signalman at Colwich had become worried when he saw the up train's track circuit indications cease to move and the down line track circuits light up at the symbol representing the crossing on his track diagram. Receiving the message from Pasturefields crossing keeper, he raised the alarm with Control at 12.32 pm. He was not able to send the 'Obstruction Danger' signal

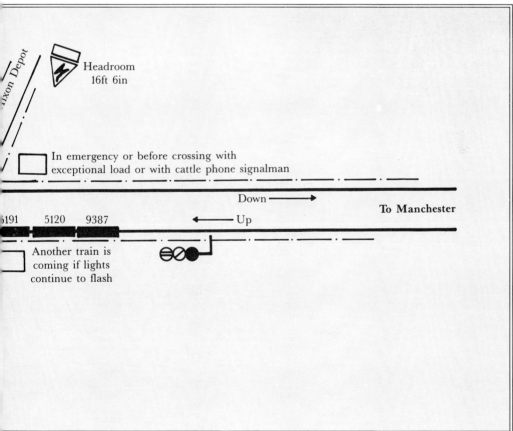

The scene at Hixon a short time after the crash had taken place. The mangled wreckage of the electric locomotive is in the bottom right-hand corner; three men were riding in the cab. Luckily, the smashed and tumbled coaches behind the engine were nearly empty, so the casualties were relatively light. The formation they took up and the distortion of the rails demonstrates the tremendous shock wave that went back through the train as the engine hit the 162-ton 'road train' at about 70 mph. The 120-ton transformer was thrown off its platform to land several yards down the track, the coaches scraping past it as they braked. The crossing, the white transformer and the dark transporter can be seen at the top centre and right of the view. (Associated Press)

to Meaford box, owing to the wires being cut, until 1 pm, when 'six bells' was sent and acknowledged.

After the disaster, which was caused in the best British tradition by both lack of imagination and thoughtlessness, the rescue work was equally British — prompt, spirited and brave. The guard of the train, 49-year-old Mr Final, leaped from his van, well supplied with flags and detonators, and ran a mile back along the up line to find a telephone that worked and to place flags and detonators to the rear of his train as a protection against a following train running into the wreck. Having telephoned Control to advise them of the crash, he then ran two miles through the fields to the south of the wreck where he placed detonators on the down line. He then ran the mile back to his train — 'I never stopped running,' he said later — making a distance of four miles which, for a tolerably unfit 49-year-old, was a feat of marathon proportions. He was still on his legs at the end of it and spent his time in helping with the rescue work. The Fire Brigade arrived within 15 minutes of being called and the first ambulance and helicopter arrived three minutes later. The first of the 44 injured were in hospital at 1.5 pm, the last of them entered Stone hospital at 3.35 pm. The remains of those in the cab of the electric locomotive were not removed until 11.10 pm that night.

The Hixon crash was foreseeable and therefore preventable. The root cause was the ineptness and lack of imagination, lack of thought, on the part of those in the Ministry of Transport and British Railways who handled the modernization of level crossings. Telephone procedure at crossings was, and remains, of paramount importance where very slow moving vehicles are concerned, yet the mention of this was hidden away in paragraph 18 of the information sent to the Chief Constable. The Ministry gave him no hint that the booklet contained something of crucial importance to all road users and, being a very busy man, he did not go through the book with a fine tooth-comb to find what, if anything, might be of interest to his men. The booklet was also sent to members of the Road Hauliers Association, but as it was fiendishly camouflaged by the sub-title 'An essential guide to railways when selecting sites' (for level crossings), the managers of firms like Wynn's and Pickford's did not think it contained anything of interest to anyone directing a road haulage operation and ignored it accordingly. The Ministry of Transport and British Railways had taken a policy decision to place safety at public level crossings in the hands of the public and had then taken totally inadequate steps to inform the public of their new responsibilities.

CHAPTER 6

Welwyn Garden
City

1935

W ELWYN GARDEN CITY SIGNAL BOX (HEREINAFTER REFERRED TO
as 'Welwyn') stood on the down side of the four-track main line, a few
feet north of the down slow line platform of the station of the same
name. It lay almost 20½ miles north of King's Cross, and was opened along
with the station on 5 October 1926 in connection with the construction of Welwyn Garden City, the Milton Keynes of the 'twenties'. The quadruple track ran
roughly north-south, and beside the up slow line on the east side lay the single
track Hertford branch, whilst alongside the down slow, on the west side lay the
single branch track from Hatfield to Luton. Neither branch line had any physical connection with the quadruple track in 1935.

Welwyn signal box housed a lever frame, facing away from the quadruple tracks,
containing 45 working levers in a 65-lever frame. On the long shelf above the
levers was a very impressive row of finely made wooden-cased instruments, eleven
block indicators with eleven bells on which the signalling codes rang out. The
single track lines were operated by block instruments of similar appearance to
those used on the main lines.

Welwyn box was merely a block post as far as the branch lines were concerned,
not a crossing place, so the handle working the 'Line Clear', 'Line Blocked' and
'Train Entered Section' indications on the Welwyn instrument was interlocked
with the instruments at Hertford and Ayot, the latter on the Luton line. Thus
Welwyn could not give a 'Line Clear' to Hatfield on the Hertford branch instrument if he had already given that message to Hertford. The train service was
very busy, taking all lines together, and it was normal for two or more bells to
ring out together. Under such circumstances it was difficult to know which bells
had rung, because the signal engineer had not found a way of making more
than about five different types of bell to produce five distinctive sounds. Besides
the signalling equipment, the signalman also operated a small telephone switch-

board, listening out for his box's code on any one of five telephones and five single-needle telegraph instruments. The last two used trembler bells and could not be confused with the signalling, single strike, bells, but their varied codes (eg 2 short, 3 long rings) to call each signalman had to be learned, and their clamour added to the potentially distracting background noise.

Before the Welwyn signalman could turn any of the main line block indicators to 'Line Clear' and thus permit a train to approach his box, the distant and home signal for that line had to be at 'Danger', as the electrical circuitry for the 'Line Clear' indication passed through contacts in the signal arm repeater instruments on the instrument shelf in the signal box and, of course, the arm repeater was operated by contacts on the signal arm itself. On the down fast line there was a track circuit which extended southwards from the home signal for 200 yards. This, the 'berth' track circuit, had a safety function. If it was occupied by a train, it prevented the Welwyn signalman from sending a 'Line Clear' indication to Hatfield box — thus, with a train standing at the home signal it was not possible to permit a train to leave Hatfield. The security of this excellent system was rendered useless in that the Hatfield signalman could pull his down fast line starting signal at any time, even if the block indicator to Welwyn was showing 'Train on Line'.

The signalman at Welwyn worked with Welwyn North box, 1½ miles to the north, with Hatfield Nos 2 and 3 boxes 2½ miles to the south, and with Hertford and Ayot on the branches. Welwyn's down fast advanced starting signal was locked at 'Danger' until released by a 'Line Clear' indication from Welwyn North. Hatfield No 2 box dealt only with up trains and those on the Hertford line, while Hatfield No 3 worked the Luton branch and all down trains on the fast and slow lines. The train service was very frequent. In all, 106 trains were scheduled to pass Welwyn signal box in an 8-hour shift — one every 4½ minutes on average — but on 14 June 1935, extra trains between 5.10 and 6.27 pm gave the Welwyn signalman no less than one every 2¾ minutes. That was a great deal of rapid-fire bell codes — each train required five — and a great many levers unceremoniously heaved over and slung back, yet all the time with thought as to what was going on. In addition to this work, the signalman maintained his own train register with a minute by minute account of bell codes received and sent, answered other signalmen's enquiries on the telephone and occasionally operated the telephone switchboard. The box was a tough one, demanding a very quick-witted, physically fit man to work it.

The signalman with whom this story is concerned, Fred Howes, began his career on the Great Northern Railway in June 1908 when he was 16. Starting, possibly at Retford, as a telephone lad, he was keen enough to take the three-month long signalling course at the Retford signalling school the following year, He graduated from there with the following recommendation from Mr Rickett, who ended his career as Signalling Superintendent, Western Division, LNER, at Liverpool Street. Mr Rickett wrote: 'Howes is a smart good lad who understands the block rules and the telegraph and should make a reliable signalman'. A man who could understand, operate and interpret the single needle telegraph with its visual morse code and its complex procedures for use could not have been stupid or slow-witted.

Fred Howes took his first signal box in July 1912 when he went to Navenby on the rural route from Grantham to Lincoln. It was a nice little box with a station to one side and and the Navenby-Bassingham lane on the other. It had a frame of 24 levers for the signals and the few points to the station yard, and it also housed the massive gate-wheel to operate the gates across the lane. He worked there for nine years before moving one step up the promotion ladder to Kirton, a few miles south of Boston on the line to Spalding. This was another rural idyll, a signal box of 22 levers, a small station and two level crossings. The one nearest the box he worked with his big, iron wheel, while the distant crossing was worked by a crossing keeper under his control. He worked here for eleven years, then moved to Ranskill, between Retford and Doncaster on the East Coast main line. This had a frame of 34 levers, a small station and a few sidings, but it had a much busier service and the trains passed at high speed. Less than a year after moving here he applied for the vacancy at Doncaster 'A' box and was appointed there in February 1933. This box had 23 levers to control up trains only on the up main and into two platform loops, with a couple of points leading to carriage sidings. Here he would have dealt with a lot of slow-moving trains and with shunting movements. After a year there, the vacancy arose at Welwyn, a Class 1 job , and he applied for it. So did five others. The three senior to him dropped out of the race for various reasons leaving Fred with the job. In May 1934 he went to learn it.

There is no doubt that it was a very different place from anywhere he had worked before, but he was an experienced man and the learning was only a matter of time. Mr V.M. Barrington-Ward, Superintendent of the Western Section of the Southern Area, LNER — a 'toughie' operator much beloved by the late Gerald Fiennes — said of Fred Howes: 'His record is perfectly satisfactory and good reports have been received from Doncaster in regard to his work'. Inspector Chamberlain of Doncaster said of him: 'He is a very careful signalman and one to consider well before making a move'. Howes' difficulty at Welwyn was that there was very little time in which to think, and the cautious Fred took five weeks to learn the job. This corresponds to two weeks on early shifts, two on late shifts and one week on nights, not only to get used to the position of the levers in the frame and the sound of the bells but also to get used to the train service and learn the sequence. The local District Inspector said that he had never known a man take so long to learn Welwyn box, and the Inspecting Officer, Lt Colonel Mount, made much of this to imply that there was something wrong with Fred Howes' brain. But this was something of a red herring. Howes did *not* take an inordinately long time to learn and take charge of the box.

Contained in the Report's innuendoes on Howes' character there was a certain amount of truth. He was certainly an unusually quiet man and therefore this dour Northerner made few friends among the quick-tongued Cockneys. Signalman Birch who taught him the job said that after spending 200 hours with him in the box he did not know if Fred was a member of the Union or not;

'sometimes he would go for an hour without saying a word'. There is no doubt that having such a silent companion in the box would have been very uncomfortable for Mr Birch, and he was thought of as 'a bit peculiar'. The Welwyn Garden City station-master, Mr Hodson, was to tell the Inquiry into the crash: 'Howes is a quiet — almost peculiarly quiet — man and it is difficult to get anything out of him at all'. Mr Hodson managed to make Fred Howes sound sinister. Inspector Hook, who examined Howes on the rules and regulations before passing him as fit to work the box, said: 'I had to drag everything out of him, he was not at all forthcoming'. But Hook had to admit that Howes knew his job, because he passed him as competent. Fred Howes worked his shifts with Signalman Horace Ball at Welwyn North, and Ball's comment on Howes was appreciative. 'He is a quiet man who gets on with the job.'

Signalman Howes took charge of the box for the first time on the night shift of 11 May 1935. On 18 May, he was on late turn when an express failed to stop at the inner home signal which was at 'Danger'. This was due to Fred having lowered the outer home signal too soon, before the driver had made a good, strong brake application. The man came on too fast and was taken by surprise at the inner home. A signalman had always to remember this when he wanted to stop a train, and had to make sure that he lowered his signals in such a way as to convey to the driver the need to stop. Rule 39a covered this technique, and Fred had infringed it, but between him and the driver the matter was 'squared up' and nothing was reported. Unfortunately for Fred, Mr Hodson had seen the incident and the man came to the box to demand an explanation — as was his duty.

Fred told him honestly enough what had happened and thought no more about it. Hodson, however, carried out his clear duty and reported the matter to Mr Warriner, District Superintendent at King's Cross. How far his zeal was motivated by a real devotion to duty and how much by a dislike or distrust of the 'almost peculiarly quiet' Fred Howes we shall never know. A formal report from Fred was required by Mr Warriner, but Fred said he had explained the matter once and he was not going to do so again — being a man of few words. Naturally enough, Mr Warriner took a dim view of this and summoned Fred to his presence up at 'the Cross'.

On 4 June, Fred took his ride to London, was interviewed by the Superintendent and told to consider himself severely reprimanded for breaking Rule 39a. He was also told that this punishment would have to go before Barrington-Ward for confirmation and that in due course he, Signalman Howes, would receive a formal, written notice of the Superintendent's decision. Fred went back to work and the days passed. The formal notice was issued on 13 June and arrived by train at Welwyn Garden City on the 15th. Mr Hodson took it to the signalbox where it lay waiting for the arrival of Fred Howes at 10 pm for the night shift.

The evening was dark and drizzling with rain, but like a good chap Fred Howes arrived in the box ten minutes before time. He opened the envelope and was sufficiently shocked or surprised by the contents to read them to his mate, Birch. Given his universally acknowledged reticence, this was indeed unusual. Signalman

Birch got into his overcoat, said, 'Don't worry, they can't hang you for that,' and left the box.

The night shift was busy with the summer train service and a few extras as well so that, on average, one train passed the box every four minutes through-out the 85 minutes leading up to the crash. Howes had been working the box on his own for five weeks (he had therefore had ten weeks there altogether), and admitted that he still had occasional difficulty in deciding which bell had rung when two or more rang together. At such moments he waited until the bell was rung a second time, not a practice to endear him to the equally hard-pressed signalmen on each side of him. He also found it difficult to keep up with the business of booking train times into the train register; sometimes he was as much as three minutes behind in this, and then the times of several trains would be entered *en masse* as intelligent guesses based on the usual running times, and until the times were entered there was no tangible record of what he was deal-ing with. A bell code was rung out and answered in a couple of seconds; the action, repeated thousands of times a day, could over several weeks easily become a reflex action needing little or no thought — yet each bell code said something important about a train and its position on the track. The act of writing down the time that a bell code was received or sent transformed the fleeting act of tapping a morse key or turning a knob into a reality by fixing the event in time and in the memory with black ink on the page of the register.

At 11.3 pm, just after a Hertford to Hatfield train had left Welwyn Garden City station, Porter Jakes telephoned the signal box, not merely to ask for a line to Hatfield on the telephone circuit but also to ask Fred Howes to run the whole errand for him. A parcel of lost property had been sent from Hertford to Wel-wyn on that train but it had not been put off — it was lost. Jakes wanted Howes to phone the Platform Inspector at Hatfield and ask him to search the train for the parcel. Fred said he would do it when he had time. At 11.15, Jakes rang to ask if there was any news and Fred replied that there was not. During this time, Fred was working hard trying to keep abreast of the train service. Jakes ought to have been supplied with a 'station to station' telephone circuit of his own, but all such enquiries had to go through the signal box switchboard. Apart from these distractions, which would have been irritating to a signalman, Fred Howes was also rather put out by the letter he had received from Mr Warriner. He had put the unpleasant business behind him a fortnight before, and now sud-denly the whole thing had been brought back to his mind. It was unsettling and the feeling of rancour nagged him — not too much, but it was there. In a man fully on top of the job these other distractions would not have been crucial, but Fred Howes was not on top of the job. He could manage it if he gave it his un-divided attention. Given time he would have become thoroughly used to the work.

The trains ran with unremitting frequency. No 823 went down followed by No 825, the 10.45 pm King's Cross, at 11.20. When Howes gave 'Train out of Section' to Hatfield No 3 for No 825 at 11.20, the Hatfield signalman at once asked 'Is Line Clear?' for No 825A, the 10.53 pm King's Cross. Howes at once gave 'Line Clear' and this train passed Hatfield No 3 at 11.21 pm. When

No 825 cleared Welwyn North at 11.22, Howes at once 'got the road' from Horace Ball for No 825A, but did not at once lower the down fast line signals. Fred Howes admitted that he did not clear the signals for No 825A 'because I was on the telephone with the porter who was asking about a parcel', but at another stage of the Inquiry Fred said that he never allowed telephone work to interfere with the signalling and would ignore the phone to attend to the bells and levers. Yet, according to his account of events, he obtained 'Line Clear' for No 825A from Welwyn North, knowing that this train was no more than 90 seconds from his down fast line distant signal, and then spent a minute or 90 seconds on the telephone leaving the signals at 'Danger' against the approaching express. That seems to me to be a very unsignalmanlike way of going on, and it may be that the shock of the crash affected his memory of events. Porter Jakes, whilst admitting that he did telephone the signalman twice about the parcel, pointed out that he had finished duty and was actually going down the road on his bicycle two minutes before the crash took place.

I believe that Fred Howes was distracted not by the porter's telephone call but by the weight of traffic. Having rung the code to obtain 'Line Clear' from Welwyn North for No 825A, he had then to go to the Luton branch instrument to obtain 'Line Clear' from Hatfield No 3 for a Luton to Hatfield empty coaching stock train. He then walked to the relevant levers and reversed them for the branch train. As he did this, up goods train No 787 passed, he sent the 'Train entering Section' bell for this to Hatfield No 2 and replaced the signals, one by one, as the train passed. Having done this and having seen the tail lamp for this train, he walked back to the block instruments to send 'Train out of Section' as he thought to Welwyn North.

It was at this moment that the fatal mistake was made. The Officers of the LNER and Lt Colonel Mount agreed that he sent 'Train out of Section' on the wrong bell and instrument, transmitting the message not to Welwyn North but to Hatfield No 3. The instruments communicating with these two signal boxes were 3 ft 6¼ in apart but a rushed and flustered man not utterly familiar with the box could mistakenly operate the wrong instrument and thereby clear the 'Train on Line' indications from the wrong track.

At the Inquiry, Signalman Howes insisted that he never sent 'Train out of Section' on the down fast line and thereby implied that Signalman Crowe in Hatfield No 3 had lowered his starting signal (which the absence of electrical locking would have allowed him to do) without any permission from Welwyn. Howes pointed out that there was no 'Train out of Section' time recorded in his train register, but as he had just admitted that he could be several minutes behind with his booking, the assertion carried no weight. On the other hand, Crowe claimed, and Howes admitted, that Crowe had telephoned him to verify that the 'Train out of Section' signal was correct. So it must have been sent.

Signalman Crowe in Hatfield No 3 had joined the Great Northern Railway in 1896 and had been a signalman for 34 years, 17 years in Hatfield No 3. He was waiting by the bell, ready to 'ask the road' to Welwyn for train No 826 as soon as 825A cleared the section. Crowe thought that No 825A would receive a signal check at Welwyn behind No 825, so when he received 'Train out of Section' for 825A after the *usual* time of running between Hatfield and Welwyn, he actually telephoned Howes and asked 'Is that "out" Fred?' Unfortunately, he did not specify to which train he was referring, thinking that this was obvious — 825A. Fred, of course, forgetting about No 825A but thinking only of No 825 said 'Yes', and Crowe promptly asked 'Is Line Clear?' for train No 826, the 10.58 pm King's Cross to Leeds passenger, mail and parcels. Fred turned his block indicator to 'Line Clear', Crowe reversed his signal levers and a minute later No 826 ran through Hatfield at 70 mph. It was eleven coaches long and weighed only 271¾ tons, a featherweight for the powerful 'K3' 2-6-0 No 4009.

As soon as he had given Crowe 'Line Clear', Fred Howes lowered his down fast line signals, his advanced starting signal having been unlocked all this time by the 'Line Clear' he had obtained from Welwyn North a minute or so before. The fact that the 'Line Clear' was showing on the Welwyn North instrument did not register with Fred, or the fact that he had been able to 'pull off' without,

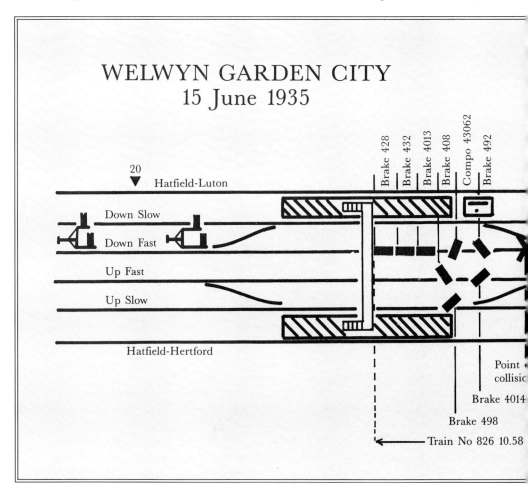

apparently, the need to go through the routine of 'getting the road'. No 825A was down to 15 mph when Fred pulled off his down fast line signals for, as he thought, No 826. The driver of 'Atlantic' 4-4-2 No 4441 took off the brakes and let the train roll, waiting to see the aspect of the starting signal beyond the signal box. Within seconds of the Welwyn home signal being lowered, the signal box indicator for the berth track circuit showed 'Occupied'. If Fred saw this it did not alarm him, although the running time for an express from Hatfield to Welwyn was 2½ minutes. He seemed to be working in a daze.

When he saw the train approaching, the fact of its crawling pace did not alert Fred to the fact that something was wrong and he did not replace the distant signal to 'Caution' behind it, but went to the window to check the doors for security and for the presence of a tail lamp. As a result, the following train, No 826, passed Welwyn's down fast distant showing 'All Right' at something over 70 mph. Seeing the tail lamp of No 825A, Fred turned back from his window to attend to the instruments and signal levers. The Luton to Hatfield empty

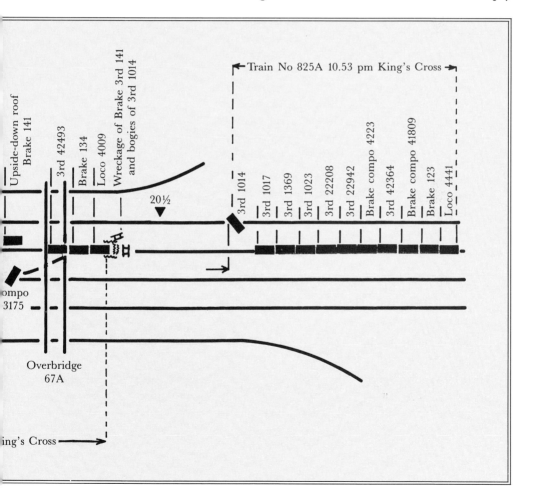

stock train was passing, he sent the 'On Line', 2 beats, bell code to Hatfield for that, noticed that he had not yet sent 'Train out of Section' for the up goods No 787 which had passed four minutes earlier and sent that code before replacing his down fast line signals behind No 825A.

The driver of No 826 had seen the Welwyn distant signal at green, but saw the home go to red just ahead of the engine. He made a full emergency brake application at once, he said. Three very long-serving and experienced guards working in No 826 said there was no brake application at all. Either way it hardly matters. Any braking was, by the time of passing the home signal, far too late to have had an effect, and 'K3' No 4009 tunnelled into the rear coach of No 825A, the 10.53 pm King's Cross, 15 yards north of Welwyn signal box, at 11.27 pm. At 11.29 pm, Signalman Fred Howes sent 'Obstruction Danger' to all the signal boxes he worked with. By that time, a taxi driver at the station had already telephoned for the emergency services and at 11.32 the first of many ambulances arrived, closely followed by the Welwyn and Hatfield fire brigades, the police, 14 doctors, nurses and first aiders. An hour later, two special trains had arrived bringing cranes, cutting gear and gangs of railwaymen. All four lines were blocked, but the up and down slow lines were quickly cleared and trains began to pass the site. Opposite the down platform the telescoped wreckage of No 826 was

The body of the first/third composite coach, eight-wheeler No 43175. This was placed third behind No 4009 on the 10.58 pm King's Cross and demonstrates the inefficiency of carriages designed with a body and a separate chassis or frame — however strong each component might be. When the impact of the collision took place, the body moved forwards on its frame and was splintered to firewood against the vehicle in front. The leading bogie of the brake van, No 4014, marshalled behind No 43175, can be seen beneath the coach, to the left of one of 43175's own displaced bogies. Modern BR coaches are built as a 'box girder' without a separate frame and are far better able to withstand end-on compression forces. (BBC Hulton Picture Library)

of the other signalman, Or so the designer hoped.

On the evening of 17 January 1918, heavy snow had fallen. The signalman at Whittington High Level switched out at 10.26 pm, pulled off his signals, wished his mates at Oswestry North and Ellesmere Junction a very good night and set off home. He left on duty at Oswestry North box signalman Edwards, a well-respected man who had worked that post for no less than 22 years, while at Ellesmere Junction (hereinafter referred to as 'Ellesmere') he left another good man, signalman Evans, who had done that job for 15 years. At 10.32 pm Edwards at Oswestry obtained permission from Evans at Ellesmere for a goods train to run through the section. The tablet was handed to the driver and the train cleared Ellesmere at 11 pm. At 12.30 am on 18 January, Evans asked Edwards for permission to run a down goods train from Ellesmere to Oswestry. Permission was granted, a tablet was removed from the Ellesmere instrument, handed to the driver and was placed in the instrument at Oswestry North after the train had cleared the section at 1.08 am. These transactions between the two men were correctly recorded in their respective train registers and were the last operations about which both men entirely agreed.

At 1.28 am Evans at Ellesmere said he had asked Edwards for a release so that he could remove a tablet from his instrument to enable down goods No 101 to run to Oswestry. Evans certainly removed a tablet from his instrument and gave it to the driver Sockett — the difficulty is that Edwards denied all knowledge of the transaction, and indeed there was no record of it in his train register. If he had been feeling very tired he could, having carried out the routine with the instrument, forgotten to make the necessary entries in 'the book' and gone back to his armchair. At 1.49 am Edwards at Oswestry asked Evans 'Is Line Clear?' for up goods No 2. Evans told the subsequent Inquiry that he did not acknowledge this bell code but went to the telephone and asked Edwards, 'Has the goods arrived?' Both men agreed on this and Evans even admitted that he had not specified which goods he meant because he thought it was obvious that he must have been referring to down goods No 101. Edwards, however, had no knowledge of, or no memory of, this train and thought Evans was referring to the goods which had cleared Oswestry at 1.08 am and therefore replied, 'Yes, long ago'.

This reply, Evans told the Inquiry, satisfied him and he then *gave the necessary release* to Edwards so that a tablet could be withdrawn from the Oswestry instrument. If Evans had had his thoughts fixed on Down goods 101, his 15 years' experience of the running times of goods trains up the bank to Oswestry would have told him instantly that it was barely possible for the goods to have arrived in 20 minutes, and impossible that it had cleared 'long ago'. He ought then to have realized that he was at cross-purposes with his mate, but in fact all this evidence of misunderstood conversations was just so much blarney. What stands out as bold as Ribblehead viaduct is the outrageous statement from Evans that, having been misled by Edwards, he gave a release to that man's tablet instrument. All the misunderstandings in the world could not have lifted the lock on that bottom slide; an electric current was required and as there was already a tablet out of the circuit it was quite impossible that the electro-magnet could have been energized legitimately. That Edwards did remove a tablet is a matter of fact, but he could only have done so after some false current was fed into the system. He gave the tablet to driver Williams, and up goods No 2 steamed away down the bank at 1.51 am.

Meanwhile, down goods 101 was labouring up the grade, a Cambrian Railways 0-6-0 with 45 wagons on a 1 in 80 bank. Fireman Dyke was busy with his shovel between the tender and the furnace door while driver Sockett kept a sharp look-out. Up goods No 2 consisted of another Cambrian Railways 0-6-0 hauling 22 wagons. The two trains approached each other on a long curve, in a cutting, in pitch darkness. Their closing speed was approximately 35 mph. As soon as driver Sockett saw the lights of the other train, he shut off steam, braked, shouted a warning to his mate — and jumped. The men on No 2 goods also took their respective headers into the snow, but fireman Dyke, preoccupied with the fire on his hard-pressed engine, was slow to react and was still on the footplate when the collision occurred. He was killed, leaving a widow and a baby son (who himself became a footplateman and was still alive in 1988).

After the crash, each driver, dazed and covered in snow, groped his way back to his engine and dug in the spilt coal to discover whether he had the right tablet, and each was thoroughly reassured to discover that he had the correct one for the section and that therefore it was the other man that was at fault. Imagine their astonishment when each went to accuse the other and discovered that they *both* had the right tablet. The 'impossible' had happened.

The collision occurred three-quarters of a mile from Oswestry North box, but signalman Edwards claimed that the did not hear the thunder of the crash and knew nothing about it until the guard of No 2 goods came dashing into the box with the news at 2.10 am. From this it would appear that Edwards had gone to sleep shortly after the departure of the up train until woken by the entry of the guard. On hearing the news, he at once telephoned Evans and, according to Edwards, Evans replied, 'Good God! Hadn't you cleared it?' To which Edwards replied, 'Certainly not. I know nothing about the goods.' With that, Edwards rushed out of his box and along the line towards the scene of the crash. On his way he met driver Williams coming back and asked him, 'Have you got the right tablet?' This was an odd question since Edwards had only handed him the tablet a few minutes before. 'Yes,' replied Williams with a bitterness that can only be guessed at, 'and so has Sockett.'

At the Inquiry, Evans denied Edwards' account of the discovery of the crash. Evans said that at 2.02 am (just about the moment when the crash occurred) Edwards had telephoned him and asked, 'Where is the Wrexham goods?' (the down goods 101). To which Evans replied, 'It is with you.' 'No it isn't,' retorted Edwards. At 2.10 am Edwards had advised Evans of the crash.

The conflicting evidence given by the signalmen, the utter lack of independent witnesses and the sheer 'impossibility' of the event caused the Inspecting Officer, Colonel Pringle, to state in his report: 'This is the most difficult case I have ever had to deal with, there is no evidence to prove what happened. I hold that both men have something to hide and that one or both of them were not working the traffic in accordance with the regulations.' Mr Sayers, the Telegraph Superintendent of the Midland Railway, was brought in to investigate the crux of the matter — how it was that two tablets could have been withdrawn, for all practical purposes, simultaneously, from a system of circuitry expressly designed to prevent that happening.

Mr Sayers found that the lineside overhead wires carrying the telegraph circuits between Oswestry and Ellesmere were immediately above the long-section tablet wire, and that weight of snow had caused the telegraph wire to be forced down into contact with the long-section tablet wire. Both these circuits used an 'earth return' system rather than a wire return circuit. Thus, if the handle of the single-needle telegraph instrument was pegged over by either or both of the signalmen, the telegraph instrument's battery could have been made to feed current into the tablet instrument circuit. As the telegraph wires had been touching the tablet wire, the signalmen would have had difficulty in working their instruments in the usual way and might have resorted to illegal means, relying on their memories and their train registers to keep a track of where the trains were. Edwards, as we have seen, had forgotten about down goods 101.

Another possibility for illegal operation, due to difficulties with the instruments during bad weather, was the use of the 'Phonophore' telephone system. This actually used the same wire as the long-section tablet instruments, and whilst the cabinet covering the live wires of this instrument in Ellesmere was locked, that at Oswestry North was easy to open. All that was required to raise a current for the tablet instrument was to fix 'jump leads' from one to the other.

Colonel Pringle recommended that the 'Phonophore' telephone circuits should be transferred from the long-section tablet wire to the telegraph wire, that a wired earth should be provided for the vital tablet circuits and that the rather poorly designed McKenzie & Holland tablet instruments be replaced by the much more robust, electrically speaking, design of Tyer & Co. Two years later this work had still not been done. As to the fate of Edwards and Evans, the Ministry of Transport report is silent. We will never know what they had done that snowy night and we never will — although one can guess. They took their terrible secret with them to the grave. And no-one answered to his widow for the death of fireman Dyke.

CHAPTER 8

Abermule

1921

DELIBERATE INTERFERENCE WITH THE SINGLE LINE INSTRUMENTS AS at Parkhall was a unique event, but there have been innumerable, reported and unreported, mishandlings of the tablet, staff or token once it was withdrawn from its instrument. In 1985, 'somewhere in the north of England', the signalman at a junction of two single lines removed one tablet from each instrument because he had two trains waiting to leave on their respective journeys — a diesel railcar to go east and a ballast train to go west. He put each tablet in its pouch, placed the pouches on the table, pulled his levers and then took the diesel railcar's tablet outside and gave it to the driver. Without checking it, the driver placed it on the driving console and went on his way. The signalman returned to the signal box to pick up the other tablet and then saw that he had given the 'westbound' tablet to the eastbound train. Thinking that he could rectify his error by driving with the correct tablet to the signalbox at the opposite end of the section, the signalman got in his car and hurried away.

The driver of the railcar suddenly laid his eye on the pouched tablet about half-way through the section. Not wanting to believe what he saw, he snatched it up for a closer look — there was no doubt about it, he had come away with the wrong one. Thinking that he could rectify his error by taking the tablet back to the signalman who had given it to him, he stopped the train, and, to the consternation of the passengers, proceeded to drive back the way he had come. On arrival at the junction, the driver found only the puzzled and impatient crew of the ballast train waiting to be allowed home.

The signalman, meanwhile, had arrived at the other end of the section. He hung around for a while, decided that the train was not coming and drove back to his own box where he found an intensely inquisitive reception committee awaiting him. Only passengers remained 'in the dark'. The tablet problem was rectified, the trains went on their respective ways and the railwaymen thought that the job was 'squared up'. Unfortunately for them, one or some of the passengers wrote to Headquarters, described their trip and asked if this was permissible behaviour.

It was this kind of tablet confusion which caused the Abermule crash. Abermule station was a pretty, stone-built wayside call on the Cambrian Railways' main line from Oswestry to Aberystwyth; it was also the junction for the sleepy little Kerry branch, but that does not concern us here. The signal box was at the east end of the down platform close to the Kerry road level crossing. In the signal box there were neither instruments nor gate wheel. The signalman went out to the lane to close the gates and he went to the instrument room, next to the booking office, to work the tablet instruments. The signal box housed a frame of 22 levers; 17 for points and signals, one as an interlocking lever for the six-lever ground frame at the west end of the layout, and four spare levers. The single track railway came from Montgomery, 3½ miles to the east, to the crossing loop between the platforms at Abermule and continued westwards, uphill towards Newtown, the next block station.

At the Montgomery end, the facing points to the passing loop were 155 yards from the signal box and worked from there, but at the Newtown end the facing points were nearly 200 yards from the box and had to be worked from the ground frame. The signalman released the ground frame's levers by reversing his interlocking lever, and a porter then set the points and operated the 'slots' on the up and down line signals protecting the junction. The signalman could pull his levers to operate either his down or up signals at the west end of the layout, but the arms would not drop unless the porter at the ground frame had taken off his controlling 'slot'. This dual control operated in regard to lowering the signals, but once they were lowered either the signalman or the porter on the ground frame could place them to danger simply by throwing his lever and replacing the 'slot' control.

On early turn in Abermule signal box on 21 January 1921 was Bill Jones. He was 60 years old and had spent all his 32 years' service at Abermule. Starting as porter in 1888, he became a signal-porter in 1891 and that was the job he was doing in 1921 except that, since 1918, he had had the grade and the pay of signalman Class 6. Working with him that day was a 15-year-old booking clerk, Francis Thompson, with two years' service, and a 17-year-old porter, Ernie Rogers, with four years' service. John Parry, the regular station-master, was on leave, and the vacancy was being covered by a reliefman, Frank Lewis. Lewis had served the Cambrian Railways for 24 years and had been a goods guard before going out as a reliefman at minor stations. He was without doubt an outsider and considerably junior in service to Bill Jones. It is interesting to surmise that there was some hostility towards Frank Lewis from Bill, the 'old hand' on his home ground, who felt that he was quite capable of looking after the station for the day without the assistance of upstart guards.

At 10.53 am, a down goods left Abermule for the four-mile run to Newtown, and the points at the Newtown end of the station were left in the 'loop to main' position. The next down train was the 10.05 am Whitchurch to Aberystwyth

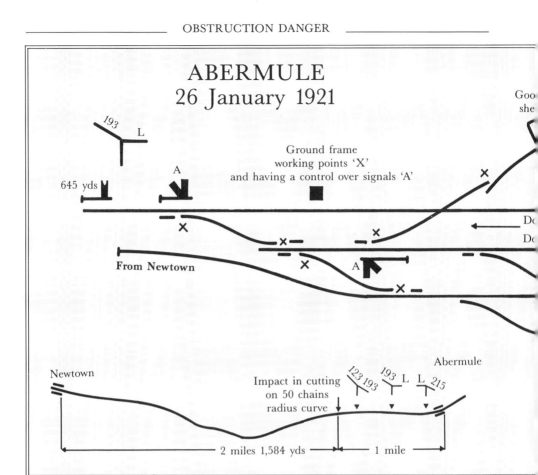

ABERMULE
26 January 1921

193 L

645 yds

A

Ground frame
working points 'X'
and having a control over signals 'A'

Goo
she

X

From Newtown

Do
Do

A

Newtown

Impact in cutting
on 50 chains
radius curve

123 193 193 L L 215

Abermule

2 miles 1,584 yds → | ← 1 mile →

Abermule station in about 1958 with old-hand signalman Bill Jones's signal box in the centre of the view. A coach is standing on the Kerry branch line. The station office housing the tablet instruments is on the left near the crossing gates. (Lens of Sutton)

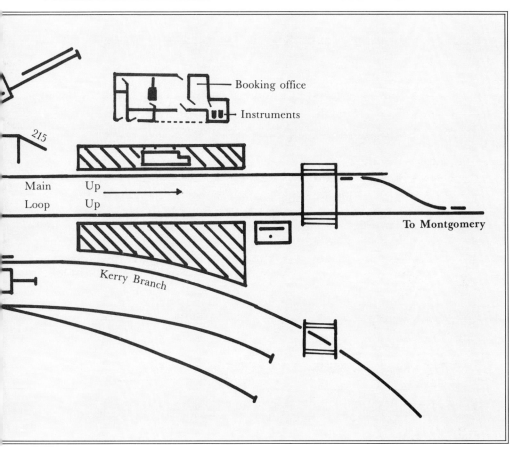

Booking office

Instruments

215

Main   Up

Loop   Up

Kerry Branch

To Montgomery

Abermule station looking towards Newtown. Relief station-master Lewis would have handed the wrong tablet to the driver of the stopping train from about this point and the train would then have left, heading for Newtown around the far curve in the line. (Lens of Sutton)

stopping passenger, due at Abermule at 11.57 am where it was scheduled to 'cross' an up express, the 10.25 am Aberystwyth. The station-master usually took his lunch-break at 11.20 am so as to be on hand to supervise the operation of the crossing movement, but on this day Frank Lewis did not leave the station until 11.35 am and was not present for the first part of the transactions over the tablets. At 11.50 am Bill Jones was in the instrument room while Francis Thompson and Ernie Rogers were eating their meal in the booking office. At 11.52 am signalman Humphreys of Montgomery 'asked the road' for the 10.05 am Whitchurch and Bill gave the necessary release for the Montgomery machine by pressing down the plunger on the tablet machine at Abermule. Humphreys withdrew his tablet, put it in its pouch and handed it to the driver of the train. At 11.53 am he sent 2 beats, the 'Train Entering Section' signal, to Bill Jones. The 10.05 Whitchurch was 3 minutes late.

Bill then telephoned Moat Lane Junction, 8½ miles away, to enquire as to the whereabouts of the 10.25 Aberystwyth and was told that the train was 'just leaving'. The up express was therefore 'right time', and Bill knew then that the express and the stopping train would definitely be crossing, as booked, at Abermule. On his way through the booking office he said to the lads, 'The fast's off Moat Lane and the stopper's left Montgomery'. As he went out on to the platform, he saw Frank Lewis talking to the permanent way inspector a little way down the yard but he did not go and tell the 'station boss' what the situation was; instead he went away to his signal box.

At 11.56 am, the bell on the Newtown-Abermule tablet instrument rang one beat. Rogers promptly answered it, acknowledged the 4 beats code which followed and 'held down' on the plunger to send an electrical release to the Newtown instrument. This was correct, except that Rogers was not permitted to use the instrument and ought to have called Lewis in from the yard — but rules have never stopped a keen lad yet. Having released a tablet at Newtown, Rogers then walked to the ground frame in order to re-set the points for the main line so that the express could enter the station on the straight run. Frank Lewis was still standing in the yard, talking. Francis Thompson went to the level crossing so that he could have the fun of having the engine pass within inches of his nose as he stood by to take the tablet off the firemen of the incoming stopping train. He, too, was forbidden to handle such things. When, at 11.59 am, the 2 beats of the 'Train entering Section' bell rang out on the Newtown-Abermule tablet instrument, there was no one in the room to hear it.

The 10.05 Whitchurch stopping train arrived in the passing loop at 12.02 pm. Thompson took the tablet from its fireman and ran with it to the instrument room, eager to operate the machine, but Frank Lewis, hearing the down train arrive, had come hurrying up the yard and, in coming through the booking hall, had actually collided headlong with the flying Thompson. This was the moment of confusion which perverted the entire sequence of the action. The young lad, knowing that he was not permitted to handle the tablet, thrust it guiltily into the hands of Lewis saying, 'Change this tablet, Frank. I'll go and see to the tickets'. But Lewis said that Thompson had said, 'Take this tablet to the down train, Frank. They're going on'. Each stuck firmly to his own account, and probably neither quotation is entirely accurate, but it seems that Lewis's variation is the most unlikely. Thompson had come running from the newly-arrived train carrying the tablet and was obviously intent on working the instrument — he was running towards the instrument room. It does not seem at all likely that Thompson would then have said 'Take this tablet to the down train', and much more likely that he had said what he claimed he had said: 'Change this tablet, I'll see to the tickets'. Both agreed that Lewis, in reply to whatever was first said, asked Thompson, 'Where's the up fast?' To which Thompson had replied vaguely, 'About Moat Lane'. Why Thompson should have said this when he knew from signalman Bill Jones that the express had passed Moat Lane eight minutes before must be put down to Thompson's fluster and lack of experience. Frank Lewis, with over a score of years' experience, took the word of a confused boy, assumed that the Controller had altered the usual crossing arrangements, took the tablet without reading its inscription, and said to the boy, 'Go and tell Bill Jones to let the down train go'.

Still these mistakes need not have been fatal. Ernie Rogers, down at the ground frame, was preparing for the arrival of the express. Only he knew for certain that it was on its way. Lewis had seen Rogers at the ground frame and assumed that, as the west-end points lay normally for the main line, Rogers was there to switch them and let the stopping train out from the loop line. Lewis hurried along the platform and handed the tablet in its pouch to fireman Evans on the engine of the 'stopper'. The fireman took it without looking at it and hung it on a convenient hook. Driver Jones did not see the hand-over for he was going round his engine with the oil-can as was the wont of old-time drivers whenever they got the chance. Ernie Rogers was astonished to see the down loop starting signal arms fall to 'Right Away', and promptly threw over the lever in the ground frame, thus dropping the counter-balance weight of 'slot' control which raised the arm to 'Danger'. He then stepped outside the hut to wave to signalman Bill Jones, asking for a release on the west-end facing points so that he could re-set them for the incoming express. He then saw Frank Lewis on the platform waving 'Right Away'. Rogers then assumed that something must have happened to stop the up express, so he went back inside the ground frame hut and reversed his slot lever. The down starting signal arm lowered once more. The way ahead into the single track section was open. The slow train started.

Frank Lewis walked back into the instrument room intending to send 'Train Entering Section' to Newtown for the slow train. As soon as he entered the room he saw the instrument's indicator and his blood must have frozen in his veins. The Newtown-Abermule tablet instrument already had its red 'tablet out' indication showing. That could only mean that Newtown had withdrawn a tablet — unless some other member of his staff had sent the 'on line' bell. This was impossible because he knew how they were disposed around the station; however, clutching desperately at straws, he telephoned Newtown and asked, 'Has the up fast left you yet?' To which the Newtown foreman replied, 'I put it "on" to you six minutes ago'. Lewis ran out of the office and on to the platform yell-ing to Bill Jones that the down train had gone to Newtown with the wrong tablet. The train was already out of sight thanks to Lewis's delay in facing facts. Bill Jones tried to attract the driver's attention by waving the arm of the up distant signal, but the train was beyond the signal and beyond all help.

The stopping train was hauled by Cambrian Railways 4-4-0 No 82 weighing 70 tons 5 cwt. Its train was made up as follows:

	tons	cwt
Cambrian 8-wheel composite No 233	23	10
LNWR 8-wheel 3rd No 260	31	00
Cambrian 8-wheel composite No 333	26	10
LNWR 8-wheel composite No 2850	19	00
LNWR 8-wheel brake van No 8396	24	00
LNWR 8-wheel brake van No 8725	24	00

One mile from Abermule the train entered a left-hand bend in a cutting which considerably restricted the driver's forward view. The engine was steaming hard on a rising grade, and the fireman was hard at work. Driver and fireman never knew what hit them. The 10.25 from Aberystwyth was hauled by Cambrian Railways 4-4-0 No 95 weighing 71½ tons. Its train was made up as follows:

	tons	cwt
LNWR 6-wheel van No 8755	13	00
Cambrian 8-wheel composite No 310	26	10
Cambrian 8-wheel tea-car No 324	26	10
GWR 8-wheel composite No 7730	27	11
LNWR 8-wheel brake van No 8093	21	00
LNWR 8-wheel composite No 3160	31	00
LNWR 8-wheel brake composite No 6109	32	00

This train was driven by John Pritchard-Jones with passed-fireman Albert Owen. They entered the cutting running downhill at 50 mph with steam shut off. At a range of 350 yards, Pritchard-Jones saw the smoke of No 82 rising in a column above the cutting top and we may justifiably surmise that his heart missed at least one beat. He braked instantly and blew his whistle, but the column of smoke continued to pillar skywards as the other engine laboured hard against the rising grade. The brakes of the express train bit hard against the wheels but not hard enough to save the situation; the 270¾ tons of the express was still making 30 mph when it rammed head-on into the 190¼ tons of stopping train also running at about 30 mph. A head-on impact of 60 mph. The total length of both trains was 252 yards before the crash; afterwards, the wreckage covered a line 180 yards long. Two engines and tenders and five coaches normally 115 yards long occupied 50 yards. The boiler of No 95 was torn from its frame. It spun round and hit the ballast facing the way it had come, while No 82, ripping its front end to shreds, climbed up over the wreck of 95. Carriages were thrown

Irresistible force meets immovable object — result chaos. The boiler of No 95, the fast-moving express train engine, is lying in front of the camera, its firebox to the right. No 82 is rearing over the tender of No 95. Notice that one shattered cylinder can be seen between the mangled frames of No 82, still dangling on its piston rod. (BBC Hulton Picture Library)

right and left, were telescoped through, crushed and disintegrated. Eleven passengers were killed on the spot, 36 were taken to hospital and of these three died later. Driver Jones and fireman Evans off No 82 on the slow train were also killed, along with the guard of the express train.

Driver Pritchard-Jones and fireman Owen had stepped outside their cab and were riding on the footsteps as the brakes ground against the wheels and the towering column of smoke came closer until the slow train came into sight around the corner. Then the two men jumped for their lives and were almost immediately buried under a hail of wood and metal as the trains met and shattered. Both men were knocked unconscious. When Albert came round he heard, among the other screams and groans, his driver's voice, calling to him. Owen crawled through the wreckage and with some difficulty located his mate. He offered to fetch a doctor but Pritchard-Jones did not want a doctor just then, he only wanted to be reassured that he was carrying the right tablet. Albert Owen went off, badly hurt, to search the wreckage and came back with the two tablets. One was marked 'Newtown-Abermule', the other 'Montgomery-Abermule'. He knelt beside

On the extreme left of the view is LNWR eight-wheel brake van No 8093. Between it and the rearing wheels of No 82 there are three eight-wheeled carriages and a six-wheeled van. Almost at 90° to the rails is the Cambrian Railways' tea-car No 324. Crushed between that and the engine is an eight and a six-wheeled coach. (BBC Hulton Picture Library)

Pritchard-Jones and showed him. 'We are all right, John; look, it was them that had the wrong tablet'. His conscience clear, Pritchard-Jones consented to his fireman going off to get help.

George Jones and Albert Evans paid with their lives and the lives of 15 others for their neglect of the most basic rule in single line work — to read the legend engraved on the tablet before setting off. The station staff at Abermule made one mistake after another, and if any one of those mistakes had not been made then the disaster would not have happened. They also were responsible for the deaths of 17 people and 36 injured through their slap-happy working and — perhaps — a little bit of jealousy.

CHAPTER 9

Thorpe-le-Soken

1931

THE ABERMULE STATION STAFF HAD VAULTED EFFORTLESSLY OVER ALL obstacles placed in their way by the rule book and common sense to produce that fearful smash, and any one man, doing his job properly, could have saved the situation. At Thorpe-le-Soken, only one man, doing his job properly, could have saved the situation. At Thorpe-le-Soken, only one man suffered from an inexplicable mental aberration and caused a collision.

Thorpe was, in 1931, a pleasant junction station in the depths of the Essex countryside. The station staff got on well together and had found the most carefree — rather than careless — way of working the place, bending — rather than breaking — the rules, although to have omitted to light the lamp in the down Clacton line starting signal for three years was a considerable fracture which might qualify for the *Guinness Book of Records*. The layout at the station was a little unusual; the double track came in from Colchester and appeared to continue eastwards through the station as double track but was, in fact, two single lines — the left-hand track in the easterly direction went to Walton on the Naze, the other to Clacton. Both rose for ¾ mile eastwards from the station to a farm crossing before the Clacton line fell steeply at 1 in 83 leaving the Walton line to continue its climb. The Walton line embankment was like a wall on the left of the Clacton line until, nearly a mile from Thorpe, the two lines swung apart, at that point the Walton line being ten feet higher than the Clacton.

The signal box at Thorpe-le-Soken was on the up platform and from there the signalman worked with Weeley, towards Colchester, to Kirby Cross on the Walton line and the Great Holland or Clacton, depending on whether Great Holland box was switched in or not. The single tracks were operated with the Tyers No 6 tablet instruments and the starting signals for each branch were locked at 'Danger' until the correct tablet had been removed from the instrument. The lever working the branch starting signal could only be pulled once after a tablet

had been removed; when the lever was returned to 'Danger' after the passing of the train, it could not be pulled again until the first tablet had been restored to the circuit and a fresh tablet had been obtained. This sounds as if every eventuality was covered, but this was not the case. There was no facing trap point in either branch line to prevent the unauthorized exit of a train from Thorpe along either route. No one thought anything of this, it was no more or less than was provided elsewhere.

On 17 January 1931, porter-signalman Appleton was on early turn in Thorpe-le-Soken box. The night was dark but clear and cold, and the station lay quiet, the dim, yellow light from the oil lamps silhouetting or lighting areas here and there. At 5.41 am, Mr Appleton gave 'Line Clear' on the down main line to Weeley for a goods train to approach Thorpe, and at 5.53 he gave Clacton a release for a tablet so that the Walton on the Naze newspaper train could leave. At 5.58 the 'Paper train' was belled 'On Line' from Clacton. Moving in the

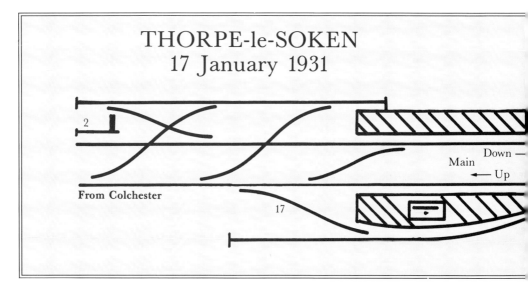

THORPE-le-SOKEN
17 January 1931

2

From Colchester

17

Down —
Main
— Up

Looking towards Walton on the Naze/Clacton from the up platform at Thorpe le Soken. What appears to be a double track is in fact parallel single tracks, the left-hand leading to Walton, the right-hand to Clacton. The double-headed train is standing on the down main line, facing Walton on the Naze with the signals raised for the Clacton direction. On the extreme right is the 'back of platform' line to Clacton whence the runaway started in 1931. (Photomatic)

dimly-lit interior of his box, Appleton acknowledged the 2 beats and 'asked the road' for this train to Kirby Cross, on the Walton branch. The Kirby Cross signalman gave the release and Appleton removed a tablet from the Walton on the Naze branch instrument. Three minutes later the newspaper train steamed into the 'back platform' at Thorpe, two six-wheeled vans hauled by a big 'B12' Class 4-6-0 No 8578. The engine stopped right outside the signal box and Porter Southgate, standing below the box window, caught the tablet in its pouch as the signalman dropped it down to him. Appleton watched as the tablet was handed

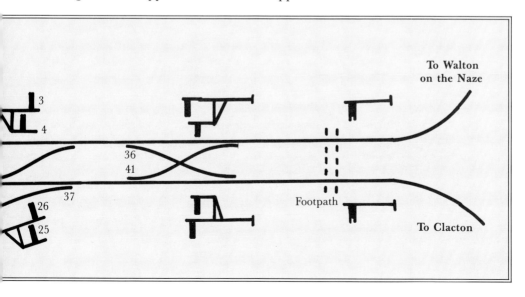

to the driver and deftly caught the Clacton-Thorpe-le-Soken tablet as the porter threw it up to him. Appleton went inside, closing the window against the cold, placed the tablet in the instrument and gave 'Train out of Section' to Clacton at 6.02 am.

Immediately Clacton asked 'Is Line Clear?' for a 'light engine' and this Appleton accepted under the 'Warning Arrangement', 3-5-5 on the bell. The signalman at Clacton would then inform the engine driver that the line was clear only as far as the home signal at Thorpe, and this permitted Appleton to continue with the shunting that would be fouling the statutory 'clearing point', the standard safety distance of 440 yards which had to be kept clear ahead of a home signal before a train could approach it.

Having given the 'Warning' for the 'light engine', signalman Appleton pulled over lever 17 so that the 'B12' could begin to run round its train preparatory to leaving for Walton. The engine drew forwards on to the up main line, the points were closed and it then ran back through the station to stop clear of points 37. The down goods train was now close to the station, so Appleton reversed lever 37 and then pulled lever No 2 to bring the goods train within the protection of his down home signal, replacing No 2 when the train had passed it. The time was 6.05 am. Appleton stood and watched the approach of the goods train, a headlamp and the red light of the fire around the cab and on the drifting smoke. He then heard the newspaper train start from behind the box but gave it no more thought than to think that it was drawing up the starting signal ready for when the signalman should set the route across to the Walton branch and lower the signals.

Appleton concentrated on the goods; when it stopped he could alter the points ahead of it to let the newspaper train proceed. One minute later, at 6.06 am, he received 'Train Entering Section' from Clacton for the 'light engine', the goods came to a stand and he turned to walk to point lever 41. Only then did he see the receding red tail lamp of the newspaper train beyond 41 points and heading back towards Clacton. The sight caused signalman-porter Appleton considerable mental anguish, so much so that instead of sending 'Train Running Away', 2-5-5 on the bell, to Clacton's signalman who might then have been able to stop the departure of the 'light engine' which had only that second been sent 'on line', Appleton ran out of his box, along the platform, waving his arms at the disappearing train and shouting, 'Where's he off to?' to no one in particular. Between 1½ and 2 minutes were wasted on these panic-stricken manoeuvres before he returned to the signal box to send the, by now, entirely futile 2-5-5. He may as well have sent 6 bells there and then.

After the 'B12' had been re-coupled to its train, guard Elliston had given the 'Right Away' to driver Sheldrake and got into his van where there were a lot of bundles to be sorted before arrival at Walton. In giving the 'Right Away', he did not actually mean the train to leave there and then but was merely conveying to the driver that the train could leave whenever the signals were cleared for it — 'everything's all right as far as I'm concerned, you go when you can'. The guard had been happy with his bundles and had given no more thought to the outside world as he felt the train jerk and start, while his driver and fireman had gone happily into an occupied single line section for which they did not have the tablet, and back in the direction from which they had just come, never once realising that they were on the wrong line or that they had passed the starting signal at 'Danger'.

The differences between the two branch lines were great. The Walton branch rose steadily all the way to Kirby Cross with only one bridge, carrying a road over the line, and two long curves, while the Clacton line fell steeply and suddenly and then ran level with the Walton branch ten feet above before passing over a girder bridge which would have boomed as the engine passed over it. All these landmarks were the stock-in-trade of an experienced footplate man, the way in which he found his way along the line — especially after dark — yet neither driver Sheldrake nor his fireman, Mr Wright, noticed. Driver Sheldrake had been in railway service for 37 years with 17 years as a driver, most of the time working out of Clacton.

The 'light engine' was a 'D16' Class 4-4-0 No 8781, running chimney first, and it entered the deep, curved cutting near Great Holland signal box as the runaway entered it from the Thorpe end. Both trains had left from their respective starting points simultaneously and they met, head-on, at the centre of the cutting close to the closed signal box. If only that box had been open! Forward visibility in the curved cutting was at best 470 yards, and the line was falling at 1 in 100 for the 'D16'. The powerful and lightly loaded 'B12' came up the hill tender first at about 20 mph, and the 'D16' was making about the same speed. In the ensuing impact, the 'D16' climbed over the 'B12's' tender and both Sheldrake and Wright were killed instantly while driver Goodridge and fireman Wilding of the 'B12' were seriously injured. The Ministry of Transport's Inspector, Lt Colonel Anderson, recommended the installation of trap points at Thorpe to prevent this accident from happening again. He was ignored.

CHAPTER 10

Fakenham

1931

F IVE MONTHS AFTER THORPE-LE-SOKEN, THE LNER SUFFERED
another single line collision, this time at Fakenham on the Wymondham
to Wells-on-Sea branch. The branch was a single track from Dereham to
Wells and was worked with the wooden train staff and paper ticket system in
conjunction with block telegraph instruments. The signalman asked 'Is Line
Clear?' on an ordinary, double line instrument, but a train could not leave his
station unless the wooden train staff was present. It could be on the engine of
the departing train, or it could be in the signal box; in the latter case the train

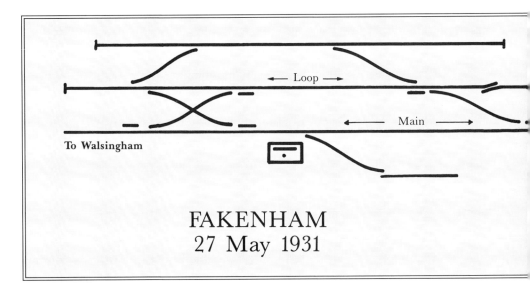

To Walsingham

FAKENHAM
27 May 1931

could depart under the authority of a paper ticket filled in by the station master or signalman authorizing the driver to proceed and confirming to him that the wooden train staff was at the station. The signal boxes working with Fakenham were Walsingham, 4.8 miles to the north, and Great Ryburgh, 2¾ miles to the south.

Coming from the south a driver met a set of facing points which could take his train into a bay platform; these points were 415 yards from the signal box and were worked by an electric motor run by batteries switched on by the movement of lever 32*. Protecting these points was a bracket signal; the higher, right-hand arm routed down the main line and was operated by No 36 lever, while the lower, left-hand arm, lever No 33, routed into the bay. Of course, levers 32, 33 and 36 were mechanically interlocked so that it was impossible to pull them unless the points were correctly set. There was also a track circuit on the bay line which, if occupied, prevented lever 33 from being pulled. The down distant and both the home signals, 33 and 36, were interlinked with the block instruments so that, if any one of them was not fully at the 'Danger' or 'Caution' position, the signalman could not give a 'Line Clear' indication to the signalman at Great Ryburgh. Immediately north of the north end of the platform the Norwich road crossed the railway on the level, and north of the crossing there was another set of facing points leading to the passing loop, used when trains had to cross each other on the single track. At the north end of this loop, some 260 yards long, stood Fakenham North signal box.

On 27 May 1931, a fine, dry day, signalman Holland was on duty on the early turn. At 9.06 am, Walsingham asked 'Is Line Clear?' for the 9.06 am Wells to Norwich passenger train, and Holland accepted this under the 'Warning' arrange-

* These had once been worked from Fakenham South box, abolished before 1931.

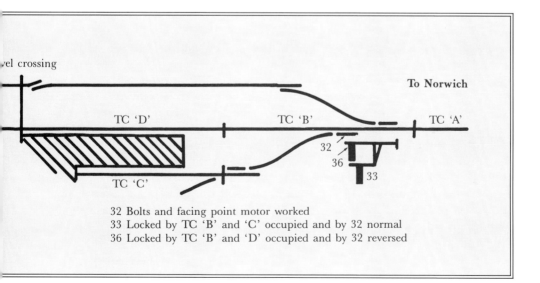

32 Bolts and facing point motor worked
33 Locked by TC 'B' and 'C' occupied and by 32 normal
36 Locked by TC 'B' and 'D' occupied and by 32 reversed

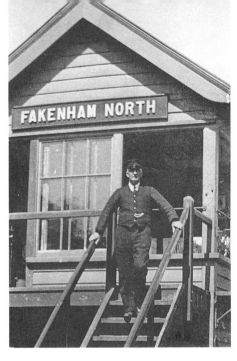

ment, 3-5-5 on the bell. The train left Walsingham at 9.20 and came down the hill through the cutting into Fakenham station at 9.28, a typical LNER country branch train consisting of three ancient six-wheeled coaches with a six-wheeled brake van behind and a couple of six-wheeled milk tankers on the back, the motive power being a stalwart of the line since way back in Great Eastern Railway days, an 'E4' 2-4-0, No 7486. Signalman Holland had already 'blocked back' outside the down home signal towards Ryburgh*, and gave the 'E4's' driver, Mr Middleton, a green flag to pass at 'Danger' the up starting signal. The driver knew what was required, went on over points 32 and stopped with the rear milk tanker clear of the points. Signalman Holland then reversed lever No 32 and lowered signal 33. The little 2-4-0 snorted and heaved its train back up the hill and into the bay line. When the track circuits were clear, Holland put the signal back to 'Danger', pushed lever No 32 normal into the frame to set the road for the down main and sent 2-1 on the bell to Great Ryburgh to 'clear the block'.

The indicator needle to show which way the points were lying, and which should be showing that they were lying correctly shut, dropped to the 'Wrong' position. Holland waited for the batteries to wind the motors round until the blades were re-set, but the needle hung obstinately at 'Wrong'. He reversed the lever and then pushed it once more into the frame. Still no correct result at the points. He therefore pulled the lever fully over to the reverse position, and the needle flicked up to 'R' (for 'reversed'). He was then able to give 'Obstruction Removed', 2-1 on the bell, to cancel the 'blocking back' bell code to Ryburgh. At once the signalman at Great Ryburgh 'asked the road' for the down passenger train, the 8.17 am from Norwich, and Holland accepted this under the 'Warning', which he was perfectly entitled to do. He then telephoned the sta-

---

* Bell code 3-3 and instrument set to 'Train on Line' to permit the occupation of the single line for shunting.

tion and asked for a porter to come to the signal box to fetch the hand-crank which would be used to wind the motor round by hand and thus close the points for the main line.

The down train left Great Ryburgh at 9.31 am. It was hauled by an 'E4' 2-4-0 No 7486 and consisted of two six-wheeled brake vans next to the engine with three six-wheeled passenger carriages behind them. The driver was A.E. Borrett and his fireman was C.R. Wrigley. The train had been standing at Great Ryburgh's starting signal for one minute before the signal was lowered, and under those conditions the driver knew that he had been accepted into the section under the 'Warning' — the section was clear but Fakenham station was blocked — and that he could therefore expect to be stopped outside Fakenham's home signal.

As his vintage train trotted through the rolling, wooded ploughlands there was bustle at Fakenham. Station foreman Youngs was loading milk churns into a brake van on the train in the bay, guard Arnold was working with his relief, guard Rycroft, stowing parcels, while on the engine driver Middleton and fireman Smith were talking to the men who were relieving them, driver Barnes and fireman Pear. The porter who had gone to fetch the hand-crank from the signal box was walking back with it towards the station when the down train approached the down homes which were both at 'Danger' — however, far from stopping, it was coasting in as if the driver was making a normal stop at the station. Middleton and Smith had got off their engine and were walking north up the platform, their backs to the down train, when the sound made them turn just in time to see No 7486 running into the bay at about 10 mph and about 25 feet from the engine they had just vacated. The two guards heard nothing but something made them look up from their work just in time to make a shout of alarm

Above *Looking towards Fakenham station, past the tender of No 7457, the latter engine's frames splayed wide at the front end.* (Austin Gill Collection)

Below *Some 'telescoping' of carriages behind No 7486 caused 12 passengers to be injured and one to be killed.* (Austin Gill Collection)

A view of the 'telescoping' taken from the bay line platform. The force of the blow has caused the buffers of the left-hand coach to bend upwards and slide over the buffers of the right-hand coach, thus directing the left-hand coach into the seating of the other. (Austin Gill Collection)

and jump out on to the platform.

The incoming train struck home at about 8 mph and drove the stationary train back against the buffers, telescoping the third coach into the second and killing one passenger. Twelve passengers and three railwaymen were injured. Both engines were derailed. Driver Borrett was 58 years old and had been a driver for 16 years with an exemplary record. He said he had first seen Fakenham's down home signals as he was passing over the M&GN line bridge about ¼ mile south of the station. He said that 'the tall one' (ie the down main home) was 'off'; 'I have seen it ever since in my mind's eye'. This was an honest enough statement — he obviously thought he saw it cleared for him and just as obviously it could not possibly have been lowered because the points were set for the bay. Had he said that he saw the bay line signal lowered, then there would have been some room for doubt, although even then the track circuit would have prevented the signal lever from being pulled. This seems to have been a case of a highly competent man seeing what he wanted to see, a true case of mental aberration.

CHAPTER 11

Sun Bank Halt, Llangollen

1945

T HE SUN BANK TRAGEDY OF 7 SEPTEMBER 1945 IS A CLASSIC CASE OF warnings left unheeded. Sun Bank Halt was 3⅝ miles from Ruabon on the double track branch to Llangollen. Turning west from the Great Western's Shrewsbury to Chester main line at Llangollen Junction, Ruabon, the line climbed at 1 in 54/80 for a mile to Acrefair before dropping almost as steeply into the valley of the river Dee along the northern side of the valley heading westwards. Immediately west of Sun Bank, the railway passed from a line cut into the hillside on to an embankment of loamy earth laid against the face of the hill for 440 yards towards Llangollen. The foot of the embankment was 10 feet above the river and 135 yards from the water's edge. It rose 40 feet above the meadows at the Sun Bank end but fell at 1 in 75 westwards. The Shropshire Union Canal, owned and maintained by the London Midland & Scottish Railway, lay on a natural terrace on the hillside, 37 feet above the embankment at the east end with the Ruabon to Llangollen county road 25 feet above the canal. The hillside rose from the water meadows on a 1 in 3 gradient for several hundred feet and was formed of a particularly hard form of slate overlaid by a moraine of clay, sand, gravel and boulders — debris left by the melting glaciers after they had carved the valley from the bedrock. Surface water running off the rocky heights soon disappeared below the surface to form underground lakes and streams in and through the permeable moraine, flowing below the canal, eroding its clay lining, and below the railway embankment to emerge in springs along its base and to permeate the meadows. Gravel and sand interspersed with slippery clay lying on glass-hard slate does not sound like the best foundation for a canal or a railway, but both survived without serious injury for a very long time, although not without signs of distress. Like the slag-heap at Aberfan.

The canal had been authorized as the Ellesmere Canal in 1793. In or around the year 1800 the canal had breached above the spot where the railway embank-

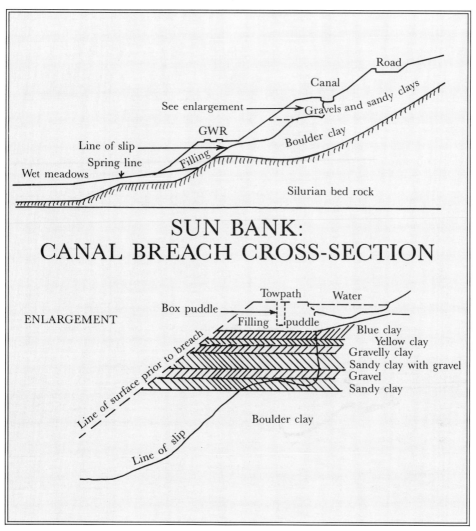

ment would be built. The resulting mudslide had formed a delta in the meadow below, and the canal bed had been cut into the hillside. In 1945, the 'kink' in the watercourse and the grassed-over delta in the field could still be seen, mute evidence of, quite literally, an underlying problem. However, matters had proceeded peacefully for a very long time. In 1847 the canal had been leased 'in perpetuity' to the London & North Western Railway. The embankment to carry the Llangollen branch railway had been constructed below the canal in 1859 and was opened to traffic on 2 June 1862. While it began lying against the hillside at the east end, it curved away as it fell towards Llangollen, until at the west end it was 200 yards from the face of the hill. There were no drains through the embankment and no drains for surface water on top of the bank. The formation was never affected by the peculiar geological conditions of the place and the icy cold, crystal springs that burst from the foot of the embankment were highly prized for tea making and drinking water by the men of the permanent way gangs charged with the maintenance of the line.

In 1921 the canal had become part of the newly formed London Midland & Scottish Railway and in 1922 four dry-stone 'counterfort' walls had been built into the face of the hill to support the canal bank at precisely the spot where it would later breach. So even then the site must have been giving cause for concern. Settlement of two bridges over the canal was such that by the 1930s both had become seriously distorted. Bridge 41 above the east end of the railway embankment was in a poor way but Bridge 42, Wenffrwd bridge, was collapsing. Sometimes the tranquil surface of the canal was excited by a whirlpool as water poured into a cavity which had opened in the canal bed. A supply of several tons of clay was always kept on the towpath for use in plugging such holes and this would suffice for a time before the vortex reappeared giving the faithful labourer, Mr Chase, more work as he attempted, single-handed, to maintain his crumbling length. In 1933 there had been a bad cave-in which he had staunched by laying sheets of corrugated iron over the hole. This seemed to be the answer and he was very pleased because for four years he had no more trouble there, then one morning in 1937 he had come along and found that the ero-

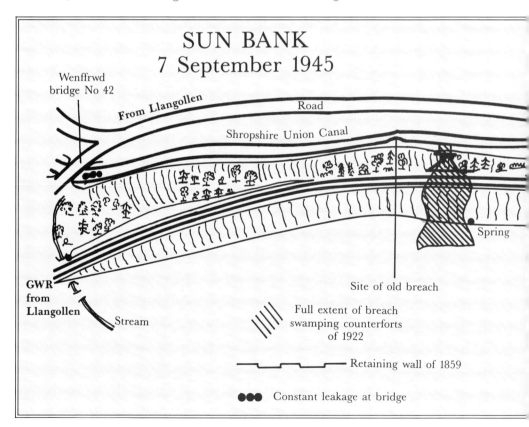

SUN BANK
7 September 1945

Wenffrwd
bridge No 42

From Llangollen   Road

Shropshire Union Canal

Spring

GWR
from
Llangollen
Stream

Site of old breach

Full extent of breach
swamping counterforts
of 1922

Retaining wall of 1859

Constant leakage at bridge

sion had been going on below the sheets and now the hole had grown so big that the iron had disappeared and there was the all too familiar vortex. Back to the spade and the pile of clay. At the same time as the 1933 whirlpool had appeared there had been a failure of the wing-wall of the Wenffrwd bridge as a hole 2 feet in diameter had opened underneath it. This little hole had a very big appetite and had swallowed several cubic yards of 'fill' before it was satisfied. In 1938 a crack 5 feet long and ⅛ inch wide had appeared along the towpath which had been corrected by digging a trench between it and the edge of the path, which was then filled with clay. Two more counterfort walls had been raised and there had been innumerable small leaks through the canal bank.

In 1939 the war had started. Plans to rebuild the crippled bridges 41 and 42 had been shelved and labourer Chase had carried on alone with his task of lengthman. In 1944 the canal had been closed to navigation but was retained as an important water supply for the local farmers, for the Monsanto chemical company at Acrefair, whose premises were authorized to abstract 11½ million gallons per day, and as a feeder to the Wolverhampton and Ellesmere Port Navigation. For six years the canal had continued, forgotten and taken for granted.

On 5 August 1945 there was an exceptionally heavy thunderstorm with continuous rainfall, at least 2 inches falling on the hill in 24 hours. One month later,

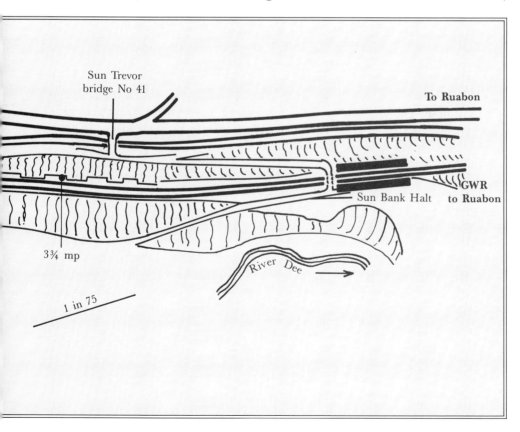

at about 3.40 am on 7 September, the canal bank breached and millions of gallons of water, falling over 40 feet, washed the railway embankment away with a breach 120 feet wide, the rails and sleepers hanging in a festoon across the gap. The power of the water was enough to wash away 3,000 cubic yards of earth, but it could not break the flimsy wires which carried the block telegraph signalling currents and the poles carrying the wires remained intact — and that was 'Sod's Law' at work.

At 4.40 am, the 3.35 am Chester to Barmouth mail and goods train left Ruabon. It was a 'D' headcode train — one where a proportion of the vehicles were fitted with the vacuum brake under the driver's control — and had an 'Is Line Clear?' code of 2-2-3. The locomotive was 2-6-0 No 6315 and the train consisted of, from the engine, 40-foot passenger brake van No 1114, 60-foot passenger brake No 75, 16 goods vehicles belonging to the GWR, LMS, LNER and SR, and a GWR 20-ton brake van.

Signalman Williams switched Trevor signal box into circuit at 4.33 am that morning. His 'Is Line Clear?' to Llangollen for the 3.35 am Chester was transmitted at 4.41 am over the wires spanning the darkness-enshrouded breach in the track. Llangollen returned 'Line Clear' and signalman Williams pulled off for the Mail. It passed him at 4.45 am. The guard of the train was Mr. F.W. Evans, aged 47, of Chester, who had been a guard since 1924 and who had worked this train all week. This is his own account of what happened:

> 'We were approaching Sun Bank Halt at about 40 mph. As I was getting ready to make out my journal and was sitting at the desk there was an impact. Then I received a number of bumps. I tried to apply the brake and then there was a terrific bump. The train had come to a stand and I went to the van door but could not open it. A fire broke out on the floor which I endeavoured to stamp out without success. I picked up my hand lamp and detonators and opened the end window and got out through that. There were rails overhanging the van and I pulled myself on top of the van using them. I pulled myself on to the rails and swarmed along and got on to the permanent way. I went back to Trevor and advised the signalman which was the first information he had had. I returned piloting the engine of the 4.45 am Ruabon to the scene of the obstruction. Ambulance and fire brigade notified. I then returned to Chester with the 8.10 am ex-Ruabon. Back of my head cut, left shoulder bruised, bump on chest so far as I know at present.'

The locomotivemen were from Croes Newydd shed. Driver David Jones, a man of 52½ years, with 35 years service on the Great Western and 25 years as a driver, was killed instantly when his engine plunged into the deep chasm at 40 mph, but his fireman, 23-year-old G.C. Joy, who had been a fireman since November 1940, had a lucky escape, cracking a bone in his left wrist and suffering from severe shock. he reported his escape laconically thus:

> 'When approaching Sun Bank Halt I was looking over the side of the engine and noticed nothing unusual as it was dark at the time. The next thing

I recollect was digging myself out of dirt and debris. I looked around but could see nothing. I then proceeded to Llangollen to report and was met by the station-master who sent me to the cottage hospital. After treatment I was sent to the War Memorial hospital, Wrexham, where I am still detained.'

Having nearly drowned in the thick mud of the breach, fireman Joy was severely shocked and dazed and in fact had no idea how he had got to Llangollen. Somehow he had got on to the main road where he was found by a Mr Robson who put him in his car and drove him to Llangollen station. Station staff here were already aware of what had happened.

Temporary (wartime recruitment) porter Humphreys had booked on duty at Llangollen at 4.30 am to meet the Mail and he waited in the darkness on the down platform for nearly half an hour in the company of shunter Sandford who caught the train each morning to go to work. When it did not come, they phoned their signalman who could offer no further information than that it had left Trevor. It was on coming out of the porters' room, having made the telephone call, that they noticed the glare of fire in the direction of Sun Bank Halt. They told their signalman who suggested that the shunter could ask the postman, who was waiting in the yard with his van to pick up the mails, to drive with the shunter along the road towards Sun Bank and see what had happened. The postman and shunter Sandford were soon back with the news that the train had 'overturned' and was on fire. At that the signalman was informed, and the police and all emergency services alerted, while porter Humphreys ran to fetch the station-master. When Humphreys got back to the station he found fireman Joy with Mr Robson. Joy was thoroughly shaken and could give no useful information, so they drove him to the cottage hospital at once.

When guard Evans arrived back at Trevor signal box, a walk of almost two miles, he was very dazed, shaken and bleeding profusely from a bad head wound. Nevertheless, he had placed his three detonators ¾ mile to the rear of the breach and he reported the situation precisely to signalman Williams who sent 'Obstruction Danger' to Llangollen at 5.34 am. The 4.45 am Ruabon to Barmouth goods was waiting at the starting signal and after placing the train in a siding, driver Lea of Croes Newydd was authorized to enter the section under Regulation 14a to examine the line. In this he was accompanied by guard Evans — who had nothing more medicinal than a mug of water — and guard Edwards who was in charge of the 4.45 am goods. They left Trevor at 5.40 am, and after exploding guard Evans's three detonators saw the smoke and flames from the train ahead. The engine was stopped and the two guards went on foot to the site. There was nothing to be done. Only the brake van was not totally destroyed by fire, and the 100-foot breach was packed with the obscene, blazing wreckage. It must have been a horrible sight for the two men, especially for the recently escaped guard Evans who knew that at the very bottom of the pile, down in the mud, was his mate, driver David Jones.

Fire had broken out at once after the engine had come to rest on the far side

of the breach, its front buried in the remaining embankment. Somehow or other it had travelled 100 feet across the mud and was embedded up to the bottom of its boiler in the quagmire. Blazing coals from the firebox were thrown out into the coal of the tender and soon the whole train was burning. An LMS 4-wheel van No 162103 marshalled next to the brake van was loaded with barrels of gas oil, and these exploded on impact, setting fire to the floor of the van and giving guard Evans an added incentive to find a way out of his brake. With the exception of the brake van, the entire train and its payload was completely destroyed.

Clearance of the wreckage presented the railway engineers with exceptional difficulties. They had a 45-ton steam crane on site later in the day but they did not dare bring it close to the breach to make lifts. Resourceful as ever, the Great Western men asked for assistance from the Army and two 8-ton Scammell winch lorries with crews were provided by the Royal Artillery Mechanical Transport

School at Rhyl and these, together with a similar lorry which was volunteered by a local timber merchant, Mr Langshaw Rowland, set to work to drag the debris out sideways from the breach into the meadow at 5 pm on the day of the crash. The nominal 8-ton pull of the winches was increased to 32 tons by wire rope tackles. From dawn till dusk and through the succeeding days and nights the Great Western engineers, the military and Mr Langshaw Rowlands and his men worked hard until all that was left was the locomotive, its tender having been pulled out sideways on the evening of Monday 10 September.

On Tuesday morning the engine's boiler, which was practically undamaged, was lifted clear of the frames by the 45-ton railway crane, but the frames and wheels could not be moved. Much spade-work was done to excavate them from the mud, and rails were laid on which to run them, but the 'engine' part of the machine could not be budged either by the crane or by the winches so that, at last, the engineers agreed, reluctantly, that they would have to cut the frames. This was done between the leading and middle driving wheels and each part then answered to the call of the combined efforts of the Royal Artillery winch lorries and an RA winching bulldozer. The breach was cleared by the evening of 12 September and work commenced to restore the railway.

The Great Western's Chief Civil Engineer, Alan Quartermaine, decided to erect a wooden bridge to carry the up line across the breach to permit the tipping of rock and ash to re-make the embankment. The Royal Artillery bulldozer pushed back into the hole as much debris as possible so that the meadow could be restored as grazing land. In store at Ruabon was timber for just such an emergency and this was now brought out. The driving of 12 x 12 inch piles using a specially adapted steam crane commenced on 10 September while the locomotive was still embedded in the breach. On the piles were fixed 14 x 14 inch timber piers as much as 40 feet tall which were to support the 14 x 14 inch beams below the rails, four beams to each rail. In one week from the start of pile driving, the single track bridge was complete. It was 120 feet long and consisted of seven spans, two of 15 feet and five of 18 feet. Train loads of rock and ash were now brought in and tipping commenced. In five days, 3,000 cubic yards of 'fill' was dropped and at 12.15 pm on 22 September the first train ran over the new bank at a speed restriction of 5 mph. The wooden bridge remained encased in the new embankment as stabilizing piling.

The speed and efficiency with which the damage was put right — in those far-off days when everything was so 'old fashioned' — was due to the superb organization of the Great Western and to the well-trained efforts of railway and Army men. The Great Western officers knew this and, as always in large or small cases of men's devotion to the job, they made sure they let the men know they were appreciated. For instance, District Inspector Thorne of Corwen worked 24 hours on 7-8 September, 22 hours on the 8-9th and from 10 to 16 hours for each of the next ten days. He received no overtime pay for this because he was 'Salaried Staff' and was paid a small allowance every week to cover the occasions when he had to put in an hour or so more than normal. His efforts on this occasion did not go unnoticed by the Superintendent of the Line and he was awarded a special payment — for which he did not ask — £20. Permanent Way Inspector Pate of Gobowen received £15 gratuity for working long hours. The GWR also acknowledged its debt to the men of the Royal Artillery School of Transport. There were two officers, five warrant officers and six sergeants involved with the Scammel lorries and the bulldozers over a period of two weeks. The officers were voted 10 guineas each by the General Manager at the Great Western's meeting and the others were granted 10 shillings for each day they had worked. The Great Western Directors' Minute stated that 'they were highly skilled in this sort of work, they had incurred very long hours, working until after dark, for which they will only receive their army pay. It was largely due to their unremitting efforts that the railway was so rapidly restored.' But there was a problem. To quote again from the Minutes: 'If the gratuity be forwarded to their Commandant it would be handed over to a military charity'. The difficulty was overcome by handing the cheque for £47 10s to a Mr H.H. Swift who gave it to Major Hemelryk who then distributed the largesse. Originally the Directors had resolved to donate £100 to the Royal Artillery Benevolent Fund, but on hearing the plea for the hard-working soldiers they split the gift and sent £52 10s to the Fund and a letter of appreciation to the mens' commandant.

The cost to the GWR of repairing the breach was £7,019 10s 8d, of which the LMS paid £1,519 10s. The cost of replacing the rolling stock came to £11,000, the GWR paying for all the wagons destroyed. Locomotive No 6315 was written off and not replaced. The farmer whose field was flooded in mud by the LMS canal failure was compensated with £103 13s by the GWR, and that Company also paid £257 to have the land ploughed and re-seeded with grass. Traders and the GPO who lost materials were compensated by the GWR. In total, the collapse of the LMS canal cost the Great Western £17,400 while the LMS incurred costs of £6,000 in repairs to the canal. In a joint report on the legal implications of the event, the GWR/LMS investigators wrote to Sir James Milne and Sir William Wood, General Managers of the Great Western and LMS respectively that 'It is undesirable to proceed with the determination of the legal liability for GW expenses in making good damage caused by the mishap. The GW Company will, however, meet the cost of making good damage to LMS rolling stock'. The idea seemed to be that with the nationalization of railways a possibility, the Companies would have ceased to exist by the time there was an outcome to a court case.

Nevertheless, this seems to be a curious attitude to adopt. The Labour government had only recently come to power, and the passing of the Act was some way off, while the actual date of nationalization was three years away. The two companies kept the lid on the affair very well. They carried out their pleasant and patriotic duty towards the Army, they gave some of their men an extra pat on the back and they made sure that the landowners were happy. With no legal argument over liability for the disaster, it remained an accident which no one could have foreseen. The only injured person who does not figure in the lists of the compensated was Mrs David Jones, widow of the driver David Jones who was killed as a result of the collapse of the canal.

CHAPTER 12

Lichfield (Trent Valley)

1946

L ICHFIELD (TRENT VALLEY) STATION LIES ABOUT 116 MILES NORTH OF
Euston on the old London & North Western main line to Crewe and is
roughly equidistant between Stafford to the north and Nuneaton to the
south. The old Midland Railway route from Sutton Coldfield to Burton and
Derby passed over the station at the south end of the platforms and a chord
line from a junction facing Crewe went round to join the latter route. The tracks
north and south of Lichfield (Trent Valley) station were double, but through
the station and for 600 yards to the north they were, in 1946, flanked by 'Slow
lines' — known as 'Platform lines' when they were alongside the station platforms. The layout was controlled by two signal boxes, No 1 on a brick pedestal
between the up and down fast lines at the north end of the platforms, and No
2 box, 535 yards to the north.

On 1 January 1946 the weather was bright, clear and freezing hard. Signalman
Williams was on the late turn in No 1 box with its 80 levers, while No 2 box
was in the hands of signalman Shone. Mr Williams was a man of medium height
and moderate weight, turning the scales at 9½ stone. He was well known for
the energy he put into swinging over the big levers, using all his weight to overcome the inertia and the friction in many yards of point rodding or signal wires.
At about 6.45 pm, he accepted the Stafford to Nuneaton stopping passenger
train from No 2 box and set the road from the up fast to the up platform line,
working facing point bolt lever 32, facing point lever 33 and the lever to operate
the trailing end of these points, No 34. He then pulled over lever 6 for the signal
routing trains into the platform.

The train steamed in hauled by 'Prince of Wales' Class 4-6-0 No 25802. The
engine weighed 105½ tons and had in tow four wooden-bodied, eight-wheeled
carriages weighing 94 tons. When the train had drawn clear of points 34 and
was into the platform, signalman Williams 'reversed the road', throwing lever

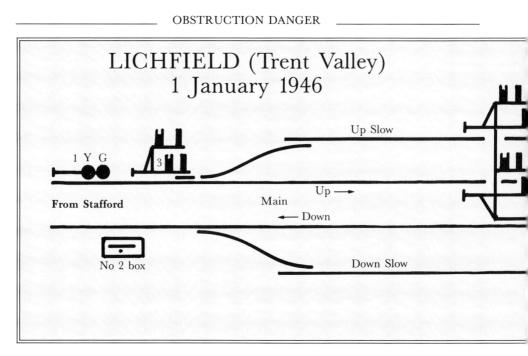

LICHFIELD (Trent Valley)
1 January 1946

Up Slow

1 Y G

3

From Stafford

Main

Up →

← Down

No 2 box

Down Slow

6 back into the frame to place that signal to 'Danger', ramming lever 32 into the frame, then lever 33 to set the facing points for the up fast line, lever 34 to re-set the trailing points and finally heaving over on lever 32 again to place the bolt in the facing points to prove that they were properly closed and to hold them tight shut. He gave the 2-1 code to No 2 box — 'Train out of Section' — for the passenger train, and was at once asked 'Is Line Clear?' for the 2.50

Looking north towards Lichfield No 1 box up home signals in 1937. The up main home signal is lowered and a 'Royal Scot' Class 4-6-0 is just about to pass over the facing points which, ten years later, were to be left set for the left-hand turn-out after the signalman had reversed the operating levers. Below the gantry, in the distance, No 2 signal box can be seen. The original station stands on the left. (E.S. Russell)

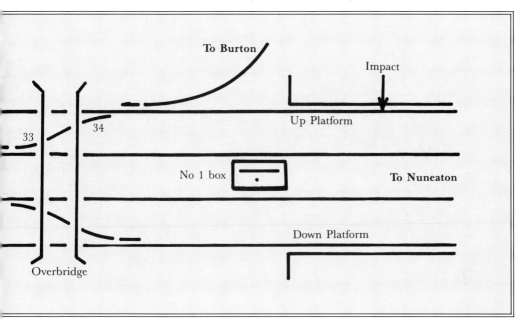

pm Fleetwood to London fish train. He 'got the road' from the next signalman to the south and pulled over the up fast line signal levers: starting signal No 5 against the railway line overbridge at the south end of the station, home signal No 4 on the gantry a little way to the north of the box, his inner distant signal, a semaphore, worked by lever No 3, and his outer distant, a colour light several hundred yards to the north of No 2 box on lever No 1.

A view of the re-sited up main home signals for Lichfield No 1 signal box on 31 March 1953. The old gantry was taken away and the signals re-sited after the crash. The up homes for Lichfield No 1 box are on the left with the up fast signal arm raised. In the right foreground is the facing point leading to the up platform line or to Burton on Trent. The corner of the signal bracket on the up slow line can be seen in the top right-hand corner of the picture (E.S. Russell)

Looking south towards the station and No 1 signal box as 46242 City of Glasgow *comes through on the down 'Caledonian' on 17 June 1957. The points from up fast to up platform line can be seen immediately to the left of the front of the engine.* (E.S. Russell)

Out in the frosty darkness under the stars, driver Reade with his 'Black 5' No 5495 hauling the fish train, was pleased to see the bright green light of the outer distant, and his fireman called across the cab that they were at last going to get a clear run. They had been stopped and checked for miles behind the stopping passenger train, and there is nothing more tedious for the driver of a fast train than to be continuously checked. The guard of the fish train saw the colour light distant signal at 'All Right', and signalman Shone in No 2 box saw the repeater for the signal, which was also his distant signal, show 'off'. He also heard the wire squeal beneath his signal box as Williams pulled No 1 box's inner distant.

On the up slow line, a very short distance ahead of No 1 box's home signal gantry, was the engine of a train for Burton on Trent. Why the engine had passed the signal at 'Danger', even by a few feet, is not known, but anyhow, driver Kendall of this train was anxiously watching the signal arms just behind and above him, hoping to see the arm for the Burton direction rise to the 'proceed' aspect. He said at the Inquiry that he could see the arms clearly silhouetted against the starry night sky and he quite definitely saw up main signal arm No 4 rise after the passenger train had gone into the platform line. He was disappointed that his route had not been cleared and he said to his fireman, 'They're busy tonight, they've pulled off again on the up fast'. Signalman Shone said that he saw the small green light of signalman Williams's up home signal, the far right-hand light of a group of five lights, the other four of which were red.

Driver Reade came up to Lichfield station at 30 to 35 mph, his train a featherweight of seven vans weighing 80 tons. He said he saw the home signal on the gantry showing a green light to the up fast line and a moment later his engine gave a vicious lurch to the left. He was thrown off his seat on to the floor and he had only just managed to get to his feet, close the regulator and apply the brake when the crash occurred. The 'Black 5' tunnelled through the fourth and third coaches of the passenger train — which was standing on the Platform line with its brakes on — splintering the wooden bodies and flinging aside what under normal circumstances seemed like massively heavy steel underframes. Half of the wooden body of the second coach shot sideways off its frame on to the platform and was found 120 feet behind the 'Black 5' when the movement ceased. The front half of this coach was rammed forward over the top of the leading coach and came to rest with the half-roof and sides fitting neatly over the engine's tender while the long solebars lay alongside the engine's running plate. Only the leading coach was not totally demolished. 20 passengers died, 21 were injured and a porter was felled by flying debris. The impact was sufficient to drive the passenger train forward, brakes hard on, for 100 yards.

So totally unexpected was the collision that signalman Williams, only a few yards from the impact, thought that the blows he felt against his box and the rattling of his levers was due to something dragging from the passing fish train and sent '7 bells' — 'Stop and Examine Train' — to the next box south, Hademore Crossing. It was only when the guard of the fish train came to his box three minutes later that he became aware of what had happened and sent the 'Obstruction Danger' code at 7.1 pm. He called upon the guard to witness that the points were set for the main line, and was so thoroughly shocked that he had to be taken to hospital. The fish train had not been derailed to cause the collision — it had taken the left-hand turn at the main platform to facing points which were lying for the turn-out.

The Divisional Signal Engineer, Mr H.E. Morgan, and his Area Assistant, Mr A.E. Matthews, arrived at the scene at 10 pm. They went at once to the

A view of a facing point bolt driven fully home through the locking port on the stretcher bar. The bolt can be seen as a projecting tongue at the bottom centre of the picture. Immediately to the left of the bolt is the second port which comes into alignment with the bolt when the points are reversed. The bolt is a very close fit in the port with only a few thousandths of an inch clearance. Note that the bolt has a cam-plate-shaped section at the far end; this runs through and drives a detection bar so that the movement of the bolt imparts a lateral motion to a rod which then makes or breaks a contact for electrical detection on the bolt. If the bolt does not go fully 'home', the electrical circuit will not be made and the electric lock on the signal lever will not lift. (Author)

The distortion of the down rod

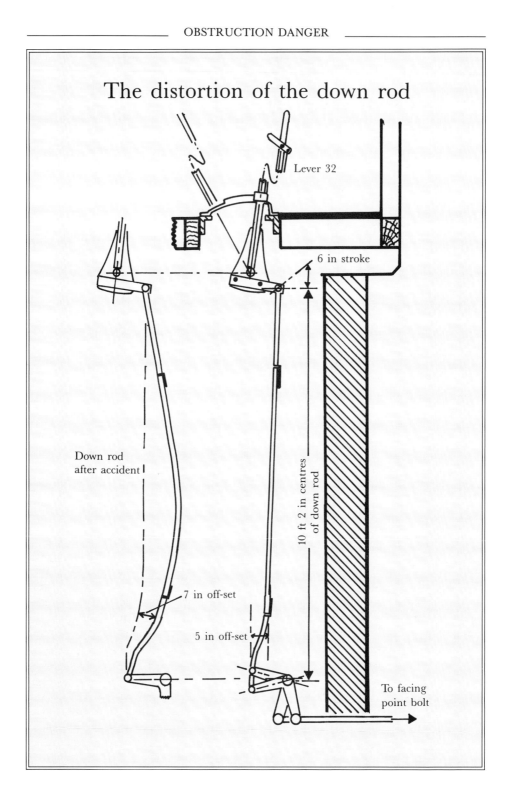

Lever 32

6 in stroke

Down rod
after accident

10 ft 2 in centres
of down rod

7 in off-set

5 in off-set

To facing
point bolt

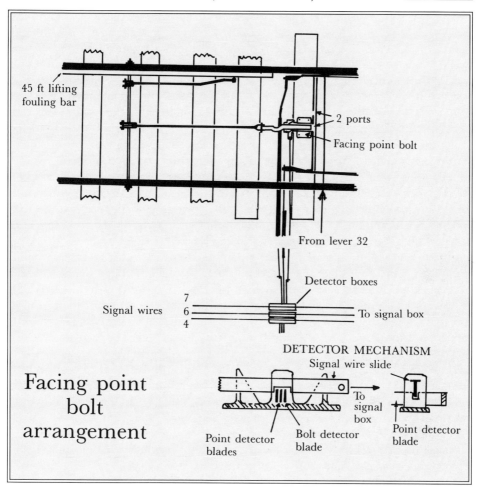

45 ft lifting fouling bar

2 ports

Facing point bolt

From lever 32

Detector boxes

Signal wires

7
6 — To signal box
4

DETECTOR MECHANISM
Signal wire slide

Facing point bolt arrangement

To signal box

Point detector blades

Bolt detector blade

Point detector blade

facing points and found that, apart from a ⅜ inch opening between the right-hand switch blade and its stock rail, the points were set for the up fast to up platform line, with the facing point bolt fully home in its port on the stretcher bar connecting the two switch blades. The detection bars attached to the switch blades and point bolt, through whose slots the signal wire slides had to pass, were in good order. The slide in the wire to No 4 signal, the up fast home, was 4 inches out of register with the notch in the detector bar connected to the switch blades, which was exactly correct because the points were set for the platform line. Under these conditions it was simply not possible for No 4 signal to have shown a green light for, when Williams pulled that lever over, the detector bar would have prevented the pull being communicated to the signal arm. The detector bars and signal wire slides for signals 6 and 7 were also slightly out of register due to the ⅜ inch opening of the points, so the signalman would not have been able to raise those signal arms either. Yet three very experienced railwaymen had stated that No 4 signal was showing a green light.

The two signal engineers walked back towards No 1 signal box, examining the point rodding as they went, and finally entered the locking room below the operating floor of the box. There they found another mystery. The down rod to the facing points driven by No 33 lever was bowed outwards towards the front wall of the box to make an arc 10 inches out of vertical at its widest part. The rod was over 10 feet long and was in three sections. The uppermost 2-foot section, attached to the lever, was made from 1¼-inch diameter, solid steel rod. The central section was an 8 foot length of channel section steel normally used for point rodding outside the box, and this was attached to 2 feet of 1¼-inch round bar which in turn was attached to the upright 'pedestal' crank, which changed the direction of thrust in the rodding from the vertical to the horizontal. The central section had bowed outwards under some extreme compression force. This bowing, together with whatever 'springiness' there was in the 100 yards of horizontal rodding to the points, would have taken up the entire 6 inches of travel imparted when signalman Williams pushed over No 33 lever. Williams had thus been able to restore the facing point lever to the frame, and the mechanical interlocking on his fast line levers had been released. He had then been able to reverse his home signal lever, No 4, which in turn had released the inner and outer distant signal levers. The fact that the detector bar would have prevented the signal wire from moving right through to the signal arm would not have prevented an energetic signalman from swinging the lever over and getting it into its notch in the frame. The wire from the box to the detector bar would have been exceedingly taut, but there is no doubt that it could be done. But what had caused the 'down rod' on No 33 lever to bow out like that?

In order to run the breakdown crane and vans alongside the wreck, the facing points had to be set for the up fast line. The switch blades were crow-barred over to close the ⅜ inch gap between the right-hand blade and the stock rail; this took the strain off the facing point bolt which was then withdrawn by pushing lever 32 into the frame. As soon as the bolt cleared its port in the stretcher bar, the switch blades slammed over for the up fast line direction and under the signal box the distorted down rod promptly took up its correct alignment. Facing point lever 33 was then reversed, and it was seen that the points answered it perfectly, and now without any slight gap in the right-hand side. The engineers then tried to re-create the faulty situation in which they had found the points. They placed lever 32 — the facing point bolt — normal in the frame (over in the row with the rest of the levers) and on reconnecting the drive rod to the facing point bolt they saw that the bolt was still engaged in its port by ¼ inch. It should, of course, have been quite clear and free of the port when the lever was placed normal in the frame. With the bolt's tip thus engaged, it was found that, albeit with considerable difficulty, lever 33 could be heaved into the normal position. Of course, with the bolt locating the port it was not possible for the blades of the point to move. The engineers looked under the box and there, sure enough, the down rod from lever 33 was bowed out, taking up the entire drive on the rodding. The engineers then pulled over the up fast line signal levers. They all came over, the outer and inner distant signals cleared to green, but the arm of the home signal, No 4, was prevented from moving because of the detector blades attached to the points' switch blades.

The next question was, 'Why did the facing point bolt not come clear out of its port when the relevant lever had moved across the full sweep of its travel?' The engineers went again to the points and had the bolt moved in and out by the movement of the signal box lever. It went in to the full amount of its travel but did not come out likewise. The examining technician put his hand on the drive rod and felt a grating sensation as the bolt was withdrawn — it was as if the rodding was being dragged over the ground. Waving to the signalman to leave the bolt at the 'withdrawn' position, he made a minute examination of the rod and discovered that the tail of the rocking shaft driving the fouling bar simultaneously with the facing point bolt was prevented from making a full turn by a pile of ballast, frozen to the ground. The tail rod grated over the stones and was finally stopped altogether when the tip of the facing bolt was still engaged in the port. There was enough 'whippiness' in the 100 yards of rodding to en-

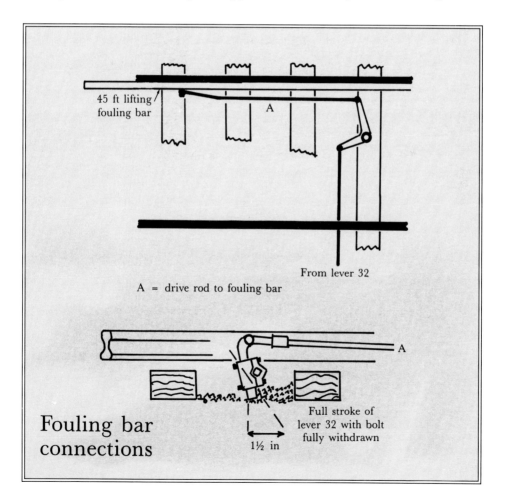

45 ft lifting
fouling bar

A

From lever 32

A = drive rod to fouling bar

Fouling bar
connections

Full stroke of
lever 32 with bolt
fully withdrawn

1½ in

able the signal box lever to complete its stroke. Signalman Williams, who always threw his whole 9½ stone, of necessity, into heavy movements, did not notice the extra effort he undoubtedly had to make in moving levers 32 and 33. Once those levers had been reversed, the mechanical interlocking was free to allow the up fast line signal levers to be pulled.

Signalman Williams did not know for certain, when questioned, whether his up fast home signal, No 4, had answered the lever — he had not checked. The lever had come over and he had left it at that. On the mechanical evidence of the detector blades, it cannot possibly have cleared. On the other hand, driver Reade on the fish train, driver Kendall on the Burton train, and signalman Shone all said that it did. Driver Reade was bound to say that he had a green off the signal, but the other two men, I believe, were mistaken and saw what they expected to see.

So that is the end of the story of the Lichfield crash — or is it? Why did that down rod off No 33 lever bend? The channel point rodding used for the central

This GWR fouling bar is similar to the one at Lichfield but with one very important difference — the GWR method of attaching the operating rod to the bar is safe. The point of attachment can be seen above the first sleeper on the right. When the signalman pulls the facing point bolt lever, the bolt is withdrawn from its port and as it moves so this fouling bar is raised and moved forward, an 'up and over' action. If a vehicle is standing anywhere along the length of the bar, its wheel flanges will be lightly touching it and therefore it will not rise. This naturally prevents the signalman from moving the facing point bolt. It can be seen from this illustration that the tail of the operating crank on the fouling bar, if it was sweeping an arc between and below the sleepers, could be obstructed by a pile of ballast, which is why the GWR did not use that method of attachment. (Author)

Going up the hill between Bell Busk and Hellifield, down trains passed a semaphore distant signal and, 848 yards further on, almost at the summit of the climb, they passed a semaphore stop signal. These two signals comprised an 'intermediate block section' known as 'Otterburn signals' which were both operated by lever No 45 in Hellifield South Junction signal box. If the signalman did not replace the signals to 'Danger' after a train had passed the home signal by restoring lever No 45 to 'normal' in the frame, the occupation by the train of track circuit No 50 which commenced 440 yards beyond the home would automatically replace both signals to 'Danger' behind the train. As the train advanced towards Hellifield station, it came off track circuit 50 and occupied track circuit 8636 which extended from Hellifield South Junction's outer home to the inner home. When the last vehicle of the train was ahead of the latter signal, alongside the station platform, track circuit 8636 was unoccupied. If at that time lever No 45 had still not been replaced to 'normal' in the frame, then the Otterburn signals would automatically clear once more.

The signalmen at Hellifield South Junction tended to let this happen occasionally; the practice was forbidden by the rules but, providing that the inner and outer home signals were at 'Danger' behind the train in the platform, there was not that much harm in allowing the Otterburn signals to work automatically. Really, the system was wrong. Intermediate block signals should not have been controlled by a signal box in advance, and they should not have been capable of being worked automatically; such working was not part of the design, and the dangers of such operation were obvious to the LMS company. When the system was installed in 1938 a rule was framed ordering the signalman to replace the lever No 45 to normal behind each train as it passed the Otterburn home

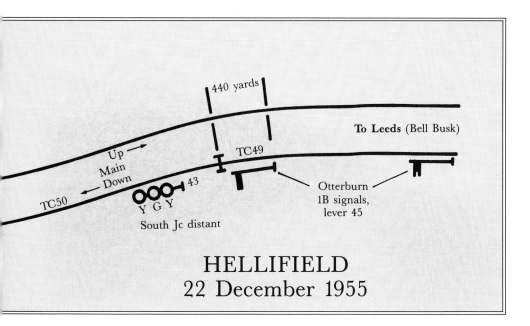

HELLIFIELD
22 December 1955

101

Above *Hellifield South Junction, looking south to the signal box with the line to Blackburn converging on the main line from the right. South Junction signal box is at the end of the platform. The inner home signal for that box with North Junction's distant signal below it can be seen beyond the box, jutting above the line of hills.* (Lens of Sutton)

Below *Looking north along the down platform towards North Junction box. The 9.5 pm St Pancras to Edinburgh train was standing alongside this platform when the 9.15 pm St Pancras to Glasgow crashed into its rear.* (Lens of Sutton)

signal. Had that been done on 22 December 1955, the crash would not have happened.

Hellifield South Junction signal box was 384 yards from the North box and the North box down distant signal was on the same post at South Junction's inner home. South Junction's down distant was a colour-light signal 1,872 yards from the inner home. North box's distant signal did not control the aspect of South Junction's outer distant, although it would have been a simple matter to make the position of North box's semaphore arm control the South box colour-light distant. Each signal was independent of the other, worked from its own signal box.

On the night or early morning of 22 December 1955, the 9.05 pm St Pancras to Edinburgh express was double headed and had a load of 12 eight-wheelers including two sleeping cars and two parcels vans which were marshalled at the rear. Following this was the 9.15 pm St Pancras to Glasgow, hauled by a 'Britannia' Class 'Pacific' and driven by Mr Blakemore of Leeds Holbeck shed. Both trains were running late from Leeds and at Delaney's Sidings box, at the foot of Bell Busk bank, the 9.05 was stopped with a defective brake on a sleeping car. The fault was too great to be rectified there, so the train went on at reduced speed to Hellifield where there were Carriage & Wagon department fitters on duty. The train arrived at Hellifield 78 minutes late. The 9.15 was seven minutes behind. Two 'C&W' men crawled in under the defective car and began to work on the brake.

The Hellifield South Junction signalman could permit a second train to approach the Otterburn signals as soon as the first train had cleared track circuit 49, which extended for 440 yards beyond the home signal. The latter was at 'Danger' owing to the occupation of track circuit 50. Therefore the South Junction signalman could give 'Line Clear' to Bell Busk. The 9.05 pm St Pancras cleared track circuit 49 at 4.33 am and 'Line Clear' was duly given for the following 9.15 pm St Pancras. The Bell Busk man pulled his down line signals 'off' and the express passed him at 4.38 am. At 4.39 am, on the other side of the summit, the 9.05 St Pancras cleared track circuit 8636, but since lever No 45 had not been restored to 'normal' in the frame at Hellifield South Junction, the arms of the Otterburn distant and home signals raised to the 'All Right' position. Driver Blakemore on the 9.15 St Pancras was one minute away from the Otterburn distant signal then and did not see the signal's yellow 'Caution' light, only the green. Two minutes later he passed the home signal also at green and shut off steam to coast down through Hellifield station at around 50-55 mph. Forty seconds after that he passed the bright green light of Hellifield South Junction's down distant signal. He had the road through the station — or so he thought.

Drifting smoke rolling off the coasting engine's chimney blotted out the view, so he did not see South Junction's home signal, but even of he had it would have been at 'All Right'. Having missed this signal, he took the precaution of telling his fireman to keep a sharp look-out for the inner home. A few seconds later there it was, its arm raised, but below it the North box distant at 'Caution'. Neither man had ever seen the inner distant 'on' when the outer had been 'off' and were taken aback. A split second later they both saw the red tail light of the 9.05 ahead. 'Whoa!' shouted the fireman. Driver Blakemore gave a full emergency brake application but it was too late to do much good.

The 'Britannia' struck the rear of the train at about 30 mph, driving the whole forward and wrecking the two rear vans, derailing them right on the spot where the fitters had been working. The sleeping car on which they had been working was pushed forward and derailed, telescoped into the coach in front with its headstocks and solebars buckled. The magnitude of the damage diminished as the shock waves were absorbed along the length of the train.

No one was badly hurt. Guard Richard Atkinson, who was travelling 'passenger' to Carlisle to pick up a southbound freight working, was taken to hospital. A cargo of day-old chicks was rescued intact from the debris — the only fatality of the crash was a guinea pig travelling in a cardboard box in the brake van of the 9.05. The Carriage & Wagon department fitter, Geoff Seeger, who was under the train attending to the brakes, had a very lucky escape from death. He was lying on his back on the sleepers with his legs across the rails (having sent his mate Clifford Stead to the engine driver to tell him not to move) when he felt an unmistakable vibration in the track. Looking round, he saw the telltale 'Catherine wheels' of sparks coming from the hard-pressed brake shoes of a very rapidly approaching train. He came out from beneath the sleeping car faster than a rabbit with a ferret after it, and dived head first under a coal wagon on an adjacent siding to give some shelter from the flying debris of the inevitable crash.

The signalman had to shoulder the blame. Not only had he not replaced the Otterburn signal lever, but he had also been slow to replace to 'Caution' and 'Danger' his own distant, outer and inner homes, thus leaving the way open for the 9.15 St Pancras all the way to the buffers of the stationary train. The signalman was worried about his wife who was ill and this, coupled with the fact that he was also dealing with a freight train on the up line, might have reduced his level of concentration. He was a very decent man who had fallen into the trap laid by the less than perfect signalling arrangements which the London Midland Region had inherited from the LMS. LMR had acknowledged this fault because a scheme for improving the system regarding the Otterburn signals had been drawn up but not implemented. When the 9.05 St Pancras arrived in Hellifield station, the North box signalman had replaced his distant signal to 'Caution' behind it. In a well-designed system, this action would have switched the outer South Junction colour light distant signal to 'Caution'. But it was not a well-designed system, and the signalman 'carried the can' for his own and the Region's failings.

CHAPTER 14

Milton

1955

T HE 8.30 AM EXCURSION FROM TREHERBERT TO PADDINGTON ON SUNDAY 20 November 1955 was filled almost entirely by members of Womens' Institutes from the Valleys. The train was formed of nine ex-GWR coaches and an ex-LMS cafeteria car, and was hauled from Cardiff by 'Britannia' 'Pacific' No 70026 *Polar Star* worked by driver Wheeler and fireman Marsh from Cardiff Canton shed. Their guard was a Treherbert man, a goods guard working as passenger guard that day, Mr Wall. Driver Wheeler was 55 years old with 40 years' service and was at that time in No 4 Link, 'Senior Vacuum Goods' which had regular turns to London including the 'Red Dragon' express, which driver Wheeler had worked in October. Fireman Marsh was 30 years old with 13½ years' service. Their route to Paddington lay on the 'Great Way Round' via Gloucester because the Severn Tunnel was closed for its usual Sunday maintenance.

The road was littered with speed restrictions, details of which were laid out in the 'Weekly Engineering Notice', better known to railwaymen as the 'K2'. Driver Wheeler had been issued with his, covering Sunday 20 November and the following week, on the previous Thursday or Friday, and he noted that on the Sunday he would be diverted through the goods loop at Liswerry, that there would be a 5 mph slack at Over Junction near Gloucester, and a 15 mph restriction on the up main line at Wantage Road. What he did not see, on the next line below, or maybe over the page, was a warning of a diversion through the goods loop at Milton, between Steventon and Didcot.

The journey went as well as could be expected with a 'Britannia'. The engine was a standard design meant to run anywhere in Britain where the tracks were strong enough to take it. It therefore had a left-hand driving position to conform to the majority view on this. Unfortunately, Western Region had the traditional right-hand drive, and all signals were placed to be sighted by a driver standing at the right-hand side of his footplate. When there was a long boiler jutting out 30 feet ahead, or even a slight curve in the track, the difference between the two positions was profound. The noise in the enclosed cab was deafening at speed, whilst the coal dust swirled, in defiance of the fireman's efforts to 'lay' it with water, causing the siren of the Automatic Train Control (ATC) to become choked during the journey.

The GWR ATC, which from 1906 until December 1947 was the only such system in daily use on any railway in the world, gave the driver an audible warning of a distant signal at 'Caution' or 'All Right'. A wooden ramp 44 feet long, with a metal contact strip along its upper edge, was placed between the rails a few yards on the approach side of a distant signal. When the signal arm was at 'Caution', the metal strip was electrically 'dead', but when the arm was properly lowered to 'All Right' it was 'live'. On the engine there was a contact switch which was raised by the ramp and thus broke an electrical circuit on the engine. This circuit was maintaining an electro-magnet which was holding shut a valve. When the circuit was broken by the raising of the contact switch, the valve opened and allowed atmosphere into the vacuum brake pipe, applying the brakes and sounding a shrill siren. The driver cancelled the automatic brake application and silenced the siren by lifting a small handle on the side of the cab ATC gear box.

If, however, the signal arm was lowered, the current in the ramp contact strip travelled to the cab electro-magnet via the contact shoe so that although the engine's circuit was broken by the raising of the shoe, there was still current to maintain the electro-magnet and hold the air valve shut. This current also rang a loud, bright, trembler bell in the cab. The GWR ATC could stop a train running at 70 mph at the first stop signal after the ramp without steam being shut off and it worked faultlessly in every respect until it was fitted to the 'Britannia' Class engines, where it was squeezed into a cab that was not designed for it. The designers placed the cab gear box down on the floorboards, close to the firehole, so that every time the siren sounded, dirt was sucked into it, eventually jamming the 'spinner' and reducing the volume of the warning note. It must be said, however, that a completely jammed siren would have no effect at all on the equipment's ability to bring a train to a stand and, furthermore, the presence of the ATC on the engine did not relieve the driver of his duty to look for signals on the lineside. The ATC was an aid, a great reassurance in fog and, if the driver failed, a very effective last line of defence.

The train was 10 minutes late leaving Swindon. Having negotiated the Wantage Road speed restriction, driver Wheeler tugged firmly at the regulator and, with the cut off around 45%, 'set sail' on what he believed was then a non-stop run for Paddington, with another speed restriction at Pangbourne. He shortened the cut off till the engine was running on 15% and making 40 mph as it ran past Steventon station, four miles beyond Wantage. At this point, fireman Marsh stepped across to his coat, hanging on the cab-side by driver Wheeler's left shoulder. He took out his watch from the inside pocket and looked at the time. It was 1.10 pm — they were still 10 minutes late. He thought that driver Wheeler would make a serious effort to regain that time after Reading so he,

Marsh, was concerned that he had a good boilerful of water. The water gauge-glass showed three-quarters full when he checked it as they passed the station. He then checked his pressure gauge and looked in at his fire. The watch, and the checking of water, fire and pressure, occupied him from passing under the bridge at the east end of the station platform until they were passing under Milton Lane bridge 1,016 yards further on, an interval of about 45 seconds as the engine accelerated from 40 towards 50 mph. As they passed the second bridge, he checked his boiler water feeds and saw that the exhaust steam injector was wasting water at the overflow and was therefore not delivering water to the boiler. He leant over the cabside to watch the overflow while he adjusted the inboard controls, and when he could not get the exhaust injector to work, he turned over to the live steam injector. From the second bridge to the home signal at Milton was a distance of 1,012 yards which would have been covered in 40 seconds as the train was accelerating. While fireman Marsh was attending to his proper duties over a period of nearly 90 seconds from the moment that the engine passed under the bridge at Steventon station, it would appear from driver Wheeler's evidence to the Inquiry that he, Wheeler, was watching his mate, not the road ahead. He could not hear the clogged siren and therefore his attention was not drawn to the fact of passing the distant signal at Caution.

When the engine cleared the first bridge, Milton's up main distant signal was standing at 'Caution' 680 yards away on the right-hand side of the track, but, at that distance, clearly visible to the driver on the left-hand side of the engine. Only later did the length of the boiler obscure the view, and even then there

The driver's view of Milton's up main distant signal from within the cab of a 'Britannia' at 360 yards. (British Rail)

The driver's view of Milton's up distant signal, leaning from the cab at 360 yards. (British Rail)

The fireman's view of Milton's up distant signal, leaning from the cab at 360 yards. (British Rail)

The driver's view of Milton's up main home signals, leaning from the cab at 515 yards. (British Rail)

The fireman's view of Milton's up main home signals, leaning from the cab at 515 yards. (British Rail)

The driver's view of Milton's up home signals, leaning from the cab at 194 yards. (British Rail)

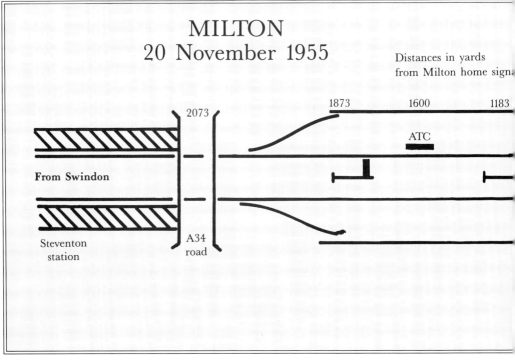

MILTON
20 November 1955

Distances in yards
from Milton home signal

From Swindon

Steventon
station

A34
road

2073

1873   1600   1183

ATC

were moments when the arm could have been glimpsed between the smoke deflector plate and the smokebox. The distant signal ramp was 417 yards on the
approach side of the signal. The ramp was passed, the signal was passed, and
neither man noticed. The second bridge was passed and the 'Danger' signals
were then 1,012 yards away, continuously visible from the fireman's side and
visible intermittently from the driver's side. In the rear van, temporary passenger guard Wall knew all about the diversion into Milton loop, and heard with
growing apprehension the accelerating rhythm of the wheels. He had not mentioned the diversion to driver Wheeler, he said, because he thought it would be
presumptuous of him to tell a main line driver his business. Now, in his van,
alarmed at what was happening, he was shy of interfering with Wheeler's driving. The handle to apply the vacuum brake was close to hand but he was concerned that, if he put the brake on just as Wheeler applied it from his end, the
train would become divided. A threadbare superstition, but even a divided train
was better than a crashed one. *Polar Star* and the ladies of Treherbert continued
to accelerate, whilst guard Wall wrestled with his conscience.

In Milton signal box, Granville Burt had been on duty since 6 am. His facing
points were clamped at the switch blades and the clamp was padlocked. He could
not alter the lie of the points and there was no hand-signalman at the site who
could have removed the clamp in order that Burt could set the points for the
straight run. District Inspector Checkley had not posted a man at the points
to instruct drivers that they would be going through the loop — as required by

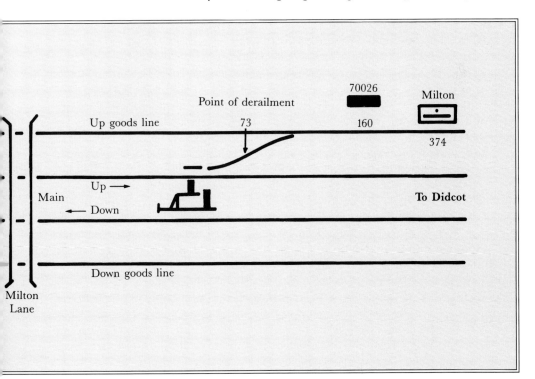

the regulations — because this diversion had been entered in the 'K2' and there-fore all drivers ought to be aware. Checkley had saved one man's Sunday over-time — something he was well known for — his desire for economy overriding his usual meticulous observance of the rules, something else that local signalmen were only too well aware of. When 70026 came through Milton Lane bridge into Burt's sight he could see that it was moving quite fast. He watched in growing alarm, but he was powerless to do anything — the signal box was nearly 400 yards beyond the points. The first driver Wheeler knew of the diversion was when he saw a 4-inch gap where the left-hand switch blades of the facing points ought to have been. He instantly made a full brake application but it was far too late.

The engine swerved left into the 10 mph turn-out at an estimated 52 mph. Up in the signal box Granville Burt stood rooted to the spot as the tragedy unfolded, like some old-time silent movie, 378 yards down the line. He saw the big engine then lurch to the right, leap the track and carve a ramp for itself along and down the face of the 18 foot high embankment. The leading coaches cascaded down after it. Calm with shock, he sent 'Obstruction Danger' to the Steventon and Foxhall Junction signalmen at 1.13 pm.

Under the intense side thrust from the trailing driving wheels as the bogie turned the engine into the reverse curve of the points, rails broke, chairs were ripped out of sleepers and whole 60 foot lengths of track were dragged sideways through the ballast. Such were the forces at work that rails weighing 90 lbs per yard were snapped like twigs, and one piece was rammed like a huge splinter between the frame of the leading bogie and its wheel, forcing the wheel along its axle, lancing upwards, shearing off rivet heads and the thick webs of the cast-iron cylinder till it all but punctured the boiler shell. A piece of fishplate was found embedded, punched into the boiler plate by this rail. The engine came to rest on the grass at the foot of the embankment and fell on its left side, seri-ously injuring driver Wheeler. The leading coach came down behind but missed the engine, which was relatively undamaged, but the second coach fell on the engine, shattered and was then crushed by the third coach falling on top of it. The fourth and fifth coaches slewed broadside across all four tracks, ripping open as they went. The cafeteria car crashed into and mounted their debris. The last four coaches were almost undamaged. Fireman Marsh was not badly hurt. He dug his mate out from the coal which had buried him and helped him out on to the grass. He then ran to get detonators with which to protect the train, and on being told that this had been done he returned to the engine, got some bars and a spanner and went to help rescue people trapped in the wreck. He worked hard and had to be ordered away after two hours.

When the feared '6 bells' tolled out at Foxhall Junction that peaceful, Sun-day lunchtime, Signalman Harold Gasson was in the box, eating his sandwiches, during his spell of duty as hand-signalman for the engineering work on the main line at Foxhall that was causing the diversion through Milton loop. He dropped his food, got on his bike and pedalled as fast as he could along the trackside path to Milton box. The journey of 3⅛ miles took him 10 minutes, but clouds of dust still hung in the air over an appalling scene of destruction. He ran up the box steps to see if Granville Burt was all right. He was strangely calm. 'There was nothing I could do, Harold,' he said. 'The points were clipped. I just had to watch.' He was worried because some of his signals were lowered due to the dragging of their wires by the wreckage, but Gasson tried to reassure him that they did not matter because the 'block' was very firmly on, but Granville was upset by them so Gasson went outside and cut the wires to return the arms to 'Danger'.

He then went down to the upturned engine. Flames were ballooning out of the overturned firebox, threatening to set light to the tender coals and the carriages above, so he wedged the doors shut and went back up the bank. Pinned under a coach frame, the heavy girders across his stomach, was a man, the only man on the train apart from the train crew. He was calling for help. Harold lay down on the track and peered into the wreckage. He could see him but could only reach him with one hand. He lit a cigarette for him, handed it through the twisted girders and then lay on the ground, holding the injured man's hand, talking to him sometimes. The man was horribly cold. Time passed. A doctor came and gave him morphia. Eventually, a crane was attached to the wrecked coach to lift it and free the man. Harold told him the encouraging news, while ambulancemen readied themselves to go and extricate the many injured. The crane eased the coach upwards, the great girders were lifted off the man's body and he died holding Harold's hand. There were 293 passengers on the train; 11 were killed and 62 were injured.

The Ministry of Transport's Inspecting Officer, Brigadier Langley, held driver Wheeler responsible for the crash after he honestly admitted that he had not seen the signals when he ought to have done so. He had been watching his mate working, he said. The Brigadier also said that guard Wall's 'inactivity showed

Twenty-four hours after the crash, coaches were still embedded in ballast and the police were still looking for survivors. (Associated Press)

a lack of judgement', which must surely be an understatement considering that a guard is on a train to supervise it, and Rule 148(b) made it clear that the guard's job was to bring it to a stand if he saw it was running into danger. The Brigadier tried to tread as lightly as possible on men's mistakes, but when one is handing out blame it might be better to share the load rather than give the entire burden to one man.

An apparent mystery surrounds the non-activity of the ATC after the 'dead' ramp of Milton's distant signal was passed. Wheeler and Marsh emphatically denied that they had cancelled the warning siren; they had not heard it and, indeed, Wheeler said at the Inquiry that he was waiting to hear either the bell or the siren. Very soon after the crash, the ATC gear was examined and it was found that the electro-magnet in the cab gear was holding the air valve firmly shut. When the contact switch at the front of the engine was moved, the electro-magnet went dead and the air valve opened. Two weeks later, when the engine was raised, a full test of the ATC was carried out and it worked perfectly, although the siren was not as loud as usual due to dust in the spinner. Why then had the ATC been unable to stop the train?

The GWR braking system, for which the ATC was designed, was somewhat different from that employed by other British companies, and subsequently British Railways. The GWR used 25 inches of vacuum to produce a more powerful brake, or to permit the use of smaller brake cylinders, and, much more important in the context of this story, they used a 5-inch diameter crosshead-driven pump to draw air from the vacuum pipes and thus mop up any small leaks there might be while the train was in motion. Most other railways used a jet of steam from what was called the 'small ejector' to do this job. By using a pump, the GWR saved a lot of coal and were able to maintain a higher vacuum than could be done economically using the small ejector method. Of course, British Railways used the small ejector method. When the brake was applied on a GWR engine, the vacuum pump's suction was automatically switched from drawing on the whole system to drawing only on the upper side of each brake piston in its cylinder, thus ensuring the maximum differential between atmospheric pressure rushing in below the piston and the vacuum above it. When the brake was applied on a British Railways 'Standard' locomotive, the small ejector continued to throw air out of the brake pipes, but the inrush of air through the driver's brake valve was so great that the amount being discharged by the ejec-

No 70026 Polar Star *is about to be turned on to its wheels by means of cables hauled around pulleys by a diesel shunter. 2-8-2T No 7239 is standing on the track to which the pulleys are fixed to prevent the rails and sleepers moving under the strain.* (British Rail)

Eighteen months after the crash, with not a steam gland leaking, No 70026 Polar Star *comes through Reading in the grand style at over 70 mph trailing a 'full digger' of 14 coaches. To slightly improve visibility from the cab, the smoke deflector hand-rails have been removed and replaced by hand-holes. There is every sign that the engine is in the finest fettle — no leaks, the fireman sitting, leaning out with a broad grin for the photographer as his boiler blows off at full pressure, and the chimney leaving a light grey smoke behind, witnessing to a really hot fire.* (Les Reason)

tor did not unduly affect the braking force. But, and this was a big 'but', the GWR ATC had an air inlet to the vacuum pipe of a diameter large enough to admit sufficient air on the understanding that the inrush was not going to be in part thrown straight out again by the continuous action of a small ejector.

On GWR engines the ATC acted with great efficiency because atmospheric pressure was allowed into the brake pipes and stayed there. On a 'Britannia', the ATC air inlet orifice was *not* large enough when there was a small ejector constantly throwing air out during braking. The Ministry of Transport carried out comparative tests with a 'Britannia' whose small ejector was working throughout the ATC braking process, and one whose small ejector was blanked off. With a load of ten coaches, including the dynamometer car, a 'blanked off' 'Britannia' was run at 60 mph over Milton's up main distant signal ramp at 'Caution'. The ATC gear was allowed to carry out its function and steam was not shut off. This train was brought to a stand in 1,599 yards, one yard short of Milton's up home signals. The other test, with the small ejector running continuously, brought the train to a stand in 3,000 yards from the dead ramp — 1,327 beyond the facing points. Needless to say, No 70026 *Polar Star*, in common with all Western Region 'Britannias' at that time, had a small ejector which worked continuously and whose ATC action was further retarded by coal dust clogging the air intake. The result of these tests was the fitting of Western Region 'Britannias' with an 'isolating element' to close off the small ejector during braking and thus bring the braking system on those engines a little closer to the 1911 perfection of the Great Western system. As driver Wheeler is reported to have said, 'It wouldn't have happened if we'd had a "Castle" '.

CHAPTER 15

Lewisham

1957

WHEN I WAS A SIGNALMAN, THICK FOG WAS A TRIAL. THE STEAM AND smoke from passing locomotives made the surrounding murk all but impenetrable, and the task of spotting a train's tail lamp became very difficult indeed. Many a winter's morning I have gone home with red sore eyes from a night hanging out of the box window straining to catch a glimpse of the red tail lamp as it fled past in a whirl of smoky fog. In such conditions I would call out the permanent way gang to 'shoot' trains at my distant signals while another member of that long-suffering fraternity would stand outside the box all night to see tail lamps and report their presence — or otherwise — to me. Until this help arrived, I would go outside and spot the light from the ground, below steam level, but even when I had a man to help, if two trains were passing he could only see the one nearest to him and I would go out to spot the other lamp. Even today, many years after I saw my last steam-hauled train disappear into a thick fog, when I go into the back yard to get a bucket of coal on a foggy night and I see the house lights streaming away into the murk, I am instantly back on the lineside with the signal box windows above me, blazing into the foggy night.

If the fog was a trial for signalmen, it was a hundred times worse for engine drivers and I was always full of admiration for their steel nerves as they went into a wall of fog at 80 mph with a passenger train, or at 25 mph with a 700-ton goods train, which took as much distance or even more to bring to a stand than an express passenger train. The drivers survived by their uncanny knowledge of the road, driving by feel of bumps and lurches, by the sequence of sounds from overbridges or underbridges as well as by keeping a check and tally on each station or signal box as they passed. Having passed a distant signal, it was vital to know to which signal box that signal belonged — some boxes had only one stop signal after their distant while others had two, three or even five. The last stop signal in the sequence was the one that gave access to the next section. If a driver thought a signal box had but one stop signal then, when that one was lowered, he would believe he was 'Right Away' and then would not be looking for the second signal which actually controlled the entrance to the next section. This might be at 'Danger'. The perils are obvious. So, all down the line for maybe 245 miles, a man had to know exactly what the road held for him, gradients, curves, stations, signals, junctions and goods loops. To drive your way through that lot, virtually blindfold, was a virtuoso performance rarely appreciated by anyone not of the footplate fraternity — and they took it phlegmatically in their rolling stride.

On the ex-GWR lines of British Railways, the enginemen enjoyed the benefits of the ATC which had spread over all double track lines of the system since its introduction on the Henley branch in 1906. In July 1931, the Hudd Automatic Warning System was given a trial on the Southern Railway and a great deal of development was carried out with the system on LMS metals. The war put a stop to these researches although, paradoxically, research into wartime radar produced smaller, very much more powerful magnets which were quickly applied to the Hudd system after the war. The Hudd system (AWS) was brought into use over the old LT&SR route between Campbell Road Junction and Shoeburyness on 1 December 1947. It did not use the metal to metal contact of the GWR system with all the wear and tear that that involved, and it further improved on the earlier system by giving the driver a visual, as well as an aural, reminder that he had been given a warning to brake.

The AWS depended on magnetic induction. On the underside of the engine, 4 inches above rail level, was fixed a permanent magnet, its north pole leading. On the track, laid between the rails 200 yards on the approach side of each distant signal — or the outer distant signal when a signal box had two — there was another permanent magnet, its south pole facing the oncoming train and its upper surface slightly above rail level. Between 10 and 15 yards beyond this was laid an electro-magnet which was only energized when the distant signal was showing 'All Right'. When the engine magnet passed over the first track magnet, a current was induced which opened a small air valve. This sounded the warning horn and began to build up a pressure on a diaphragm which, after three seconds, would force the main air valve open and begin to apply the brakes. However, the electro-magnet would be reached in far less than three seconds and, if it was energized, the current induced would close the small air valve and thus stop the process. If, however, the second magnet was 'dead', the process of braking would go on until the driver lifted his cancelling lever. Not only did this stop the horn and the automatic braking process, it caused the hitherto all-black circular indicator to break into a chrysanthemum-shaped, yellow and black display which would remain in sight until the next track magnet at 'All Right' was passed.

British Railways developed their standard AWS system from the Hudd, the BR device being basically the same but with some small refinements. The Management seemed very reluctant to install the system, and in spite of several

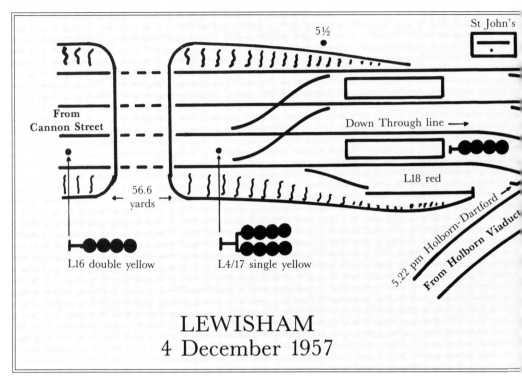

5½

St John's

From
Cannon Street

Down Through line ⟶

L18 red

56.6
← yards →

L16 double yellow

L4/17 single yellow

5.22 pm Holborn-Dartford

From Holborn Viaduct

LEWISHAM
4 December 1957

accidents that might have been saved by the presence of AWS — and much public hand-wringing after these events — by 1957 only a few engines running on the East Coast main line had been equipped to test a small number of track magnets. The system had been in use for years with great success on the Southend line, and one can only wonder why it was not installed on the other, very intensively used parts of London's rail network to give some assistance to drivers and some additional security to the passengers whose lives depended, especially in fogs, on the steel nerve and route knowledge of the footplatemen. Was this reluctance due to a shortage of investment funds, and was it negligence on the part of Government that the funds were not provided? In the very heavily used sections of London's suburban railways, was it expecting too much of flesh and blood never to make a mistake at any one of thousands of signals over millions of man-hours and millions of train miles?

St John's Junction, Lewisham, is on the main line of the old South Eastern Railway, 3¾ miles south-east of London Bridge station, ¾ mile from New Cross. From New Cross, the four-track main line ran in a cutting spanned by several road bridges until, at St John's, it was on an embankment. At the junction, the North Kent line continued straight on as a double track while the quadruple main line swung away southwards, passing beneath a steel girder bridge. This bridge carried the Holburn Viaduct to North Kent line railway, and the junction of this line with the North Kent was also controlled from St John's signal box. About 950 yards down the main line, towards Ashford and the coast, lay

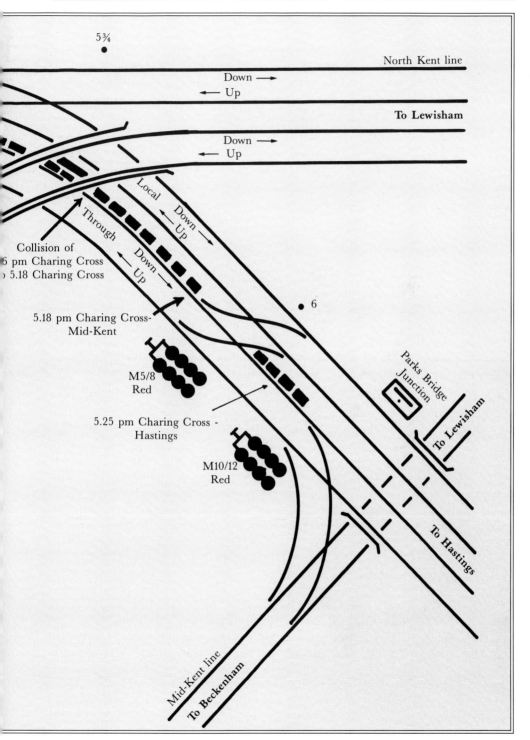

5¾

North Kent line

Down →

← Up

To Lewisham

Down →

← Up

Local

Down →

← Up

Through

Collision of
6 pm Charing Cross
5.18 Charing Cross

Down →

← Up

6

5.18 pm Charing Cross-
Mid-Kent

Parks Bridge
Junction

M5/8
Red

To Lewisham

5.25 pm Charing Cross -
Hastings

M10/12
Red

To Hastings

Mid-Kent line

To Beckenham

Parks Bridge Junction where a double track curve left the Down Through lines to drop down to a junction with the mid-Kent line to Beckenham. Trains on the Down Through line requiring to go down to the mid-Kent line had to cross over the Up Through line on the level at Parks Bridge Junction.

Trains passed St John's and Parks Bridge Junctions from Cannon Street, Charing Cross and London Bridge, so the area was the most intensively used piece of railway in the world. Over a 24-hour period, there were an average of 46 trains an hour passing St John's, and during the rush hour, 5.01 pm to 6.01 pm, one train passed that signal box every 45 seconds. On the Down Through line during that hour, 20 trains were scheduled to pass. St John's Junction was worked by two signalmen in a 54-lever signal box, one dealing with the up trains, the other with those on the down roads. Each man had a booking lad who maintained a 'second by second', accurate, written record of the sequence in which trains were described to the signal box from places in the rear, and also the times at which each train passed the box. Owing to the archaic system of train signalling then in use, these boys were absolutely vital to the safe working of the box. Parks Bridge Junction, with 50 levers, was also worked by two men, but on 4 December 1957 they had no booking lad. The Southern Region had not provided one, let alone two, and as a result the Parks Bridge Junction signalmen were operating an intense service of trains without a written record of what trains were approaching them or what trains had passed by. They were relying entirely on their memories and the vast experience they had gained over many years' service to keep an inherently unsafe system safe.

At the core of the problem was the type of train describer in use. These were designed by Mr C.V. Walker in the 1880s and were entirely unsuitable for the traffic of 1957. Two 'Walker' instruments were required to convey the necessary information about a train from one signal box to the next. One instrument showed

A train describer of the type in use between Lewisham St John's and Parks Bridge Junction. Each train's description is indicated by the pointer, but only until another train is described when the first description is lost. This archaic system required a constant, written record of the indicated sequence of trains. There was no one to keep such a record in Parks Bridge Junction box on the fatal night. (Author)

what type of train was approaching, the other showed which route the train was to take. The signalman transmitting the information did so by pulling forward the handle above the desired description and then released the pointer by pushing back the lever at which it had stopped; the pointer was driven by clockwork and rotated around the dial in a series of audible clicks until it was arrested at the new position. The booking lad would then record the new message and the time it was received. This was essential, because every two to three minutes, in the rush hour, a fresh description would be 'clocked on' and the previous description was lost. Without a booking lad to keep the tally, the signalman had to remember what had been described, and at Parks Bridge Junction there were six pairs of describers to watch besides actually moving the signal levers and looking after the telephone enquiries. There were no bell signals and the trains ran box to box with only the descriptions to warn the signalmen. If a man forgot a description, or if he missed seeing a description, his mental picture of the traffic approaching was, potentially, dangerously flawed. This was the case at Parks Bridge Junction on 4 December 1957 when the men were working without booking lads.

The trains were controlled along the tracks by electric colour-light signals of the four-aspect variety as intensely bright as those of 1989. These signals were installed with the 'third rail' electric traction during 1927-29; some worked quite automatically with the occupation of the track circuits ahead, but those at St John's and Parks Bridge Junctions were semi-automatic. Each signal was set to 'green' by the signalman reversing its lever, and each signal aspect automatically changed to 'red' by the action of the track circuits as the train moved along the track. The signalman could reverse a signal lever when track circuits permitted, and that signal's aspect would change from 'red' to 'yellow', 'double yellow' or 'green', depending on the aspects of signals ahead and the occupation of track circuits. A train standing on the rails held the signal immediately to its rear at red — 'Danger'. The signal next in rear of this would then be at 'single yellow', the next one back was then at 'double yellow' and the one behind that would show 'green'. There was no AWS installed.

At 12.30 pm on 4 December 1957, Driver Trew and his regular fireman, C.D. Hoare, booked on duty at Ramsgate motive power depot to work the 12.55 pm express to Charing Cross, non-stop except for the Ashford call. The day was even then foggy in the London area and the approaches thereto, traffic was delayed somewhat and driver Trew brought his train to a stand at Charing Cross at 4.10 pm, 23 minutes late. He was a very experienced man with 45 years' railway service, 18 as a driver. He handed his engine over to a 'ferry' crew and he and his fireman hurried away to the canteen for a quick cup of tea — the late arrival had cut their meal break short — before riding 'on the cushions' round to Cannon Street. They hurried and did not eat anything because they did not want to be late at Cannon Street and thus delay the departure of their back working, the 4.56 pm to Ramsgate.

At Cannon Street, however, there was no sign of their train. The engine, Bullied 'Pacific' No 34066 *Spitfire*, had been seriously delayed by the ever thickening fog. It had left Stewarts Lane shed, tender first, at 3.15 pm for the journey to the carriage sidings at Rotherhithe on the Bricklayers Arms branch, a trip which had taken the engine over the steel girder bridge at St John's, down on to the North Kent line before reversing back, past St John's box and finally on to its train in the carriage sidings at 4.45 pm. The engine had then hauled the carriages up the steep gradient to the main line where a pilot engine was attached to draw the coaches and the locomotive into Charing Cross. The fog had become dense, traffic was disrupted and the empty train did not arrive in the terminus until 5.55 pm.

For over an hour, driver Trew and his mate waited on the end of the platform hoping for their train to arrive. He felt he had to wait, for, if he went away to the warm somewhere he would not have been on hand when the train arrived and he would have caused further delay thereby. While he and Hoare waited, they saw other trains leaving, and we must now turn our attention to certain of them, beginning with the 5.05 pm Cannon Street to Hastings express.

This left at 5.43 and comprised eight coaches behind a 'Schools' Class 4-4-0 with driver Frewin and fireman Emery who had ridden up from Hastings 'on the cushions' for the working. They had taken note of the foggy conditions on the way up and were acutely aware of the particularly dense fog in the cutting between New Cross and St John's. Fireman Emery therefore made up a big fire before leaving Cannon Street and fired coal into the furnace only as far as London Bridge before closing the firebox doors and giving all his attention to looking out for signals. The engine was working only moderately — quarter regulator and 25% cut off — for a speed of 35 mph. There would be no need to fire any more coal till the train was clear of the complicated junctions and the worst of the fog. Fireman Emery saw signal A42 at the country end of New Cross station platform from a range of 40 yards. He reported promptly to his driver that it was showing a double yellow and driver Frewin at once closed the regulator and touched the brakes, asking his mate to continue to keep a sharp look-out because the next three signals, L16, L17 and L18 — semi-automatics controlled from St John's Junction — were all placed on the fireman's side of the line they were travelling on, the Down Through. The signals were sited on the 'wrong' side of the track because in clear weather this gave the driver the most distant view of each owing to the curvature of the line. In the cutting these signals could only be seen that evening as the engine's front buffers drew level with them — a range of 33 feet in the case of a 'Schools' Class engine. This was fireman Emery's evidence at the Inquiry, and Colonel Wilson, conducting the investigation, seemed not to be pleased. He pounced on Emery with, 'You could not see it until the last moment? A great, blazing colour light and you could not see it?' Fireman Emery remained quite unmoved at what seemed like an attempt to browbeat him. In the event, Frewin and Emery took their train warily past St John's, under the flyover and past Parks Bridge Junction until they were brought to a stand by a signal at Hither Green a short distance beyond.

Following them on the Down Through line was the 5.16 pm Cannon Street to Orpington electric multiple unit (emu). Signalman Presslee in St John's signal box 'clocked it on' to Parks Bridge as 'Main line' on one describer, 'Main electric' on the other. This was done as the train was passing New Cross. The 5.16 pm Cannon Street passed St John's at 6.03 and was brought to a stand by signals at Hither Green immediately in the rear of the 5.05 pm Cannon Street. Following close behind the 5.16 was the 5.25 pm Charing Cross to Hastings diesel-electric multiple unit (demu). There was no provision on the ancient Walker describers to describe such a train, and it had to be transmitted as 'Main line — Main electric'. Because Signalman Presslee was sending a second description identical to the one that had so recently been sent on that describer, he allowed the pointer to swing twice round the dial hoping that the prolonged clicking of the clockwork-electric escapement would draw attention to the slightly unusual fact.

Signalman Beckett at Parks Bridge Junction admitted that he probably did not see the second description and thus did not know of the second 'main line' train which was approaching. This train passed St John's at 6.08 pm and came to a stand at signal M10 at Parks Bridge Junction, out of sight of the signalman in the dense fog (although it would have been indicated in the track circuit diagram). Two minutes after Signalman Presslee had described the 5.25 pm Charing Cross demu forward as an emu, he had to describe the 5.18 pm Charing Cross to Hayes emu. This was transmitted as 'Mid-Kent — Main electric', the new description wiping out the earlier indication. Signalman Beckett did see this and duly noted in his head that the next train on the Down Through line required to take the right-hand junction at his box and go down on to the Beckenham line. He was unable to set the road for this movement because there was a train approaching on the Up Through line and because there was a train stationary on the down Mid-Kent line just ahead of the junction. As the 5.18 pm Charing Cross to Hayes emu was drawing to a stand at Parks Bridge M5 signal, behind the 5.25 pm Charing Cross to Hastings demu, the driver from the latter train, having waited three minutes at signal M10, was about to carry out Rule 55 by means of the signal-post telephone. He rang signalman Beckett and reported: 'I am the 5.25 Charing Cross to Hastings standing at your signal M10'. To this Beckett replied, according to the driver, 'All Right'. Beckett said of this conversation that he had not heard clearly what was said owing to the noise of the diesel engine, and after taking the message was still under the impression that the train at M10 wanted to go on to the Mid-Kent line.

No sooner had he put the phone down than the driver of the 5.18 pm Charing Cross to Hayes phoned from his signal-post telephone to report his position, but signalman Beckett said at the Inquiry that he had no recollection of any such message. Messages from all the signal-post telephones were answered in Parks Bridge box on one hand-set which did not advise the signalman as to which signal-post telephone was in use.

At 6.13 pm, the situation at Parks Bridge Junction was that the signalman was misled by his equipment. He could see on his diagram that there was a train at signal M10 which, he was convinced, required to take the branch line when in fact it wanted to go on down the main line and in fact, had he known this, he could have allowed it to proceed. Behind this train there was, standing at signal M5, the real branch train, of whose presence signalman Beckett was blissfully unaware. The rear end of the 5.18 Charing Cross to Hayes was stationary in dense fog only 138 yards ahead of the red light of signal L18 at St John's. Signals L17 and 16 to the rear were correctly displaying their single and double yellow warning aspects respectively, so the train was adequately protected. The tragic fact was that it need not have been standing there at all.

Back at Cannon Street, driver Trew was thoroughly chilled when, at 5.55 pm, he climbed aboard No 34066 and this fact could go a long way towards explaining what was to happen. It is also true that, apart from a cup of tea, he had not taken any food for several hours, all this due to his railwaymanlike desire not to cause any delay and thus exacerbate an already very difficult situation. He noted that water was relatively low in the tender, due to the time that the engine had taken to run from Stewarts Lane; there was not enough for the non-stop run to Tonbridge, so Trew warned the platform inspector to advise Sevenoaks that he would be stopping there to fill the tender. He was not in any way concerned about this; there was plenty of water to get to Sevenoaks, he would stop and get more there — fine.

He started his train at 6.08 pm, the fog becoming denser as he proceeded. All his signals were at green up to and including A42 at New Cross which Fireman Hoare spotted for him when it was close to the front of the engine. Driver Trew had the train well under control at 30 mph and after 'getting the green' at A42, Hoare did a round of firing in preparation for the long climb to Knockholt summit with 410 tons behind. What happened to driver Trew in the next 45 seconds will never be known. In the cutting, the fog was particularly thick leaving him in complete darkness unrelieved by the bright yellow lights of the signals L16 and L17 because they were on the fireman's side. They were visible only from 30 feet but, had they been on the driver's side, he would have had them coming out of the murk at him to help him maintain his orientation. That they were not on his side of the engine was due to the fact that they were sited for best viewing in clear weather.

Driver Trew was in complete darkness with no forward vision as the engine, an easy-riding 'Pacific', slipped smoothly along at only 30 mph without any passing landmarks. It was almost as if it was not moving. Driver Trew had been chilled and he was 62 years of age — did the warmth of the cab, his comfortable seat and the gentle movements of the engine comfort his body and lull his mind? Just for a few seconds? For whatever cause, his defences were down for about 45 seconds and the two warning signals, L16 and L17 were passed by unremembered. He was not asleep, but 'lost' a vital 1,000 yards in that featureless fog. As he approached St John's station lights, he called out to his mate, 'What have we got?'

Hoare popped his head over the side and to his horror saw the red-hazed fog at the end of the platform. He yelled his warning and the brakes were instantly applied, but before they could take effect 34066 crashed into the rear of the 5.18 Charing Cross. The 'Obstruction Danger' signal was sent from St John's Junction at 6.20 pm.

Looking back towards Lewisham St John's signal box and London. The 4.56 pm Cannon Street approached the flyover and collided with the rear of the 5.18 pm Charing Cross to Hayes on the down through line, the third track from the right, which resulted in the steam locomotive's tender falling against and displacing the over-bridge's central support. (Crown Copyright)

The 5.18 Charing Cross had been standing on the rising gradient with its brakes on, so the impact was that much worse. No 34066 forced its smokebox into the rear of the tenth coach, telescoping the ninth coach over and around the eighth. Motorman Skilton of Caterham was driving the emu and felt a jolt from the rear which suggested to him that he had been hit from behind. He did not think it was very serious until he got out and walked back. The rear three coaches

After its central supporting column was knocked away by the tender of No 34066, the Lewisham flyover sagged over the Kent Coast main line. It was the crushing weight of the bridge on the carriages beneath that caused most of the fatalities in the Lewisham crash. (NRM)

of his train were wrecked, and the leading coach of the Ramsgate train had been crushed against the engine's tender so that both coach and tender had been thrown to the left which such violence that they struck the central girder supporting the railway overbridge, dislodging the support and bringing the steel girders down on to the coaches. The shock wave of the crash travelled through the ground and was felt by a man working in a garage 400 yards away.

Two minutes after the collapse of the bridge, the 5.22 pm Holburn Viaduct to Dartford emu was moving slowly on to the bridge, going towards a signal at 'Danger'. Its driver saw the state of the track and was going slowly enough to be able to stop, but even so the leading coach was leaning at a sharp angle on the distorted rails above the wreckage below. The first calls for the emergency services were made by people living by the lineside. The ambulance service was called at 6.22 pm, the police at 6.23. An ambulance already on the road was diverted to the scene and arrived at 6.25, and the first one from the depot was only five minutes behind. In the darkness and dense fog, the true extent of the disaster became known only gradually and more and more resources were poured in. Householders along the line took the injured into their homes and came on to the line with tea, coffee, food, blankets and bandages, the latter made from torn-up sheets. The Salvation Army arrived, the WRVS and St John's Ambulance Brigade. The last of the wounded were in hospital by 10.30 pm. There had been nearly 1,500 people in the electric train and about 700 in the steam-hauled train. In all, 88 passengers were killed. The guard of the electric train was also killed and one other passenger died in hospital; 67 other passengers received injuries which did not require hospital treatment.

Gangs of men with breakdown vans and cranes from Ashford, Bricklayers Arms, Nine Elms and Stewarts Lane took 24 hours to disentangle the wreckage. The moveable coaches were towed away and the 350-ton steel girder bridge had to be cleared. Some outside help was called in to assist Southern Region men; the bridge was shored up and gangs of men worked continuously in a shift system for 36 hours to flame-cut the bridge into sections small enough to be lifted away. They worked beneath the bridge, not knowing if it would collapse on top of them as it was dismantled.

Driver Trew was, of course, utterly shattered by what had happened. He was taken to Lewisham hospital suffering from 'severe shock', to use the calm, formal language of the official report into the disaster. The following morning, 5 December, he 'made his own way home' still suffering from 'severe shock'. Whether he was given a companion for this potentially hazardous journey the official report does not mention. At home he retired at once to bed where he lay for weeks in a state of shock bordering on nervous breakdown.

Two days after his return home he was interviewed by the Ashford District Motive Power Superintendent, concerning the accident. This proceeding seems to have been lacking in sensitivity and, indeed, this gentleman had to leave the house shortly after he arrived 'because driver Trew's nervous tension was acute and he seemed on the point of breaking down', again quoting from the calm language of the report. Twelve days later he was visited by the police who informed

Clearing up the wreckage the next day, the overbridge supported on timber struts. (Crown Copyright)

him that he was to be charged with manslaughter. He was still very ill and it was not until 10 January 1958 that his doctor agreed that Colonel Wilson, heading the Ministry of Transport Inquiry, could question him about the incident.

On 21 April, Mr Trew attended the Old Bailey on a charge of the manslaughter of William Reynolds, guard of the 5.18 pm Charing Cross train. Mr Trew pleading 'Not Guilty'. He answered the questions put to him in a weak, hesitating voice and made frequent use of a bottle of smelling salts which he held all the while in a shaky hand. Even so, he was painfully honest in his answers to questions put to him by the prosecuting counsel, Mr Christmas Humphreys.

Q. What right had you to approach a red light at 20 to 25 mph?
A. I had no right at all.
Q. Why did you approach St John's at 20 to 25 mph?
A. I was expecting a green. I have never been stopped at St John's in all the time I have been driving.
Q. You had no right to assume that the signal would be green?
A. No.

Mr Trew's defence counsel said to the jury that 'Trew was not blinding along uncaring what happened to his passengers or his train. He got into a cutting of blackness and darkness and did not know where he was. As soon as he saw the lights of St John's he called out to his mate, "What have we got?"'

The judge told the jury that to be guilty of manslaughter 'the facts must be such that in the opinion of the jury the negligence of the prisoner went beyond a mere matter of compensation between subjects and showed such a disregard for life and the safety of others as to amount to a crime against the State and deserving of punishment. . . if you come to the conclusion that he failed to take precautions and that his driving amounted to such gross recklessness, negligence and disregard for passengers then it ought to be regarded as criminal.' The jury then retired and returned after four hours. It is easy to imagine what the suspense was doing to Mr Trew. The jury reported that it could not agree on a unanimous verdict either way. The case was then dismissed and a re-trial was ordered for 7 May. Mr Trew was going to have to stand trial twice on the same charge.

In Ramsgate there was tremendous support for Mr Trew. A petition with 10,000 signatures went to the Home Secretary, R.A. Butler, asking for 'mercy for Trew'. When he appeared again at the Old Bailey on 7 May, he had given evidence at the formal inquiries spread over months, each time having to re-live that ghastly moment when, for the first time in 45 years, he had made a mistake. Waiting, between inquiries and trials, he can hardly have had the terrible business out of his mind. Now, on 7 May, his health was suffering and the evidence against him was withdrawn. Mr Christmas Humphreys said, 'I must repeat that it is only on the proved medical and mental condition of the defendant and the real danger to him of a further trial that I ask leave to offer no evidence against him'. The judge discharged him and Mr Trew walked from the court a free man.

Had he been treated fairly? The signalling system was at fault and essential staff had not been provided. Why had the AWS not been installed on the busiest stretch of railway in the world? All these matters had contributed to the disaster, but only Mr Trew was saddled with the blame and only Mr Trew was brought to trial — twice — for the death of a fellow railwayman.

CHAPTER 16.

Dagenham East

1958

THE AFTERNOON OF 30 JANUARY 1958 SAW THE FOG CONTINUING TO drift around the Thames estuary and the situation deteriorated as night fell so that by 6 pm a driver on the south or north bank of the river was lucky if he could see lights beyond the end of his locomotive's boiler. On the Fenchurch Street to Southend route, he would not have been able to see the end of the boiler of his engine. The consensus was that visibility was down to 10 yards.

The line from Barking to Dagenham East was quadruple, the up and down local lines being used, as a rule, by the 'tube' trains of London Underground although the Southend steam services did use them occasionally. The up and down through lines were the exclusive preserve of the Southend and Shoeburyness steam services. After Barking Junction, the signal boxes we are concerned with were Upney, Becontree and Dagenham East station. There was an intermediate block section between Becontree and Dagenham East called 'Heathway signals', worked from Becontree box, so there were, in effect, four signal boxes in the 3¼ miles from Upney to Dagenham East and they were all needed during the rush hour periods; outside those times Upney and Becontree were switched out. During the morning and evening peak periods, 6.45 am to 9.45 am and 4.15 pm to 7.15 pm, the signalmen in those boxes handled 117 trains — 39 per hour.

On the through lines, the steam trains were signalled by traditional semaphores with normal block signalling. The signalmen at the boxes mentioned, Upney, Becontree and Dagenham East, could not give 'Line Clear' to the box in the rear unless the home and distant signals were at 'Danger' and 'Caution' respectively and the 'berth' track circuit was clear. The levers working the starting signals at these boxes were released for one pull only by 'Line Clear' from the box ahead, and the home signal could not be pulled unless the starting sig-

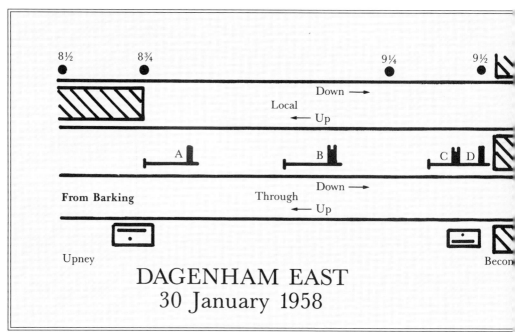

DAGENHAM EAST
30 January 1958

nal lever was normal (at 'Danger') in the frame. The Hudd AWS was installed at the distant signal of each box so the whole line seemed to be very efficiently locked against accidents and, indeed, it worked at high pressure for many years without incident.

Upney signal box on late turn that 30 January 1958 was manned by signalman Tinson who was 45 years old with 12 years' railway service, 2½ of them at Upney. Becontree was manned by porter-signalman Sass, 36 years old with less than one year's service and only 5 weeks as a porter-signalman. Dagenham East was manned by signalman Andrews, 49 years old with 34 years' railway service. Because of the fog the trains were running late, and Upney box was still open at 7.15 pm when it ought to have been switched out. In Becontree box, porter-signalman Sass had completed a twelve-hour day at 7 pm and was understandably keen to close down and go home. This was not difficult, in spite of the constant procession of trains, because the old LMS (LT&SR section) regulations were still in force which permitted a box to be switched out when there was a train in the section. All that was required was that the block indicator of the section in advance of the box being switched out should agree with the indication shown on the block indicator for the section to the rear of the box being switched out. Thus the man in advance knew of the presence of a train in the section.

The trains were running 'block and block', to use the railway vernacular. The 6.15 pm Fenchurch Street was standing outside the home signal at Dagenham East from 7.19 until 7.24 pm because the 6.10 pm Fenchurch Street was ahead. At 7.14 pm signalman Tinson at Upney asked 'Is Line Clear?' to porter-signalman Sass at Becontree for the 6.20 pm Fenchurch Street. Sass 'gave the road' at 7.16

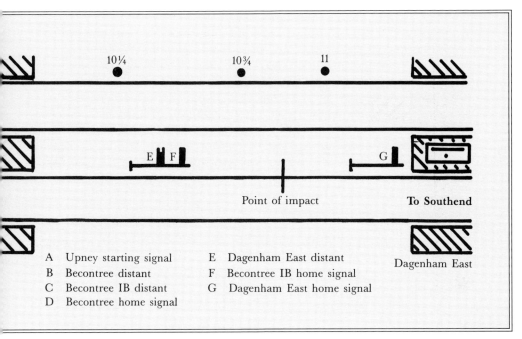

A   Upney starting signal
B   Becontree distant
C   Becontree IB distant
D   Becontree home signal

E   Dagenham East distant
F   Becontree IB home signal
G   Dagenham East home signal

pm and at 7.17 pm the 6.20 passed Upney very slowly because the driver had had the distant signal at 'Caution' against him. Signalman Tinson sent 'Train out of Section' to Barking at 7.17 pm and was at once asked 'Is Line Clear?' for the 6.35 pm Fenchurch Street. Tinson 'gave the road' and the train came to a stand at his home signal at 7.23 pm because the 6.20 was of course occupying the section between Upney's starting signal and Becontree. At 7.24, signalman Andrews in Dagenham East gave 'Train out of Section' to Sass for the 6.15 pm Fenchurch Street. Porter-signalman Sass immediately 'got the road' from Andrews for the 6.20 pm and lowered his signals. Having done that he at once sent 'Train Entering Section' to Andrews. The train had not actually reached Becontree but Sass had to do this if he was to switch out — the instruments had to have the correct showing after he had 'turned the switch'. As soon as signalman Andrews had placed the indicator to 'Train on Line', Sass sent 7-5-5 to both Tinson and Andrews; both men replied and with that Sass threw the switch to take Becontree box out of circuit, leaving Upney and Dagenham East in direct communication. The time was 7.24½.

Signalman Tinson then lowered his home signal to bring the 6.35 pm inside the protection of the home signal, intending that it should wait at his starting signal until the 6.20 pm had cleared Dagenham East. This he was entitled to do by the special regulations applying to his box. At 7.26 pm, as the 6.35 pm was slowly approaching through the fog, Tinson was asked 'Is Line Clear?' by Andrews for an up train. Tinson 'gave the road' and then went to his window to watch as the 6.35 passed by. Riding in the last coach the guard called out, 'Are all the boxes in?'

'No,' replied Tinson, 'Becontree's switched'.

The tail lamp could just be seen as the train dragged its tail into the fog at 7.27½. At 7.29 pm, the up train was sent 'on line' by signalman Andrews. Tinson 'got the road' from Barking and cleared his up through line signals. Having done that he went outside for a pee and when he came back at 7.31 pm he discovered to his amazement that the track circuit between the signal box and the down starting signal, which had been showing 'occupied' with the 6.35 standing on it was now showing 'unoccupied'. In a panic, and somehow hoping that perhaps the track circuit was not working, he dashed outside and along the line for 40 yards in the desperate hope that the train was still there. He saw nothing and could hear nothing — he had to face facts, the train had gone. Back in the box at 7.36 pm he sent the 'Train Running Away' signal, 4-5-5 on the bell.

Passed fireman R.S. Barnes was driving British Railways 'Standard' 2-6-4 tank No 80079 at the head of the 6.35 pm Fenchurch Street. He was aged 25, a Tilbury man who had joined the railway service aged 16 in 1949. He had become a fireman the following year and had had 5½ years' experience of working over the line as a fireman. In July 1957 he passed his examination in the rules and engine knowledge to become a driver and was then classed 'passed fireman' and eligible to take on driver's duties when required. In the six months between July and January he had driven over the line 13 times but never in a fog. He now found himself in a real 'pea-souper' where the bright electric lights of the passing 'tube' trains a few yards away were no more than glimmers in the murk and he was trying to spot oil lamps on signals as much as 21 feet tall. Such lamps are at their brightest from a range of at least 100 yards; the closer one gets, the less they show so that in dense fog they are invisible when they are at the most favourable range. As one gets closer still, the acute angle of view, looking up at them, renders the light dimmer and dimmer.

The starting signal arm and lamp at Upney were 21 feet above the rails and the Inquiry concluded that Barnes either forgot that it existed or else he was looking for it and missed it in the blinding fog. Barnes naturally enough emphatically denied that he had done any such thing. He said he had seen the green light of the signal. If the signalling had been carried out as stated by all three signalmen concerned then that signal could not possibly have been cleared. There was, however, one other possibility. If porter-signalman Sass had not sent the 'Train on Line' signal to Andrews for the 6.20 pm Fenchurch Street then when he, Sass, had turned his block switch to take Becontree out of circuit, that 'Line Clear' on the Becontree — Dagenham East block instrument would have been transferred to the instrument in Upney, now in direct contact with Dagenham East. This would have allowed signalman Tinson to clear his starting signal for the 6.35 pm. This in itself is a large 'if' because it would have been easier for Sass to carry out the routine in the correct rather than the incorrect way.

The second big 'if' concerns signalman Tinson. If he pulled his starting signal lever merely because a 'Line Clear' indication suddenly showed up on his instrument, without his having received 'Train out of Section' or without having exchanged 'Is Line Clear?' bells with Dagenham East, he would have been behaving against all his training and instincts. He knew the section ahead was occupied, for he stopped the 6.35 for that very reason. Because he knew that Sass was switching out, he would have known what the 'Line Clear' had meant had he seen it come up on his instrument at that time when he had not asked for it. The Inquiry decided that Barnes had forgotten or missed the starting signal and had thus driven past it at 'Danger'.

A quarter of a mile after passing Upney's starter, the AWS magnet applying to Becontree's down through line distant signal gave Barnes the 'All Right' and he put on steam. From the near dead stand at Upney to the crash at Dagenham it was estimated that the average speed was 25 mph, so the top speed was much higher. The 6.20 was moving at about 5 mph when it was struck, and by looking at the damage caused it was estimated that No 80079 was running at 25 mph when the impact occurred. Owing to the poor visibility, Barnes did not see the tail lamp of the 6.20 until he was very close and his brake application had only a few seconds to work. Neither he nor his fireman, S.G. Fryer, was badly hurt, and as soon as they could they got down and did their best to protect the other lines; Barnes went back to tell his guard so that he could go to the rear with detonators while fireman Fryer ran forwards to tell the signalman. A minute after the crash, at about 7.35, an up London Transport train ran into the wreckage, but the train was travelling slowly and little harm was done.

People living close to the lineside heard the noise of the impact and dialled 999 for all emergency services. No 80079 had tunnelled through the rear three coaches of the 7-coach train, and, of the 1,000 passengers on the two trains, ten were killed and 72 were taken to hospital injured. Signalman Andrews was 650 yards from the scene and knew nothing of the crash. At 7.36 pm he received the 4-5-5 code from Upney and replied to this with 'Obstruction Danger' which was the only reply he could give to that code when the section was occupied. It was not until 7.40 pm, when Fryer came rushing into the box, that he knew that the line was actually obstructed.

Later on, passed fireman Barnes came into the box. Signalman Andrews gave both men tea and asked Barnes what happened. 'Did you go by Upney's starter at "Danger"?' Andrews was by far the senior man, he knew that Sass had carried out the switching procedure correctly and that therefore this was the only explanation. Passed fireman Barnes denied he had done so, saying, 'No, of course not. He [the Upney signalman] pulled us up at the starter and pulled it off — you know, the starter alongside the little cabin by the bridge'. Andrews was adamant about this and repeated it in front of Barnes, describing where all three of them had been standing in the box when the conversation took place.

The significance of Barnes's remark was immense and damning. It showed that he had mistaken Upney's home signal for the starting signal — he was one signal adrift in his tally of signals — so that when the home signal (which he took to be the starting signal) was lowered, he naturally believed he was 'Right Away'. As an illustration of the degree of precision a driver needs in his knowledge of the road, this example cannot be bettered. One can only feel sorry for poor Mr Barnes.

CHAPTER 17

Welwyn Garden City

1957

AFTER THE 1935 CRASH AT WELWYN GARDEN CITY STATION, THE 'Welwyn' block system of electrical controls was installed there (and gradually all over the country) to prevent such a rear-end collision happening again. Before a 'Line Clear' could be sent to the box in rear, the home and distant signals had to be at 'Danger', the berth track circuit had to be clear and it had to have been occupied and cleared by the previous train. But although human ingenuity can invent such clever devices, human frailty can drive a coach and horses — or an engine and coaches — right through them.

In 1957, Welwyn Garden City station had an enlarged layout. In 1944, a connection had been laid from the south end of the Hertford line platform to the up slow line, and from then onwards southbound Hertford line trains used the up slow while the old branch line became a goods loop. Also at that time an enlarged goods yard had been built on the up side of the line. The lever frame in Welwyn Garden City signal box (hereinafter known as 'Welwyn') installed in 1926 had 65 levers, but the new layout required 81 so extra levers were added to the frame. Welwyn's up fast line signals were spread over a 2,700 yard length of track from the up distant just south of the viaduct to the north of the station to the up starting signal well to the south of the station.

When trains were running very close together, as was frequently the case, the driver of an up train might receive a 'Caution' from Welwyn's up distant signal because the preceding train had not cleared Hatfield, then a few seconds later that train would clear and the Welwyn signalman could lower all his up fast line signals, outer home, inner home and starter, but the station's footbridge blocked the view of the starting signal so the driver of the checked train would have to go at reduced speed for maybe ¾ mile until he could see the starting signal under the bridge.

In September 1956, an 'inner distant' signal was placed below the inner home on the same spot and spare lever No 31 was used to operate it. The signal was on the approach side of the footbridge so drivers could see it from several hundred yards away. If they had received a check at the outer distant, on passing beneath a bridge by the outer home they could then see the inner distant cleared for them and could therefore put on steam much sooner than would otherwise have been the case. This type of signal was by no means unknown elsewhere on ex-LNER lines, and seems to me, as an ex-signalman, to be a very good idea, but many very experienced drivers disliked the Welwyn example and called it a 'hurry up' signal. They would have preferred a 'banner repeater' in that position, but the AWS was installed and was not placed at 'banners', while any distant signal could be provided with a magnet. The Welwyn inner distant was considered to be misleading, some men actually thought it was Hatfield's distant and their annoyance may have built on the traumas of the past to create a certain suspicion about the efficiency of the signals and the signalmen at Welwyn.

On 7 January 1957, Signalman Betteridge took over the early turn in Welwyn box at 6 am. He was 56 years of age with ten years' experience in that box. With him he had his very capable 19-year-old booking lad, M. Winter. Down at Welwyn North box, on the other side of the great viaduct, was relief signalman Dolby, aged 64, with nine years as a reliefman at the end of a lifetime of signal box work. The morning was dark with some drifting mist. As the sky lightened, just before dawn, signalman Dolby could see the parapet of the viaduct 310 yards away while signalman Betteridge could see signal lamps 200 yards from his box. As usual, the tracks were well filled with trains, three of which concern us here. Driver Gray on Train 111, an overnight express from the North, had an engine fitted with the new AWS gear. He passed Welwyn North box at 7.01 am and saw Welwyn Garden City's up fast line distant signal at 'Caution' when he was half-way across the viaduct at a range of 250-300 yards. His AWS horn sounded, he acknowledged this and his 'all-black' display changed to the black and yellow 'chrysanthemum'. The preceding train had not cleared Hatfield, so signalman Betteridge had not been able to clear his signals. As Train 111 passed the outer home, Betteridge was able to 'get the road' for it and he 'pulled off'. The AWS bell rang at about the same time as the inner distant light came into view, the AWS display reverted to 'all-black' and driver Gray put on steam. The inner distant, with its magnet 200 yards on the approach side, had saved several minutes.

When train 111 passed Welwyn North, signalman Dolby sent 'Train out of Section' to the man at Woolmer Green and was at once asked 'Is Line Clear?' for a stopping passenger train. Dolby 'gave the road' to Woolmer Green and 'asked the road' on the up slow line to signalman Betteridge in Welwyn box. This was done because the up fast line was still occupied by the express, and to keep the stopping train running he had to turn it on to the slow line. The facing points from up main to up slow were at the south end of the viaduct and were worked from Welwyn North box by means of hand-generated electricity. Semaphore signals on a 'bracket' situated just south of the viaduct controlled movements over the points: Welwyn North's up main starting signal to the right,

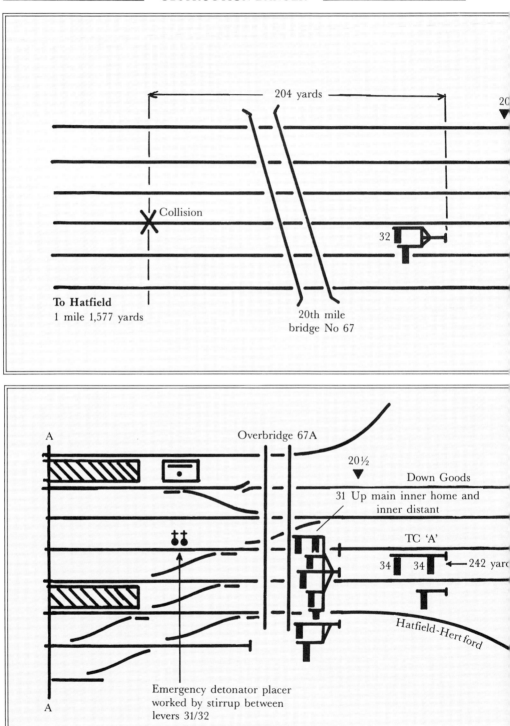

204 yards

20

Collision

32

To Hatfield
1 mile 1,577 yards

20th mile
bridge No 67

A

Overbridge 67A

20½

Down Goods

31 Up main inner home and
inner distant

TC 'A'

34   34   ← 242 yard

Hatfield-Hertford

Emergency detonator placer
worked by stirrup between
levers 31/32

A

WELWYN GARDEN CITY
7 January 1957

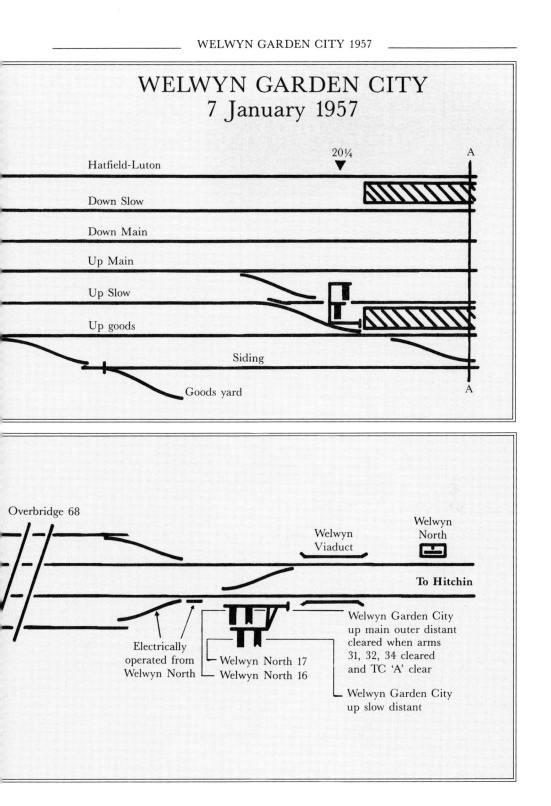

Hatfield-Luton

Down Slow

Down Main

Up Main

Up Slow

Up goods

Siding

Goods yard

Overbridge 68

Welwyn Viaduct

Welwyn North

To Hitchin

Electrically operated from Welwyn North

Welwyn North 17
Welwyn North 16

Welwyn Garden City up main outer distant cleared when arms 31, 32, 34 cleared and TC 'A' clear

Welwyn Garden City up slow distant

Welwyn North signal box and station, signalman Dolby's post on 7 January 1957 when the up Aberdeen sleeper, hauled by Owen Tudor, came out of the tunnel and passed the station at something over 60 mph. This view taken in August 1970 is looking towards the tunnel. (Mr J.Macfarlane / Author's Collection)

up main to up slow line starting signal to the left, each with an outer distant signal for Welwyn Garden City below. The stopping train, No 1565, passed Welwyn North at 7.05 am and driver Thurston was able to see the left-hand green light routing him to the up slow line when he was half-way across the viaduct. Both distant signals were showing yellow lights. He went in over the turn-out at 7.06 am.

As Train 1565 cleared on to the slow line, so Train 111 cleared Welwyn Garden City and Train 113, the 7.10 pm Aberdeen, passed Woolmer Green. Dolby 'got the road' on the up fast line for this and cleared his signals at 7.06 am. The Aberdeen was a train of 11 coaches hauled by a Class 'A2/3' 'Pacific' No 60520 *Owen Tudor*, which was not equipped with AWS gear. The train passed Welwyn North box at 7.11 am and both its driver, Mr Knapp, and its fireman, Mr Tyers, had seen the Welwyn North distant signal at green. Fireman Tyers saw no more signals after that and could not corroborate his driver's claim that Welwyn Garden City's up main distant was also showing a green light. Unless some malign person had been standing at the foot of the post holding the signal in the 'All Right' position *after* signalman Betteridge in Welwyn box had given 'Line Clear' to Welwyn North, it was impossible for the signal to be showing a green light. It had been at 'Caution' when Train 111 had passed it, the driver had checked his speed and, as Train 111 was still in the section to Hatfield when Betteridge gave 'Line Clear' to Dolby for Train 113, he could not have operated the distant signal's lever — the electrical and mechanical interlocking would have prevented this. However, driver Knapp was convinced that the signal had been cleared for him.

In Welwyn box, at 7.11, signalman Betteridge received 'Train Entering Section' from Welwyn North for No 113, received 'Train out of Section' for No 111 from Hatfield and had to decide what to do. He had the stopping train at the up slow line platform which was running late, and the Aberdeen sleeping car train 1½ miles away which was running early. The stopping train had a full load of commuters anxious to get to work on time, and the only way they were to be satisfied was if their driver and fireman were given a clear road. Betteridge had had this problem in mind since 7.02 am, and had been keeping an eye on the situation. As the bells clanged out he knew what he was going to do. He set the road from up slow to up fast, pulled the signals and, following the stan-

Looking north from the down platform at Welwyn Garden City in September 1970. Just above the bridge, the arm of the up main inner home signal is raised for the passage of the up 'Flying Scotsman'. This was one of the signals passed at 'Danger' by Owen Tudor *in January 1957. The 'Deltic' is opposite the spot on the down main line, immediately to the left of express, where the impact occurred in the 1935 rear-end collision.* (Mr J.Macfarlane/Author's Collection)

dard practice at Welwyn under these circumstances, he operated his detonator-placing machine on the up fast line to the rear of the points. The up fast line signals were all at 'Danger', except for the starting signal which had been cleared for the stopping train. This was a six-coach train with a 1929 vintage, wooden LNER brake-third at the trailing end, the brake van portion incorrectly marshalled at the leading end; the three coaches ahead were British Railways steel vehicles and the front two were, again LNER wooden-bodied carriages. The locomotive was a powerful 2-6-4 tank of Class 'L1', No 67741 from Hitchin shed driven by Mr Thurton. He appreciated the understanding of the situation shown by signalman Betteridge in routing him 'out main line' and, once clear of the points, he accelerated hard in an attempt to make up time.

Driver Knapp on *Owen Tudor* was running at about 60 mph. Up until Welwyn viaduct the night had been only moderately misty but, he said, as he got half-way across the viaduct he ran into a patch of thick fog which prevented him from seeing Welwyn's up main distant signal until he was about to pass it. He was quite certain he had seen a green light. The train was in plenty of time, so he closed his regulator and let the engine coast. Smoke from the chimney went rolling down the fireman's side of the engine. For no reason he could give, driver Knapp did not see the outer home signal at 'Danger'; he said he was looking out for it but missed it. This did not worry him unduly because he had had the distant at 'All Right', he said. As he approached the inner home signal, smoke suddenly filled the enclosed cab so that he could see nothing. Had his engine been fitted with the AWS he would have received a warning horn from the magnet connected with that disliked inner distant.

He ran by the inner home at 60 mph, then his engine ran over the detonators as it passed the signal box. Neither he nor his fireman heard the explosion, while the smoke in the cab was still so thick that he could not see the station's electric lights as he passed. Having cleared the station, the cab cleared of smoke and ahead driver Knapp saw a red light which he took to be the tail lamp of a train. Above the lamp there was a signal at green — Welwyn's starting signal cleared for the stopping train — but Mr Knapp made no report of seeing this. He dismissed the red light as belonging to a train on the up slow line and kept rolling. At the last minute, fireman Tyers, who had been sitting quietly, relying on his driver whom he could see was facing forward, apparently watching the road, suddenly realized that there was a red light on the line and yelled 'Whoa!' Driver Knapp gave a full emergency application of the brake.

When the Aberdeen train had occupied the outermost track circuit — 'CA' — the corresponding red indicator light had come on in the illuminated diagram in Welwyn box. Betteridge was at once alerted because the train had arrived at that point too quickly for one which had been given a 'Caution' indication by his up main distant signal. His immediate concern was to replace the 'slow to fast' crossover points and this he did as soon as track circuit 'BD' cleared after the passing of the stopping train. The latter was occupying track circuit 'CD' going up to the starting signal when the Aberdeen train burst through the bridge a few feet to the north of the signal box, making 60 mph. Betteridge had not seen it occupying its successive red lights across the diagram because he had been attending to the crossover, but now he knew it was a runaway as the detonators exploded and the coaches drummed by. The booking lad, M. Winter, was at the window with a red light but no one saw and the train disappeared up the line.

Betteridge sent 4-5-5 to Hatfield No 2 and stood by to throw his starting signal to 'Danger' as soon as he could. His difficulty was that he did not know whether the stopping train had passed it or not. To have thrown the signal to 'Danger' before it had gone by it would have been disastrous. Luckily, driver Thurton had made a very smart getaway and was running at around 35 mph when the collision took place. He felt a surge forward and then a fierce pull backwards as the impact severed the brake hoses to bring the automatic brake into action. The rear two coaches of the semi-fast were overturned and wrecked. The brake-third, marshalled with the passenger compartments trailing, took the force of a 25 mph collision and disintegrated, although only one poor soul was killed and 25 were injured. Six coaches in the Aberdeen were derailed but remained upright and were kept in line by the strength of the buckeye couplings. Driver Knapp, taken completely by surprise, was severely shocked, but guard Blott on the stopping train had a lucky escape. He was riding in the rear van but, having seen a door handle not properly turned further along the train, had walked forward to attend to it. The guard of the Aberdeen train walked back towards Welwyn to protect the rear and, finding a shunting engine at work in the yard, told the driver what had happened and sent him back along to sidings to raise the alarm. Signalman Betteridge sent 'Obstruction Danger' to Hatfield Nos 2 and 3 and to Welwyn North at 7.18 am.

The 'Welwyn' block system of controls between Welwyn Garden City and Welwyn North boxes was meticulously checked and found to be in perfect order.

'A2' Class 'Pacific' Owen Tudor on its side a mile south of Welwyn Garden City station on 7 January 1957 after running past signals at 'Danger' to collide with the rear of a local commuter train. The train's 'buckeye' couplings have managed to prevent all but the first two coaches from overturning, thus saving many casualties. (BBC Hulton Picture Library)

Betteridge could not have given 'Line Clear' to Dolby for train 113 unless the distant signal had been at 'Caution'. After that it could only have been cleared by malicious interference from the lineside. An elaborate experiment involving 60520 *Owen Tudor* being run at 60 mph past several signal boxes, including Welwyn, proved that Betteridge had definitely put his warning detonator on the line before the Aberdeen train arrived and that the noise of the explosion, as heard in the fully enclosed cab of the engine, free-wheeling at 60 mph, was not particularly loud. The Inquiry concluded that the collision was due to driver Knapp's oversight, and there the matter should have rested, but rumours began to circulate, and legends and fairy tales arose concerning the alleged malfunctioning of Welwyn Garden City's up main distant signal, and in spite of the overwhelming scientific evidence some of the drivers at Peterborough's New England shed were determined to prove the contrary — even if it meant fabricating the evidence.

Significantly, none of these rumours mentioned the one, proven occasion when that signal suffered a 'wrong side' failure. On 14 March 1956, during a lineside fire, certain electric cables lost their insulation, made bare-wire contact and gave a false feed to the signal motor which then raised the signal arm while the stop signals to which it applied were still at 'Danger'. This was seen and duly reported by driver Denleye of Peterborough. The wires were replaced and that was the end of the matter; there were no complaints until after driver Knapp into the rear of the stopping train.

On 8 March 1957, almost exactly three months to the day after the crash, relief signalman Dolby was on early turn in Welwyn box with relief signalman Harris in Welwyn North box. There was a slight haze around 7 am but no one denied that visibility was at least 500 yards. At 7.15 am, driver Crisp of Peterborough brought coal train No 1063 past Welwyn's outer distants, both of which he reported as being at 'Caution', turned in on to the up slow line and brought his train to a stand at the outer home signal at 7.22 am. At 7.20 am, up passenger train No 1603 passed the up main distant signal for Welwyn at 'Caution' followed at 7.29 am by local passenger train No 1593 whose driver found the distant signal at 'All Right'. Signalman Dolby returned the signal to 'Caution' behind this train, gave 'Train out of Section' at 7.31 and was at once asked 'Is Line Clear?' by Harris for the Aberdeen, Train 113. Dolby 'gave the road'. He could not have pegged 'Line Clear' unless his signals were properly at 'Caution' and 'Danger'. A down local passenger train had disgorged its passengers at Welwyn's down platform and the empty coaches had to be shunted to the up side to form a working back to King's Cross. Train 1593 was still in the section to Hatfield, so Dolby could not lower his signals for the Aberdeen. He decided to make use of the time by crossing the coaches to the up side, within the protection of the inner home signal, and the Aberdeen could wait at the outer home. He was perfectly entitled to carry out this movement at that time, so he pulled the various crossover points which irrevocably locked the levers for the main line signals.

Signalman Harris, having obtained 'Line Clear' from Dolby, hurried to clear his signals for the Aberdeen. He knew that the train had passed his outer distant at double yellow, but he hoped to be able to give the driver a green light on the inner distant and felt sure that he had 'got the signal off' in time. He was surprised to see the engine come out of the tunnel rather more slowly than usual. The engine was 'A2/3' No 60514 *Chamossaire* hauling ten coaches; it was driven by Mr Fowler and fired by Mr Kingswood, both of New England, Peterborough, shed. At the Inquiry, these men were able to be very precise about the aspect of Welwyn's up main outer distant signal. Fireman Kingswood could not see the signal from his side so he asked his driver what aspect it was showing. Fowler called out 'Right Away' and Kingswood saw him look out again, after this, to make sure that it was showing green. Satisfied, the fireman busied himself with his work until he heard his driver call out, 'They are on here!' He looked out and saw the inner home signal at 'Danger'. Fireman Kingswood told the Inquiry that they were running at 60 mph at that moment, the brakes were applied and the train came to a stand a little way beyond Welwyn station, 390 yards from where driver Fowler had first moved the brake handle. His driver told him that he had not seen the aspect of the outer home signal because it had been obscured by the smoke from a coal train standing at it.

In Welwyn signal box, Dolby had been replacing the crossover levers after transferring the empty coaches from the down to the upside when he saw, by the lights in his diagram, that the Aberdeen had passed his outer home at 'Danger'. He at once pulled his detonator lever and checked the signal arm repeaters — everything was in order. *Chamossaire* came through the bridge, well under control as far as Dolby could tell, at about 25 mph, exploded the detonators and came to a stand 290 yards further up the line. When fireman Kingswood came into the box Dolby told him he had passed two stop signals at 'Danger'. Kingswood retorted that his driver had seen the distant showing 'All Right' and added, 'We have not forgotten driver Knapp'.

'Nor have we,' replied signalman Dolby. Fireman Kingswood told the Inquiry later that he formed the distinct impression that Dolby was sceptical of both Knapp's and Fowler's claims.

At the Inquiry, driver Fowler said that he had never experienced any trouble with the up main distant signal at Welwyn until that morning, but he knew men who had and he named New England drivers Crisp, Lupton, goods guard Houghton and a Hitchin man Squires. All these men were brought in and questioned. Driver Crisp denied any knowledge of any irregularity with that signal, and driver Squires said the same but pointed out that he had reported the inner distant for being cocked up out of the proper, horizontal, position. This had been due to an over-tight wire and was promptly rectified. Guard Houghton said that on 26 January 1957 he was in his van at the back of the coal train and had seen Welwyn's outer distant at 'All Right' when he could clearly see the outermost signal at 'Danger'. The track was dead straight, but even so his story was incredible because from the spot where he said he saw this he was one mile from the home signal; furthermore, the driver of this train, when traced and questioned, denied any knowledge of such an event. He had had the distant signal in view constantly and it had never shown anything but a 'Caution' aspect.

Driver Lupton's story was more elaborate. He stated that on three occasions during the week 12-17 November 1956, when he was working coal train No 1063, he had seen Welwyn's up main outer distant at 'All Right' and had subsequently been routed from the up main to the up slow at Welwyn station. On the Thursday or Saturday of that week, when returning 'light' to Peterborough, he had stopped on the down slow line outside the box at Welwyn and had gone to see the signalman to ask him what was wrong with the distant signal. The signalman had told him that he was blocking the platform line for a passenger train and asked him to move his engine on into the goods line. Thinking that the signalman was trying to get rid of him and his awkward questions, he drove into the loop and did not get back to the box. Such was his concern for safety that he did not report the faulty signal to anyone until after driver Fowler's contretemps at Welwyn on 8 March.

The guard of driver Lupton's train was traced. He said he knew nothing at all about the matter. When the journals he had made of the trips that week were examined it was found that his train had only once been routed from up fast to up slow at Welwyn station, on a Wednesday. The signal box registers at Welwyn and Hatfield No 2 bore this out. Furthermore, if the Welwyn signalman had pulled his distant signal for a 'main line' run, he would have had to ask

'Is Line Clear?' from Hatfield before being able to clear his signals. If he then threw the signals back to 'Danger' and altered the points after the train had passed his distant signal, he would have had to (a) send the 3-5 'Cancelling train' code to Hatfield No 2 and (b) obtain 'Line Clear' for that train on the up slow line. All this would have been booked at Hatfield, even if not at Welwyn. There were no such entries. In the face of such evidence, driver Lupton had to admit that he had been wrong on important details in his story, but he refused to back down on his claim that the outer distant signal had been 'off' when the stop signals were 'on'.

Driver Fowler had passed at 'Danger' the outer home signal for Welwyn. This had two, co-acting, arms on a lattice mast. The lower arm was 16 ft 6 in above rail level, the upper arm 36 ft tall; the conformation was thus to enable the signal to be seen in spite of the brick arch bridge on its approach side. Fowler said he missed the signal because of smoke from the coal train No 1063, but driver Crisp said that his engine was not giving off any smoke and in any case it could not possibly have obscured both arms. The last piece of damning evidence in a barrage of damning evidence was that from the guard of the Aberdeen, W.K. Henderson of Edinburgh. He had worked regularly over the East Coast main line for 11 years, and on 8 March was travelling in the brake compartment of the last coach. There had been several checks south of Hitchin, the train had not been travelling very fast and he had been watching the vacuum gauge in his compartment at every application of the brake. His train approached Welwyn Garden City, he stated, at about 40 mph when the brake went on about 100 yards north of the signal box — just about as the engine was passing the inner home signal. The vacuum gauge never fell below 10 inches of mercury, there was no emergency stop and in fact he thought the train was making a normal stop such as he would have expected after so many signal checks. When he looked out he was surprised to see that the train was not alongside Welwyn station but some way up the line, having been brought to a stand in a short distance without the need of a full brake application.

So that was the end of the clumsy, engine shed conspiracy to denigrate both the signals and the signalmen at Welwyn. In his concluding remarks, Lt Colonel Wilson wrote: 'Driver Fowler, in order presumably to excuse himself and driver Knapp for having passed signals at "Danger", sought to show that the outer distant was dangerously unreliable by mentioning the names of several other New England drivers and one goods guard...every one of those second or third-hand stories was thoroughly investigated and found to be imaginary or irrelevant...I am not altogether convinced of the honesty of the evidence of driver Fowler who, if his evidence were true, made a remarkably rapid stop from a speed of 60 mph in 390 yards when he caught sight of the inner home at 'Danger' having failed to observe the outer home for no good reason. Driver Lupton's statements became confused when it was proved to him that he was turned from up main to up slow line on one day only of the November week in question and guard Houghton who was brought to give evidence at driver Lupton's request was plainly untruthful'.

The drivers' demonstrations was not fruitless, however. The inner distant signal to which they objected so passionately was removed, and the semaphore bracket signal at the south end of Welwyn viaduct was removed and replaced by a four-aspect colour light signal with a left-hand junction indicator. The provision of Automatic Warning System receivers on all locomotives was given top priority. Rightly or wrongly, the drivers had lost confidence in the signalling on the up line at Welwyn, and the system had to be altered. With the removal of these old signals, the ghost of driver Knapp's crash was exorcized, and there was no more trouble at Welwyn Garden City station.

CHAPTER 18

Chapel-en-le-Frith

1957

IT WAS PITCH DARK AND RAINING HEAVILY AS FIREMAN RON SCANLON cycled to the engine shed at Edgeley, Stockport, on the early morning of 9 February 1957. In the drivers' lobby he met his regular mate, driver John Axon, impatient to be away. 'C'mon Ron,' he said, 'we want to get finished.' The day being Saturday, there was an obvious need for early-turn men to finish their turn as soon as possible. In the famous railway phrase, 'every train's an express train upon a Saturday'. They booked on together at 5.30 am, were told that their engine was 2-8-0 No 48188, already prepared for the road, and off they went to find it. At the shed exit signal Ron Scanlon telephoned the signalman. '8188 light to 'adwoods, Bobby. 6.11 Buxton'. The shed signal was 'pulled off', they drove to the sidings, picked up their train and set off for Buxton, high in the Derbyshire hills.

The engine was in good condition with 38,000 miles to its credit since a heavy intermediate repair at Horwich in April 1955. On the six miles of 1 in 100 steepening to 1 in 60 from Edgeley No 1 box to Disley, and from Whaley Bridge to the summit at Bibbington's Sidings nearly 2 miles from Buxton, gradients of 1 in 60 for miles were no trouble to the engine which steamed well under the expert shovelling of fireman Scanlon. The only slight fault was a very stiff regulator handle and a small blow of steam from the steam brake pipe where a union was made between it and the driver's brake valve.

At first they drove through heavy rain but as they climbed the rain ceased and beyond Whaley Bridge the sun came out to give all the promise of a lovely, spring day. John Axon viewed the hills with particular satisfaction for he knew the area well both from the footplate and on foot. He had always taken great pleasure in walking the fells — he had met his wife Gladys as the result of a country ramble that had gone wrong. Axon was then a young fireman on an engine at Hope and he had seen two young ladies standing on the platform looking very forlorn. They had missed the last train home to Stockport, and got home on the footplate of Axon's engine. Soon after that, John and Gladys were doing their rambling and their courting together over the hills of Edale.

When Axon, Scanlon and 48188 reached Buxton, the sun was shining out of a clear, blue sky and the day was indeed spring-like. They left their train in the sidings and took the engine to shed. Ron Scanlon cleaned his fire, ashpan and smokebox — with a little friendly help from his mate — they took coal and water and turned the engine ready for the journey home. The blow from the steam brake pipe was a nuisance — it came out about 2 ft from Axon's face when he was seated — so he made out a repair card and Scanlon took this to the fitters when he went to their lair to make a can of tea. He came back with a good strong brew and a fitter carrying a 1½ inch spanner with which to tighten the union nut. The nut took a quarter turn to tighten it sufficiently to stop the blow and the fitter, feeling that the joint was wrong somehow, suggested that it might be wiser to 'fail' the engine and get another. This would have made for delay, and John Axon wanted to get finished — it was a beautiful Saturday, after all. The three men continued chatting on the sunny footplate, talking about what they would do when they booked off. Scanlon was looking forward to watching Stockport County play at home and Axon was going to have a couple of hours in bed to make up for his 4 am start — he was going to a dinner dance that evening with Gladys, they both liked dancing and he wanted to be on top form.

The line out of Buxton towards Stockport rose at 1 in 66 for nearly two miles to Bibbington's Sidings signal box. From there it fell at 1 in 70/58 for seven miles to Whaley Bridge with insignificant intervals of 1 in 150 falling through Dove Holes and Chapel-en-le-Frith stations. Between the latter place and Whaley Bridge the line went through some reverse curves which required a speed limit of 50 mph. After Whaley Bridge the line rose very briefly at 1 in 214, then fell at 1 in 124 followed by a level stretch for a combined distance of 1½ miles to New Mills. From there to Disley, 2½ miles, the gradient rose at an average of 1 in 308 before commencing to fall at 1 in 60/100 for six miles to Edgeley No 1 signal box.

Trains were given rear-end assistance out of Buxton up to Bibbington's Sidings. The bank engine was not coupled to the train and stopped at the 'bank engine stop board' 400 yards short of the summit while the train engine came to a stand at its stop board, 100 yards beyond the summit. There the guard would get down from his van, walk to the front of the train and then walk back towards the van, pinning down wagon hand brakes as he went until there were sufficient pinned down to give the driver the brake power he required to bring his train down the fierce, falling grades to Whaley Bridge. The guard lifted each wagon brake handle off its rest and levered it down tight with his 'brake stick', placing a pin through a hole in the guide above the handle to keep the lever hard down. For a train such as the one John Axon was handling, about 16 wagons had to be pinned down.

John Axon's guard was Alfred Ball who came forward while they were waiting to leave Buxton sidings and gave John the load of his train: 24 of coal, 5 of wood pulp and firebricks, 2 of pig iron, 2 empty tanks and the 20-ton brake van for a total weight of 650 tons. The engine and tender together weighed 125 tons, making a total weight of 775 tons. The only brakes on the train were the engine's steam brake, the tender hand brake and the brake van hand brake, for a total brake force of 93 tons, 12 per cent of the weight of the train. With 16 wagon brakes pinned down, the brake force was 164 tons, or 21 per cent of the total weight. The 'Is Line Clear?' bell signal, 1-4 or 3-2, would have informed the signalman that the train was what the railway called 'unbraked' freight. Standing alongside John Axon's train was the 8.45 am Rowsley to Edgeley, a slightly heavier train of unbraked freight, hauled by an ex-LMS 2-8-0 with driver Butler, fireman Bradshaw and guard Creamer in the van, all friends of Axon and Scanlon. The Rowsley pulled away at 10.47 and Creamer waved a cheerful goodbye to the two men as his van trundled slowly past their cab. The banker went to the rear of the train and was soon blasting away up the two-mile incline.

At 11.05 am, dead on time, John Axon started his train in true 'Saturday morning' style, 48188 in full forward gear with the second valve of the regulator open and the bank engine blazing away in the rear. Boiler pressure, which had been carefully kept below the maximum 225 psi while the engine was standing, quickly came up to the mark and with that the steam brake pipe joint began to blow again. Scanlon tied some rags tightly around it to diffuse the hot vapour and keep it away from Axon's face and hands, but of course this could have no effect and the blow of steam became stronger by the second. As they approached Bibbington's Sidings distant signal, Axon, who was watching the increasing jet of

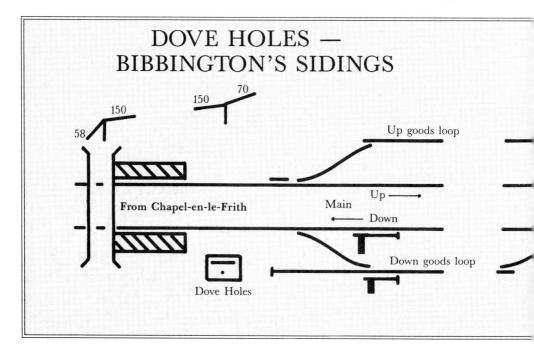

steam with considerable anxiety, said, 'We'll make it into Bibbington's and get assistance from there'.

They never made it. Within seconds, the 1⅛ inch diameter steam pipe was blown out of its socket in the driver's brake valve. It was nothing less than an explosion, and instantly the cab of the engine was filled with high temperature steam as the huge boiler began to discharge its pressurized contents through the pipe. The men were forced outside the cab by the blast from where they screwed the tender hand brake on hard; this exerted a brake force of 8 tons on the tender's wheels. Conditions in the cab were intolerable. Both men stuck bravely to the engine, but even with an overcoat wrapped around his head neither Scanlon nor Axon could stay on the footplate long enough to grope for and locate the regulator handle in the scalding fog. Scanlon took a long, heavy fire-iron from the tender and the two men supported each other on the outside of the cab as they tried to move the regulator with the bar. The handle was stiff to move owing to a tight valve at the smokebox end and, even worse, the regulator was of that confoundedly stupid LMS design which required that, when the second or main valve had been partially opened, it had to be opened fully before it could be closed. The men had to knock the regulator wide open before they could even start to knock it shut. And all the time they were clinging to the cab-side and trying desperately to wield the unwieldy fire-iron, their powerful engine roared away towards the summit while the bank engine shoved manfully from behind.

They were close to the top, running at about 20 mph, when Axon told Scanlon to jump off, to pin down brakes and to tell the guard that they were running

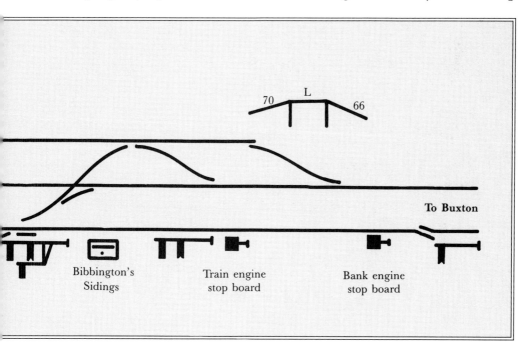

away. Scanlon jumped, fell, picked himself up and began to lift wagon brake handles off their rests as they passed by. He dropped a few but the train was travelling too fast for him to press and pin the levers down hard. He gave up and ran back to warn Alf Ball. 'Alf! Alf!' he yelled, 'get your brake on — we're away!' Alf was well aware of what had happened and was standing bravely at his post, levering the wheel of his hand brake round to put as much pressure as possible on the van's wheels — 16 tons maximum. He had been standing in his van, watching the bank engine, listening to the bank engine working against the buffers of his van, waiting for the time when his train stopped so that he could pin down brakes. The banker had dropped away but the train did not slacken speed and this, Alf said later, made him instantly aware that all was not well. 'This man's failing to stop — there's something wrong ont' engine.' Even after Scanlon's shouted warning, Alf Ball stuck to his post, loyal to John Axon, determined to give him all the support he could.

Ron watched his mates disappear over the brow of the hill, horrified. He ran back to the bank engine and said to driver Robinson, 'He's gone over the top on second regulator. The steam brake pipe has burst. We tried to close the regulator with a fire-iron but we couldn't get it shut.' Scanlon climbed on to the banker and they drove forward to the signal box to ask what had happened. The signalman, with ten months' experience of working the box, told them that the telephone had 'gone dead', and with that they realized that there must have been a crash. They could do nothing, the signalman crossed the engine to the up line and, very sadly, Scanlon, Robinson and the bank engine fireman made their way back to Buxton.

The 8.45 am Rowsley had entered the half-mile goods loop from Bibbington's to Dove Holes station at 10.55. A passenger train had passed, then the Dove Holes signalman had let the freight out on to the down main line behind it. Driver Butler took his train out of the loop with extreme care, and though he started at 11.09 it was 11.12 before his 38 wagons were clear of the loop points. At that the signalman sent 'Train Out of Section' to Bibbington's and was at once 'asked the road' for the 11.05 Buxton, John Axon's train. This Dove Holes accepted at once. The train passed Bibbington's Sidings signal box at 11.16. It had not stopped to pin down brakes, it had entered the 10 mph turn-out at something over 20 mph and the cab and tender were engulfed in a roaring cloud of steam. The signalman did not find these circumstances unusual or alarming but, noticing that the train had no tail lamp, he sent 'Train Passed Without Tail Lamp', 9 bells, to Dove Holes. The Dove Holes signalman acknowledged this and was then supposed to stop the train for examination. Guard Ball had not placed a tail lamp on his van while the bank engine was, in effect, the last vehicle of the train and, once he knew the train was a runaway, he either forgot about the lamp or left it off deliberately to trigger the signalling regulations and have the train stopped at Dove Holes.

The Dove Holes signalman knew that the 11.05 Buxton had been placed in the down loop at Bibbington's to clear the road for another passenger train so he maintained the signal at his end of the loop at 'Danger' and paid attention to the points and signals on the up line. An up freight would run to the up goods loop at Dove Holes. Having dealt with this over an interval of 30-45 seconds, he looked towards Bibbington's to see how the down freight was getting on, and to his great shock he saw the big 2-8-0 proceeding rapidly towards him down the 1 in 70 incline — and with the points set as they were, it was heading directly at his signal box. Even more remarkable was the sight of clouds of steam emanating from the cab and what appeared to be the driver clinging to the cab-side with one arm and waving his free arm violently.

It was a split second of enormous stress for the signalman. If the engine continued undiverted it would crash through his signal box, if he pulled the points for the main line it would be tipped down a 1 in 58 gradient into an already occupied section. I have no doubt that he ought to have left his signal box with some urgency and left the engine and train to run to earth off the end of the loop. This would doubtless have flattened his signal box and caused some damage to Dove Holes station, but the alternative, to 'let it out main line', went against all the signalling regulations and indeed good sense, for there was a train in the section ahead. However, he pulled the points and allowed the train out on to the main line. The runaway passed Dove Holes station at about 28 mph at 11.17 am.

The Dove Holes signalman said at the Inquiry that he took this action 'so as to give the driver the chance of regaining control of the train on a more favourable gradient'. This was a phrase which the Inspecting Officer, Brigadier Langley, seized upon throughout his report. One can only wonder where these 'favourable gradients' were. Axon knew only too well the gravitational pull of those inclines. He had 775 tons of train and only the tender and guard's hand brakes with which to stop — a total brake force of 24 tons, 3 per cent of the train's weight. The only uphill sections in the entire route to Stockport were the insignificant length of 1 in 214 immediately after the Whaley Bridge and the 2½ miles rising at an average of 1 in 308 from New Mills to Disley summit. After that it was all downhill to Stockport. Brigadier Langley calculated that, in spite of an estimated speed of 80 mph at Whaley Bridge, John Axon's train would have been brought to a stand by the 1 in 308 rising gradient half a mile before the summit. This would have been the case, he said, providing that the train had not been derailed on the curves between Chapel-en-le-Frith and Whaley Bridge.

Why John Axon did not jump off his engine at Bibbington's and there warn the signalman to send 'Train Running Away' to Dove Holes will remain a mystery. The Dove Holes signalman would have had a better, more positive warning in that way, although his actions may not have been any different. John may have stayed with his engine like the Captain of a sinking ship, out of a sense of responsibility; he had to see the job through, he had to warn the signalman at Dove Holes to get out of his box — hence his waving arm — 'GET AWAY, GET AWAY!' He gambled that he might survive the 25-27 mph derailment which would inevitably take place, but I do not think it ever crossed his mind that the signalman would panic and tip him down that 1 in 58 incline. When he saw

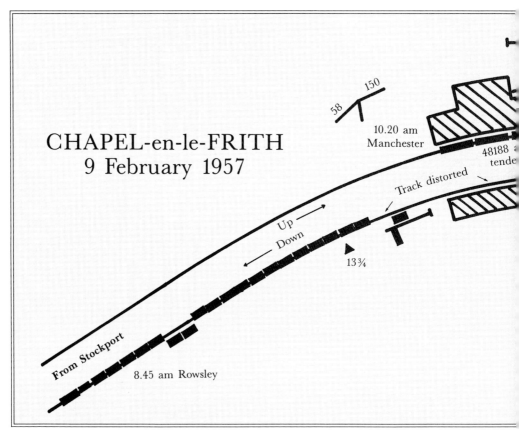

CHAPEL-en-le-FRITH
9 February 1957

150
58
10.20 am
Manchester

48188
tende

Track distorted

Up
Down

13¾

From Stockport

8.45 am Rowsley

that he was being 'sent out main line', why did he not then jump before speed increased further? Perhaps he was willing to risk jumping on to relatively soft ground beyond the loop trap points but not on to the steel rails and solid sleepers of the main line. We shall never know.

The Dove Holes signalman did not send the 'Train Running Away' code to signalman Howe at Chapel-en-le-Frith as he ought to have done, but instead telephoned. What passed between the two men is not recorded but it is certain that Dove Holes did not communicate his optimistic feelings about 'favourable gradients' to signalman Howe because Howe became instantly aware that he was about to witness a rear-end collision of terrific force. The 10.20 am Manchester to Buxton two-car diesel unit had arrived at Chapel at 11.17 and could proceed no further owing to the up freight train in the section to Dove Holes. At 11.18, as the passenger train's guard was entering Chapel signal box carrying out Rule 55, Howe had received the full import of the message from Dove Holes.

The 8.45 am Rowsley had just emerged from Eaves tunnel, 1,325 yards up the line, travelling at about 18 mph. Signalman Howe rapidly told guard Dutton that a runaway was following the train which had just come into sight and told him to get his passengers clear of the rail car and off the station. It is obvious

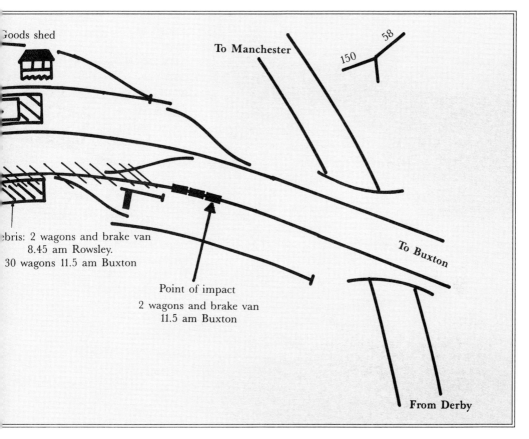

Goods shed

To Manchester

58

150

To Buxton

bris: 2 wagons and brake van
8.45 am Rowsley.
30 wagons 11.5 am Buxton

Point of impact
2 wagons and brake van
11.5 am Buxton

From Derby

from this that both Howe and the Dove Holes signalman knew there was going
to be a rear-end collision at Chapel-en-le-Frith. Dutton rushed out of the signal
box to start work, but two locomotive men had already begun the evacuation
after some rapid and extremely perceptive thought. Driver Robinson and his
fireman had been sitting in the front seat of the rail car, going to Buxton, when
they had seen the Rowsley emerge from the tunnel. They had watched the train
draw near and had then seen a great gust of smoke billow suddenly from the
tunnel mouth. Instantly they had realized that another train had entered the
tunnel at the far end and, weighing up the situation in a second, they had begun
to hustle the passengers off the train even as Dutton came running along the
platform. The passengers were off the premises when the crash occurred. The
railwaymen stayed on the platform to do what they could to mitigate the force
of the collision by alerting the crew of the Rowsley.

Driver Butler came down the wicked 1 in 58 gradient with the utmost caution, his 800-ton train well under control at no more that 20 mph. He had taken
8 minutes for the 2 miles from Dove Holes. As the engine came clanking alongside the down platform, guard Dutton and driver Simnor from the railcar shouted
a warning and pointed back towards the tunnel. The enginemen were puzzled

No 48188 leans against the platform of Chapel-en-le-Frith station as if exhausted after its furious, downhill gallop. On the platform is its tender which is lying on the site of the signal box it demolished. (J.M.Bentley)

The heavily laden wagons behind 48188 leaped over each other to form this huge pile, 30 feet tall, after their 55 mph progress was brought to a sudden stop by the impact with the rear of the 8.45 am Rowsley. (J.M.Bentley)

In spite of the beating it received, 48188 was fit to be towed on its own wheels down to Edgeley loco depot. (J.M.Bentley) and did not understand. Fireman Bradshaw on the Rowsley told Butler that 'something was up' and they were both looking back, puzzled, when 48188 shot out of the smoking tunnel mouth at an estimated 55 mph, bore down on the Rowsley and collided with guard Creamer's van at a closing speed of nearly 40 mph.

The brake van of the Rowsley and the last three wagons of that train were completely crushed, killing Mr Creamer. The blow drove the 800-ton Rowsley train violently forward for 285 yards before driver Butler could bring it to a stand. It was intact and on the rails except for four wagons near the front which were squeezed sideways by the shock wave travelling through the train, caused by the terrific forwards pressure coming from the rear-end collision. A quarter-mile of track was badly damaged. A thick pall of coal and lime dust blotted out the scene, but as it cleared the thunder-struck onlookers began to see more and more detail, like the curtain rising on a stage after a scene change. 150 tons of coal were heaped across both tracks, and 33 wagons were piled to a height of 30 feet with guard Creamer's van at the bottom of the pile. It took more that 30 hours to reach his body.

John Axon was dead. His locomotive was lying on its right side, chimney against the platform, buffers touching those of the diesel railcar. The latter was only slightly hurt and, indeed, worked back to Manchester under its own power. The steam engine's tender had risen into the air at the moment of impact, had snapped the massive drawbar connecting it to the engine and, turning through 180°, had crashed into the base of the tall, stone-built signal box. The tender now lay on the platform while the signal box was largely rubble down on the tracks of the station's goods yard. Signalman Howe, who had remained at his post to send 4-5-5 to Whaley Bridge, was in the box when it was struck. He was flung out of a window, landed 20 feet below in the sidings amongst the falling debris and lived to tell the tale. The other exceedingly lucky man was guard Ball. As his train smashed into the back of the Rowsley, wagon after wagon running up the growing pile with a noise like thunder, he lay on the floor of his van with his arms around the hand brake pillar. One supposes that he might have been praying. The terrible momentum which was causing loaded coal wagons to turn somersaults was gradually used up until the second wagon from the van was only derailed, the wagon next to the van was also derailed leaving only the brake van standing demurely on the rails with brave guard Ball alive and relatively well inside.

John Axon had ridden to his death on the fairest of days. He had stayed at his post with the bravery of a soldier under fire, had gambled with his life to save others — and had lost. His courage was recognized by the posthumous award of the George Cross on 3 May 1957. Sad to say, the courage of Alf Ball in sticking with his train to support Axon was not even mentioned in the official report on the tragedy. Brigadier Langley found no one to blame for what had occurred, neither did he voice any criticism of the Dove Holes signalman's actions. The crash was the result of the failure of the steam brake pipe union which, according to the report, could not have been foreseen.

The joint in question consisted of a 1⅛ inch copper pipe to which was brazed,

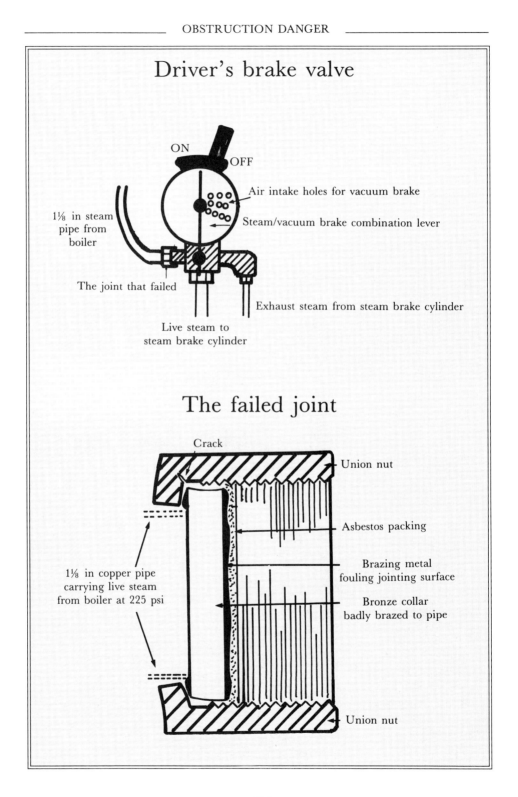

Driver's brake valve

ON

OFF

Air intake holes for vacuum brake

1⅛ in steam pipe from boiler

Steam/vacuum brake combination lever

The joint that failed

Exhaust steam from steam brake cylinder

Live steam to steam brake cylinder

The failed joint

Crack

Union nut

Asbestos packing

1⅛ in copper pipe carrying live steam from boiler at 225 psi

Brazing metal fouling jointing surface

Bronze collar badly brazed to pipe

Union nut

a short distance from the end, a collar. An asbestos washer was fitted around the stub-end of the pipe, above the collar. The collar and washer were forced into steam-tight contact with an internal seating by the union nut. A metallurgical examination of the pipe showed that the collar had not been properly brazed to the pipe, that the brazing was not continuous around the circumference of the collar and that some molten brazing metal had run on to the seating face of the collar so that the latter was not of an even thickness. Under these conditions it was next to impossible to obtain a steam-tight joint, and excessive force had been used to tighten the nut which had begun to crack. The whole joint was severely stressed and the weak brazing began to give way under the strain. Every time the nut had been tightened, the collar was that much nearer being broken off the pipe until, perhaps at Buxton, the collar had torn away and merely turned with the nut rather than been tightened. After that it was only a matter

Part of the cab controls of an ex-LMS 2-8-0, No 48348. The long handle of the steam regulator is pointing directly at the driver's brake control. The 1⅛ inch pipe carrying boiler pressure steam to the brake valve is seen here lagged with a white material and curving past the driver's hand to the union joint between pipe and valve. It was this union which failed on No 48188. (Author)

of time before footplate vibration and the force of 225 psi within the pipe did their work to blow the joint away.

The Inquiry discovered that this joint had been reported as blowing ten times in as many weeks between 12 November 1956 and 9 February 1957. When this performance was compared to 18 other ex-LMS 2-8-0 locomotives, this complaint was seen to be five times more frequent on 48188 than on the others. Yet, in the words of the Official report, 'this was not sufficiently numerous or unusual to attract attention'. The report went on to state that the Chief Mechanical Engineer of the London Midland Region had taken *'prompt action'* to redesign the joint and 'it is anticipated that the conversion of these joints will be completed *within the next four years*'. While this very prompt action was being carried out, it was decreed that all these joints should be examined at the next 'X' day examination, and that thereafter they would be checked every 40-48,000 miles 'so as to ensure that any fault is readily detected'. With the awards for bravery and these comfortingly prompt actions, the remarkable case of the Chapel-en-le-Frith runaway was officially laid to rest.

CHAPTER 19

Arklestone Junction

1958

ARKLESTON JUNCTION LAY ABOUT 6½ MILES WEST OF GLASGOW CENtral station, and 1½ miles west of Paisley on the line to Gourock. The line was quadruple with a double track branch to Renfrew. On the Glasgow side of the signal box, the 'slow' lines were on each side of the 'fast' lines, but in front of the box, there was a junction which changed the slow lines' position so that both of them lay together to the north of the fast lines. The Renfrew branch junctioned with the up and down slow lines just west of the signal box. A gantry of five signals for down fast and down slow line trains was situated 200 yards west of the box, on the approach side of a road overbridge, and the right-hand post, carrying the arm routing trains from the down fast to the down slow line, was immediately above the up fast line. The signal box was a timber-built structure of Caledonian Railway design housing a 65 lever frame, Tyers block instruments of the simple, two-position type, and an illuminated diagram. Signalman Holmes was in charge of this complicated, busy junction on the early shift on 20 May 1958.

At 8.08 am, the Gallowhill Sidings trip — a 'J' Class 0-6-0 pushing a brake van — came from Paisley along the up slow line and was routed via facing points No 50 and trailing points No 48 to the up fast line. The driver, passed-fireman Murray, who had been in that grade for a year, had not previously worked the Gallowhill trip as a driver but had done it a number of times as a fireman. His fireman was passed-cleaner Peden, 19 years old, who had three years' railway service but had never worked this 'trip' before and whose knowledge of the signals was slight. Riding in the brake van was guard Christie, with only a short railway service. The entourage shunted along the up fast and came to a stand on the Glasgow side of the big gantry to await the signalman's hand signal that the route was set to the sidings on the far side of the tracks.

As soon as the engine was clear of facing points 50, signalman Holmes reversed

The wonderfully ornate ex-Caledonian Railway timber signal box at Arkleston Junction on 12 November 1966. (Jack Kernahan).

them so that they lay for the up slow line in order to allow him to give 'Train Out of Section' for the engine and van. This he did at 8.10 am. He was then immediately asked 'Is Line Clear?' for the 7.15 am Gourock to Glasgow passenger train and he returned 'Line Clear'. At that moment he set the road from down fast to down slow line for the 8 am Glasgow to Gourock passenger train. This was a crossing junction movement where the down train would cross the up fast line, and to protect the crossing movement from any runaway moving down the up fast from the direction of Glasgow, the interlocking demanded that point 48 be reversed so as to divert any such runaway to the up slow and thus prevent it from slicing through the crossing movement. Having set the points, signalman Holmes cleared the signals for the down train, including No 42 which was on the gantry immediately above the up fast line. He had also cleared the up slow line signals for the Gourock to Glasgow train and at 8.12 am the latter was only half a mile away.

A 2-6-4 tank speeds past Arkleston Junction from Gourock; the signal box is behind the last coach of the train. Gallow Hill sidings are on the left and the points leading into them can be seen, gleaming, in the distance. (Douglas Hume)

Arkleston Junction in 1966 after some reduction in the layout. This was taken from the road bridge behind which was the gantry of signals which confused passed-cleaner Peden. The 'J15' Class 0-6-0 ran along the second track from the right towards the signal box and met the 2-6-4 tank on the right-hand track opposite the signals in the middle distance. The impact forced the 'J15' back the way it had come until it stopped beneath the road bridge. The locomotives were remarkably little damaged, but the wood and steel coaches were shattered. (Jack Kernahan)

When signal No 42 cleared, passed-cleaner Peden took this 4 foot long arm, placed as a 'right turn' indication for main line trains, to mean that the road was set for a left-hand turn across the tracks to the sidings. He did not look to check the points but simply called 'Right Away!' to his mate. His mate, Murray, happily took him at his word and, without checking, set off. Murray thought that his mate must have seen the signalman waving them back to the box because he could see that the road was not set to the sidings. He apparently did not see that signal No 42 had been cleared. In the brake van, guard Christie was messing around with tail lamps 3 minutes after his train had come to a stand and took no notice when it began to move back the way it had come. Later, he defended himself for not keeping a look-out by saying that the speed of events had overwhelmed him. Passed-fireman Murray steamed his train back towards the signal box unaware that the Gourock to Glasgow train was approaching — even if he had seen it, there was no reason for him to be concerned since he was on the up fast while it was on the up slow. At points 48, however, he was inexorably diverted into a collision course with the rapidly approaching passenger train.

On the passenger train — eight coaches hauled by a Class '4' 2-6-4 tank — driver Johnston was also unaware of the situation. Driving from the left-hand side, he could not readily see objects to the right of his boiler. It was the frantic gestures of signalman Holmes — who could see everything all too clearly — that made him look sharp. He saw the errant 0-6-0 just before he hit it, so that the instant brake application he made had no time to have any effect and his engine struck the 'J' Class almost head-on at about 40-45 mph. The men on

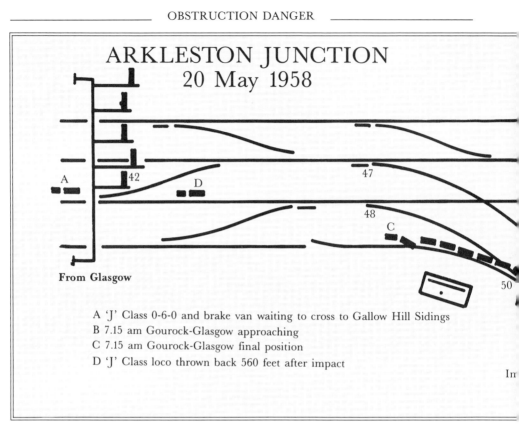

ARKLESTON JUNCTION
20 May 1958

A
42
D
47
48
C
50

From Glasgow

A 'J' Class 0-6-0 and brake van waiting to cross to Gallow Hill Sidings
B 7.15 am Gourock-Glasgow approaching
C 7.15 am Gourock-Glasgow final position
D 'J' Class loco thrown back 560 feet after impact

A composite photograph showing the damage to the 7.15 am Gourock-Glasgow. This view shows the first and the third coach of the train; the second coach has been 'lost' in the making of the composite print. (Daily Express)

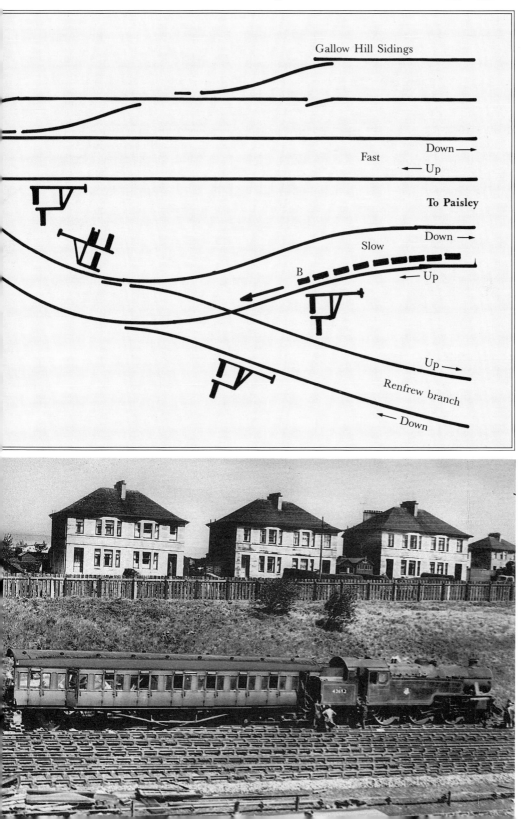

Gallow Hill Sidings

Fast

Down →

← Up

To Paisley

Slow

Down →

B

← Up

Up →

Renfrew branch

← Down

the goods engine also saw their peril a split second before the impact and jumped left and right off the engine. The big tank engine weighed 80 tons and had 226 tons of train to back that up. The 0-6-0 weighed 80 tons. It was a very unequal contest, and the passenger tank won 'hands down', batting the engine and van back the way it had come for some 560 feet, its cylinders smashed and coal from the tender filling the cab to a depth of 2 feet. The tank engine's bogie was derailed and the front end damaged, but most hurt was done to the leading coach, a wooden-framed vehicle with steel panels. The shock of the blow crushed the leading end against the bunker of the engine, wrecking one compartment, while the blow from the bunker set the whole body back along the underframe so that the trailing end of the coach smashed into the coach behind it, wrecking four compartments. In all, 97 people were hurt and 26 were detained in hospital. Guard Christie, who had taken no part in the proceedings, was still sitting in his van when the collision occurred and was given a severely bumpy ride as his van suddenly reversed direction and accelerated up the line at 40 mph.

CHAPTER 20

Ince Moss

1958

T HE INCIDENT AT INCE MOSS SHOWS THE DANGER OF ASSUMING THAT everyone else is doing their job properly and thereby allowing one's own defences to slip. At 11.30 pm on Sunday 16 February 1958, passed-fireman Firth booked on duty at Farrington engine shed, Preston. He was given the job of driving a Class '5' 4-6-0 to Liverpool Edge Hill. His foreman was aware that he did not know the road on the branch from Wigan to Liverpool, so he had arranged — so he told Mr Firth — for a pilotman to accompany him from Wigan. Mr Firth, with a passed-cleaner for a fireman, set out southwards and had an uneventful journey for the 14½ miles up to Springs Branch Junction No 2 box where he was brought to a stand right outside the engine shed. Naturally enough, Mr Firth thought that this had been done to enable the pilotman to come aboard, but the signal was eventually cleared without the pilot putting in an appearance, so Firth drove away past Springs Branch No 1 box and around the curve on to the branch line. He had worked over this line as a fireman but had never officially learned the route as a driver and so he could go no further.

He stopped his engine a few feet before reaching the home signal of Ince Moss signal box and, telling his young fireman to stay where he was on the engine, Mr Firth got down and walked 220 yards to the 'relief cabin' where crews of locomotivemen waited to take over their trains. Here he knew he would find a telephone. Later on, Mr Firth was as puzzled as anyone else as to why he did not drive that extra distance, a fair walk in the dark but nothing much for the engine to cover. Had the engine been that extra one-eighth of a mile further on, it would have given the driver of the next train a better chance.

In the relief cabin, speaking on the telephone to Springs Branch engine shed foreman, he discovered that Farrington had made no arrangements at all but that, if he was to go back to his engine and wait, a pilotman would be sent out to him. He walked back to his engine, climbed aboard, took the brake off —

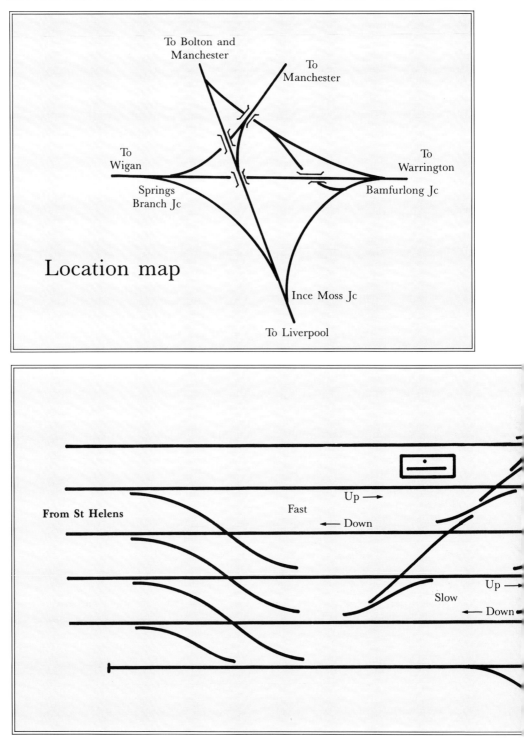

To Bolton and
Manchester

To
Manchester

To
Wigan

Springs
Branch Jc

To
Warrington

Bamfurlong Jc

Location map

Ince Moss Jc

To Liverpool

From St Helens

Fast

Up →

← Down

Up →

Slow

← Down

and waited. Expecting that at any moment a pilot would appear out of the night and that then they could go on their way, Mr Firth did not place any detonators behind his engine. This was unfortunate, because in any case no one was going to appear for 15 minutes at the earliest. Detonator protection is a driver's personal contribution to his own safety and will prove its value should a signalman fail in his job. Mr Firth, like all drivers, placed his life in the hands of the signalmen that night.

In Springs Branch No 1 signal box, signalman Bond and relief signalman Davies were in charge, Bond looking after the St Helens branch among other things. He had sent Class '5' 'on line' to St Helens No 3 at 1.40 am, Monday 17 February, and felt no concern at the length of time it was 'in section' because all six signal boxes between Springs Branch and St Helens No 3 were switched out to make a 7½ mile long section. He became concerned at 2.04 am, however,

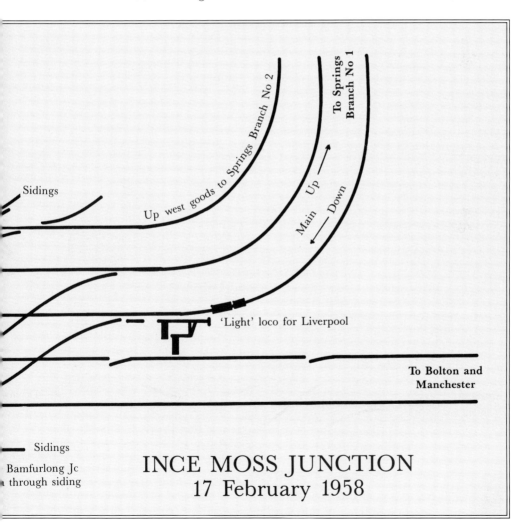

INCE MOSS JUNCTION
17 February 1958

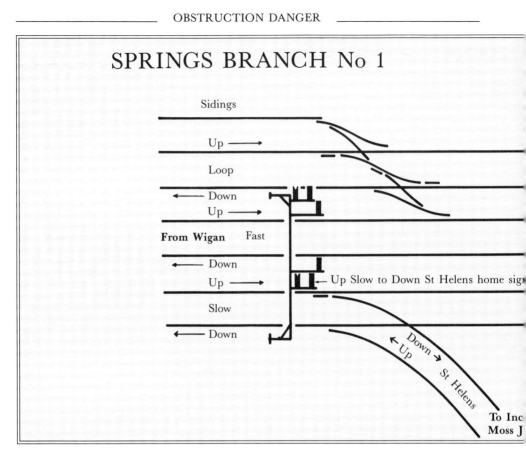

SPRINGS BRANCH No 1

Sidings

Up ⟶

Loop

⟵ Down

Up ⟶

From Wigan Fast

⟵ Down

Up ⟶ — Up Slow to Down St Helens home sign

Slow

⟵ Down

⟵ Up Down ⟶

St Helens

To Inc
Moss J

when Springs Branch No 2 box asked 'Is Line Clear?' for the 2 am Wigan to Liverpool express. At 2.06 am the train was standing at his junction home signal and still signalman Carman in St Helens could not be roused. Mr Bond had sent a polite 'one beat' without effect, and, after an interval, sent a long but tactful 'waker up' — 1-5-5, 'Shunt Train for Following Train to Pass'. There was no reply to this either, and signalman Bond, not wanting the be a nagger, did no more for the moment.

All this time, 26 minutes, the 'Black 5' had been standing out of sight 600 yards around the bend on the branch line while signalman Carman was sitting by his fire in St Helens No 3 box 'reading a cowboy book', to use his own words. He had worked the box for seven years, lived eight miles from it and, on night shift, had to cycle to and from home. Each night and morning of the previous week he had done this, and on Sunday he had cycled home at 8 am and cycled back to work at 6 pm. At 1.40 am he had answered Bond's 'on line' and, there being very little traffic to attend to, had returned to his book by the fire. So engrossing was his book that he never heard the 1-5-5 code although the bell was only 10 feet away, but he said he did hear a noise outside at that time which he assumed was the engine going by. He did not look to see the tail lamp but simply sent 'Train Entering Section' to Huyton and 'Train Out of Section' to

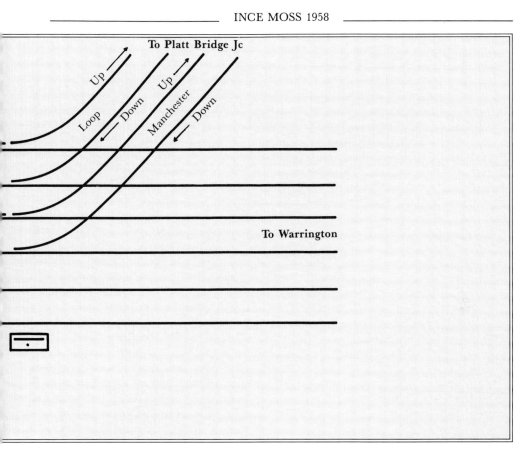

Springs Branch No 1.

Signalman Bond pounced on the bell, 'asked the road' and 'pulled off' for the passenger train at 2.11. Driver Shufflebottom opened the regulator of his 2-6-4 tank and got his seven-coach train briskly under way. He was running at 25 mph around the branch curve when, at a range of 30 yards, he saw the red tail lamp of the 'Black 5'. He braked at once but there was not sufficient space in which the brakes could take effect, and the tank engine hit the tender of the 'Black 5', pushing it forward about 100 yards before both trains stopped. Doubly unfortunate, the home signal for Ince Moss, which was of course cleared because the box was switched out, was on a tall post so as to be easily seen by drivers as they came on to the branch, so Shufflebottom had every reason to believe he was 'Right Away'. The driver of the 'Black 5' paid with his life for omitting to place detonators to the rear of his engine, and the guard of the passenger train died from his injuries three days later. The foreman at Farrington had failed to make the promised arrangements for a pilotman and the foreman at Springs Branch depot either could not or merely did not provide a man when requested; all this had caused the engine to be hanging about on the line, and the long hours and miles of cycling undertaken by signalman Carman did the rest.

CHAPTER 21

Lunan Bay

1958

THE TALE OF THE LUNAN BAY CRASH, IN WHICH NO ONE WAS VERY much hurt, could be classed as 'light relief' in the context of this book. The nature of the mistakes that were made were actually farcical, and I can only surmise that the Scottish railway hobgoblins had bewitched half a dozen men purely out of spite.

On 2 September 1958, the 7.09 am from Edinburgh to Aberdeen left on time. The engine was a 'V2', and, from the engine, the formation was eight coaches, one eight-wheeled van and two ten-foot wheelbase 'Fruit' vans at the rear. Because of the two short wheelbase four-wheelers, the train was restricted to a maximum speed of 60 mph. When the train left, the usual telegraphic advice was sent to Dundee: engine number, names of train crew, load and formation. All that the message did not say was that the rearmost vans were of the short wheelbase variety; however, it did state that they were 'ten-tonners', which amounted to the same thing.

The train came to a stand on the down through line at Dundee a few minutes late. The Edinburgh enginemen uncoupled their engine and went to the shed without seeing the fresh men. The Edinburgh guard spoke to his relief, Mr Kessack of Aberdeen, but he did not tell him anything concerning the train. After the Edinburgh man had gone, guard Kessack went to the rear and checked that the tail lamp was in place before getting into his nice, comfortable seat in the brake van. The Dundee Train Reporter, Mr Robertson, shouted across from the platform all the information contained in the train advice telegram from Edinburgh, and then walked to the front of the train to shout the same message across to the driver, Mr McRobb — 'eleven including two ten-tonners for 328 tons'. Driver McRobb, a sixty-year-old with 21 years' experience as a Dundee driver, denied that he had been told about the 'ten-tonners', but said to the Inquiry that he assumed there must have been some small vans in his train because the weight of 'eleven eights' would have been much more than 328 tons. Mr Robertson said that while he had not specifically mentioned 'short wheelbase', he had mentioned 'ten-tonners', which came to the same thing.

The train steamed away from Dundee having lost over 10 minutes at the station. The bewitching was already under way, for the train lost a further minute over 16 miles of dead level track to Arbroath where it arrived 16 minutes late at an average from Dundee of only 41.7 mph. From Arbroath, the line climbed for 2½ miles at 1 in 100/180, then down through Letham Grange and up over a slight rise before dropping at 1 in 100 towards and beyond Inverkeilor station. Driver McRobb's engine was in good fettle and, believing that the maximum speed on this section of the line was 70 mph, McRobb allowed speed to rise to 70 in order to regain some lost time. Down through little Inverkeilor station he swept in grand style at the full 70 mph. The local ganger and the signalman watched the train streak through and saw the two little vans oscillating rapidly at the rear; neither man was alarmed, they had seen it all before. Going on down the bank, however, the rearmost of the two vans became derailed 'all wheels' and was hauled over the sleepers at 70 mph and maybe a little more. The engine was going very well, and driver McRobb felt nothing amiss then, nor as the engine attacked the 1½ mile 1 in 100/90 rising gradient towards Lunan Bay.

Half a mile before Lunan Bay station there was a steel girder underbridge on the line, spanning a road below. Between the down and up lines was a low girder, and this the derailed van struck. The van leaped into the air, cleared the girder and fell to earth again. The end-on blow between wagon and girder caused the coupling hook to half straighten so that when the van hit the ballast, the coupling slipped off. The two vans parted company, the vacuum brake pipe parted and an automatic application of the brakes throughout the train began. But, in the meantime, the train had rushed on up the bank, leaving the shattered remains of the van blocking both lines.

The train passed through the arch of a bridge and came to a stand just short of Lunan Bay station, 920 yards beyond the wreckage. Having 'lost the vacuum', driver McRobb sent his mate, passed-fireman Marr, back to find the guard to discover what had happened. Both men walked to the end of the train and discovered that the last vehicle had two coupling chains hanging on one draw-hook, but was lacking a tail lamp. It was obvious to them that the complete lack of a vacuum pipe had caused the brake to go on, and to enable the train to get under way once more they walked back to the couplings between the four-wheel and the eight-wheel van. Here they uncoupled the vacuum pipes and placed each upon its 'stop'. The vacuum could then be re-created, the brake released and the train could go on its way. The spell these very experienced men were under had completely blinded them to the blindingly obvious — that they had lost a van! And the bewitchment had yet a great deal further to run.

The signal box at Lunan Bay station was switched out, but the porter-signalman came out of the station office on to the platform when he heard the train come to a stand. As the 'V2' steamed through, fireman Marr shouted to him, 'We've lost a vacuum pipe — phone Montrose and ask them to have a new one wait-

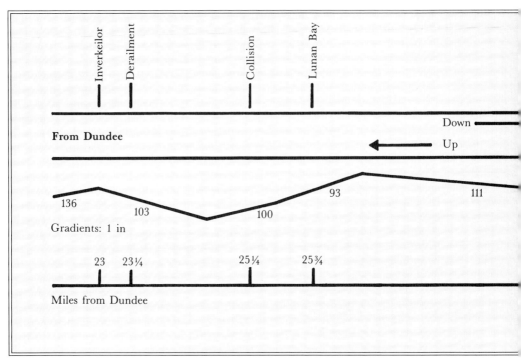

Inverkeilor | Derailment | Collision | Lunan Bay

Down

From Dundee

Up

136
103
93
111
100

Gradients: 1 in

23   23¼   25¼   25¾

Miles from Dundee

Lunan Bay station and signal box — with painted-on curtains? This view is down the 1 in 92 gradient towards Dundee and the spot, about 900 yards away, where the last van of the 7.9 am Edinburgh to Aberdeen was left behind, its absence unnoticed by the train crew even after they had examined the rear of the train. The errant van was struck by the following 7.30 am express from Edinburgh. (Jack Kernahan Collection)

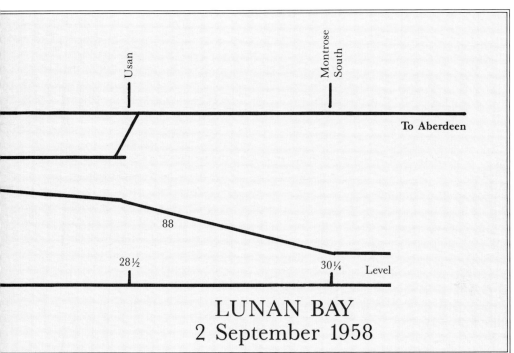

Usan

Montrose
South

To Aberdeen

88

28½

30¼   Level

LUNAN BAY
2 September 1958

Lunan Bay station looking towards Aberdeen on 29 May 1955. The station closed to passengers on 22 September 1930 but remained open for the occasional coal truck or horse box until 18 May 1964. The signal box closed the following month. A remote, rural and utterly peaceful location — but accidents can happen anywhere. (Mr J.L.Stevenson)

ing'. The signal-porter shouted an acknowledgement and stared after the last van with its ragged stump of vacuum brake pipe, not realizing that it was not carrying a tail lamp. Meanwhile, on the engine, driver McRobb was struggling with some nagging doubts which had somehow managed to pierce the Scotch mist surrounding his brain. He asked his mate how the pipe could have been torn away. His mate was unable to suggest a cause and, still puzzling, they drove on up the hill.

A mile beyond Lunan Bay, the gradient changed to 1 in 120 falling, steepening to 1 in 110, 2 miles in all, down to Usan station where McRobb braked to 10 mph to allow his fireman to take the tablet for the signal track section ahead to Montrose. The signalman, Mr Middleton, stood on the platform to hand over the tablet in its hooped pouch. He had been told about the mysteriously missing vacuum pipe and stayed on the platform to have a good look as the van came slowly past. Sure enough, there was the ragged bit of rubber pipe bound with a brass clip to the steel 'swan neck'. Satisfied at having witnessed the phenomenon, he went back to his box, sent 'Train Entering Section' to Montrose South box and 'Train out of Section' to Inverkeilor. So keenly interested had he been in the vacuum pipe, that he too had not noticed the lack of a tail lamp. As soon as the Inverkeilor signalman received the 'train out', he asked 'Is Line Clear?' for the 7.30 am Edinburgh to Aberdeen express. Usan 'gave the road', Inverkeilor's signals were cleared and away went the train, hauled by another 'V2' Class 2-6-2.

Signalman Pert was on duty in Montrose South box, a man of 64 summers, 40 of them spent in the service of the railway. He had received the message about the vacuum pipe and had informed the Carriage & Wagon Department. The train arrived at 10.24, about 3 minutes after passing Usan and 3 minutes after Usan had given 'Line Clear' to Inverkeilor for the 7.30 Edinburgh. Pert saw the tattered vacuum pipe and also saw that there was no tail lamp — but instead of at once sending 4-5 to Usan, 'Train Passed Without Tail Lamp', he telephoned Inverkeilor to ask how many vans were on the rear of the 7.9 Edinburgh. Probably because the train had gone through Inverkeilor at 70 mph or more, the signalman there said 'one' — he had not seen the pair. The Usan signalman was also on the circuit and he chipped in with a confirmation that there was only one van — as of course was the case after the rearmost van had been left in the section between Inverkeilor and Usan. Signalman Pert then gave 'Train Out of Section' for the 7.09 Edinburgh and gave the release for another tablet from Usan's machine for the 7.30 Edinburgh. The signalman at Usan, hearing that Pert had not seen the tail lamp on the 7.09, remembered that he had not seen it either, but he said nothing about this to Pert nor — more to the point — to the man at Inverkeilor.

While these phone conversations were going on between the signalmen, the 7.30 Edinburgh was storming away up the 1 in 90 from Inverkeilor to Lunan Bay and working to such good effect that 30 mph was reached in a mile . At the same time at Montrose, the guard of the 7.09 Edinburgh decided to take a stroll to the rear of his train to watch the C&W men fit a new vacuum pipe.

As he walked around the end of the small van his bewitchment was broken and, in his own words, 'I very nearly dropped when I discovered I had a tail lamp missing and an extra coupling hanging on the hook of the rearmost vehicle. I shouted to the platform foreman to get on the phone at once to Montrose South box and let them know we had left a vehicle in the section'. Pert was advised and he sent 'Obstruction Danger', 6 bells, at about 10.27. This would have been about the time that the engine of the 7.30 Edinburgh hit the wreckage of the van. Driver Fraser's forward view at that spot was restricted by the curvature of the line. His firemen, Mr Morrison, had just fired a round of coal and put his head over the side to watch the line ahead when, at a range of about 100 yards, he saw the van lying across both tracks. He yelled a warning and his mate braked at once but it was too late to avoid a collision, which took place at about 20 mph.

All the men involved with causing this accident were well respected workers who had never been known to make a mistake. That a couple of men should fail is commonplace and understandable, but that five — or six, if one counts the Inverkeilor man — should fail simultaneously and in such a spectacular manner is truly remarkable, and seems to be best accounted for by occult explanations!

CHAPTER 22

Crayford Spur 'A' and Polmont East

1959/1962

TO PREVENT A SIGNALMAN FROM GIVING A SECOND 'LINE CLEAR' before the train for which the first 'Line Clear' was given has passed through the section, there were two systems of interlocking in use, the so-called 'Welwyn block' and the Sykes 'Lock and Block' patented by William Robert Sykes (1840-1917) on 23 February 1875. The Sykes system linked the train, the signals, the signalman and the signalling instruments through electrical and mechanical means. A precise routing of actions had to be observed by the signalmen at both ends of a section in order to be able to obtain a release for the lever working the signal controlling the entrance to the section. If the routine was not followed exactly it was not possible to pull that signal lever. However, it was necessary to provide a way out of all this tight locking to cater for the occasions when, having given 'Line Clear' for a train, that train did not proceed as intended due to some failure. Each Sykes instrument was provided with a key, hanging on a chain from a hook on the front of the instrument shelf below the instrument, and by the simple act of insertion into the keyhole on the instrument and a flick of the wrist, the entire system of rail-mounted treadles, clever machinery and electrical circuits could be set at nought. Signalmen were instructed to use the key, 'Provided no train is in the section, that such a release is absolutely necessary and can with safety be given'.

The key was the Achilles' heel of the system and its improper use led to at least four collisions — at Battersea Park Junction in 1938, at South Croydon in 1947, at Barnes, and at Crayford Spur 'A' box on 17 February 1959. The other box involved with the latter was Crayford Creek Junction. As can be seen from the diagram, the layout was quite complicated and the intricacies of the track were intensified by the large number of trains passing over it. On the early shift that day, signalman Miller was working the 31-lever Crayford Creek Junction and signalman Blandford was in the 15-lever Crayford Spur 'A'. Signalman

Miller was 64 years of age with 32 years' service as a signalman, 15 of them at Crayford Creek Junction. Signalman Blandford was 31 years old, and had been a signalman for four years, two of them in that box. The job was a very busy one, with a train passing each box every 2½ minutes at peak periods. To make life even more difficult that morning there was a fog which reduced visibility to 50-80 yards.

At 10.45 am, signalman Miller in Crayford Creek box gave Blandford 'Line Clear' for an up train of empty coaches which was to reverse into his, Miller's carriage siding. At the same time, Miller also gave 'Line Clear' to Slade Green for the 9.25 am Charing Cross to Dartford passenger train. Slade Green sent this train 'on line' at 10.27, just as the empty coaches were reversing into the sidings. Miller was intent on the coaches and peered into the fog, anxious to glimpse the guard's wave which would signify that the empty train was 'inside', clear of the main line. As a result of his concentration on this movement, he hardly noticed the 9.25 Charing Cross electric multiple unit slip past in the fog and did not send the 'Train Entering Section' signal to Crayford Spur 'A' box. At 10.29 Miller was able to close the siding points and send 'Train Out of Section' to Crayford Spur 'A' for the empty coaching stock train. Signalman Blandford did not at once acknowledge this 2-1 code but one minute later, just as in Crayford Creek box the Slade Green down line bell rang one beat, Blandford sent his acknowledgement, 2 pause 1, to Miller at Crayford Creek.

This was the precise moment when signalman Miller became confused. He forgot that this 2-1 was the acknowledgement from Crayford Spur of the 2-1 he had transmitted one minute previously for the empty coaching stock train, and instead understood that Blandford was sending 'Train Out of Section' for the 9.25 Charing Cross. Signalman Miller pressed both bell plungers at once, to Slade Green and Crayford Spur 'A'. The bell in Crayford Spur box did not ring out because Miller had not pressed the plunger properly, but the Slade Green bell rang and the signalman there then asked 'Is Line Clear?' for the 9.40 Charing Cross to Gillingham passenger train. Signalman Miller gave a 'Line Clear' release to Slade Green's down starting signal.

Down at Crayford Spur 'A' box down home signal, the driver of the 9.25 Charing Cross was waiting patiently for the signal arm to be raised. There was nothing unusual about waiting here, with the junction and Dartford station just ahead, so he did not go to the box to carry out Rule 55; he could see the signal box dimly through the fog about 50 yards away, and he thought therefore that the signalman could see him. But signalman Blandford was still waiting for the 9.25 Charing Cross to be advised to him, by bell, as 'Entering Section'. He was completely unaware of its presence at his home signal.

Signalman Miller, meanwhile, was wondering why he had not had a reply from Blandford to his one beat 'Call Attention' signal. After a short interval he telephoned him and asked, 'Have you taken that down one?' (meaning 'have you given me "Line Clear" for the 9.40 am Charing Cross?'). Signalman Blandford looked at his block instrument, saw that it showed 'train on' with the hook off the plunger — the correct position if a train had been accepted — and, thinking

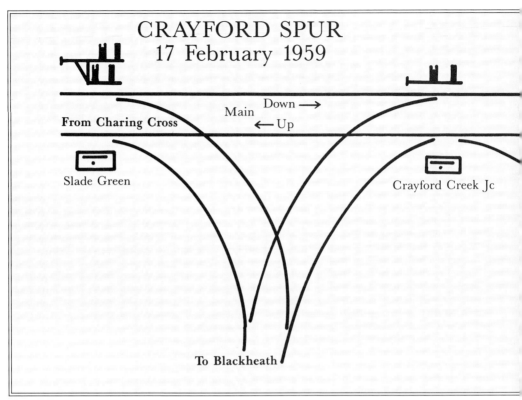

CRAYFORD SPUR
17 February 1959

Main Down →
From Charing Cross ← Up

Slade Green

Crayford Creek Jc

To Blackheath

that the 9.25 Charing Cross was the train in question, replied, 'Yes I have'. To this Miller replied, 'Well, I haven't got your plunge' (meaning, your release has not lifted the lock on my starting signal). Signalman Blandford promptly replied, 'All right, I'll give you another one', and so saying he quickly slipped the key into its lock on the instrument, turned it and was then able to give a second 'Line Clear' to Miller at Crayford Creek.

Miller cleared his down line signals at 10.53 and at 10.56 the 9.40 Charing Cross hit the back of the 9.25, injuring 70 people. Apart from showing that nothing is foolproof, this story also demonstrates the vital importance of asking precisely worded questions when making enquiries from box to box. When the words become part of the safety system, the form of words used should be as precise as the interlocking.

In the accompanying diagram of 'Box B', track circuit AT 1 is the 'berth track circuit'. Under the modernized system of lock and block known as the 'Welwyn' block, the signalman cannot give a second 'Line Clear' until the train for which the first 'Line Clear' was given has passed over that track circuit and the home signal — signal No 1 in this case — is again properly at 'Danger'. Track circuit 'A', when occupied, will lock the block instrument and prevent 'Line Clear' being sent to the box in rear — box 'C' — and it will also lock signal lever No 1 in the 'Danger' position. Furthermore, it will lock facing point bolt

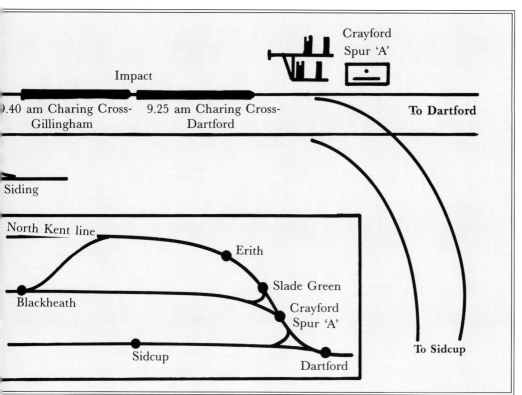

lever No 4 so that the facing points cannot be altered from whichever position they are in as the train approaches. Track circuit 'B' will lock levers 2, 3 and 4 while it is occupied by a train or vehicle. Now it was sometimes the case that a track circuit relay remained in the 'occupied' mode after the train had cleared the rails of that circuit, thus continuing to lock some point or signal lever or preventing the signalman from giving 'Line Clear' to the box in rear.

Obviously delays to trains would result from such situations, and signalmen

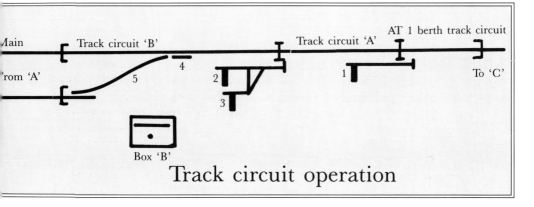

Track circuit operation

do not like delaying trains — whatever engine drivers might think to the contrary. There was a temptation therefore for the signalman to circumvent the operation of the relay if it was known that it was 'playing up' and the piece of track was not in fact occupied by a train or vehicle. The massive relays, weighing several pounds, encased in a glass box, were usually easy of access, and to prevent delays to trains during a track circuit failure, the signalman might 'tip the relay' — turn it upside down to reverse its faulty setting — whilst waiting for the technician to come and rectify the fault. Perfectly sound signalmen have been known to do this from time to time in a fit of misplaced enthusiasm for keeping the trains running without delay. I have done it myself, twice in 14 years, but the feeling of having created a hole in the signalling safety defences was more uncomfortable that the disappointment of stopping trains to instruct a driver to pass a signal at 'Danger', and I very quickly ceased to use this technique.

What can happen when a track circuit relay is tipped is well illustrated by the rear-end collision at Polmont East, Falkirk, on 5 February 1962. Polmont East signal box was 1½ miles west of Bo'ness Junction, 650 yards east of Polmont Junction and nearly 4 miles east of Falkirk High station on the very important Glasgow Queen Street to Edinburgh Waverley main line. It controlled a double track route with a down goods loop entrance. Early in the morning of 5 February, signalman Allison was on duty. He was 27 years old with 5 years' service. At about 1.11 am he noticed that his down main berth track circuit — TC 547 — was showing occupied when it was not in fact occupied. He attributed this to the wet weather and did not take any action under Regulation 25 (a) (ii).

Polmont East signal box seen from the station platform. (Stuart Sellar)

As he could not give 'Line Clear' to signalman Hamilton at Bo'ness, the latter would have to stop each down train, if the Regulations were followed, and inform the driver and guard of the circumstances and tell the driver to pass his starting signal at 'Danger'. The track circuit 'dropped in and out' (showed 'occupied' and 'unoccupied' alternately), and Allison mentioned this odd behaviour to Hamilton only as a matter of curiosity. When he needed to give Hamilton a 'Line Clear', he tipped the appropriate relay on its side for just long enough to enable Hamilton to pull his starting signal lever. He did not call his Signal & Telegraph Department lineman because — well, one just does not call the lineman out of bed at 2 am just to see to a track circuit failure. Hence the dodge with the track circuit's relay.

Just before 7 am, signalman Allison was joined in the box by his relief, 22-year-old signalman Gentleman who had started on the railway as a booking boy and had been a signalman for nearly five years. At about the same time, 6.57 am, signalman Allison gave 'Line Clear' to Hamilton for a fully vacuum braked goods train — 3-1-1 on the bell — the 5.25 am Niddrie to Glasgow. Signalman Allison opened the relay cupboard door, tipped the relay and gave the 'Line Clear' before replacing the relay. The block instrument's needle went over to 'Train on Line' as soon as the track circuit resumed its 'occupied' aspect. The cupboard door was closed and the two young men resumed their conversation, the goods train was not entered into the train register and was promptly forgotten.

After briefing him on the failure, Allison left Gentleman in charge and left the box around 7.08, just about the time that signalman Hamilton sent the 2 beats of the 'Train Entering Section' signal for the vacuum goods. Perhaps the clatter of Allison leaving, maybe the shouted 'cheerios', prevented Gentleman from hearing the bell — maybe it was never sent — but Gentleman did not 'book' it and was unaware of the approach of the train. As soon as his mate had left the box, he telephoned Bo'ness Junction to ask Hamilton to ask the lineman to attend to the track circuit failure and also to agree that the system so far adopted to keep the traffic moving should continue. While he was on the phone, the goods train arrived at his outer home signal, 880 yards away, hidden behind the arch of a bridge and the slightly curved track. At 7.10 am, in anticipation of Bo'ness asking 'Line Clear' for a down passenger train, Gentleman opened the relay cupboard and tipped the relay on its side. Just as he blinded his track circuit device, the freight train occupied the berth track. Its presence was not indicated on the signal box diagram and the block instrument's needle remained at the normal 'Line Blocked' position, not at 'Train on Line'.

While signalman Gentleman was busy with his relay, signalman Hamilton was relieved by signalman Fairgrieve. Hamilton told him about the track circuit failure and how the working had been conducted. Fairgrieve, who was 59 and had been a signalman for 39 years, was non-committal and said something to the effect that he would see how the instrument worked for him. Hamilton was leaving the box at 7.11 just as the Lochmill signalman asked 'Is Line Clear?' for the 6.50 am Edinburgh to Callander express, 4 beats on the bell. Fairgrieve 'gave the road'. He saw that the block instrument needle for the section ahead to Polmont East was hanging in the 'Line Blocked' position and considered himself perfectly justified in 'asking the road' for the passenger train to Gentleman — and under normal circumstances he would have been correct in this. Gentleman, knowing nothing about the 5.25 Niddrie standing half a mile away at his outer home signal, and having blinded his one defence mechanism, pegged his instrument to 'Line Clear'. Fairgrieve cleared his down main line signals. The time was by then 7.12. At 7.18, Fairgrieve sent the 'Train Entering Section' signal, 2 beats on the bell, to Gentleman, Gentleman 'got the road' from Polmont Junction and cleared his down main signals.

Driver Stanners was running 50 minutes late with his goods train when he was brought to a stand by Polmont East's outer home at 7.10. After a minute he sent his mate, fireman Grant, to the signal post telephone to carry out Rule 55, but Grant had been unable to contact the signalman. There were two buttons on the wooden case of the phone; he had pressed first one and then the other, had pressed each one several times in rapid succession and several times long and slow, but all without success. Driver Stanners had done the same but neither man knew that a special code of 'five short rings' was necessary to call the Polmont East signalman, and there was nothing in the vicinity of the telephone to advise a train crew of this. Even if the men had known the code, it is doubtful if the signalman would have heard it because the phone bell in the signal box was out of order and only buzzed.

The driver was on the point of sending fireman Grant to the signal box when the signal cleared. Driver Stanners had only a light train of 18 wagons and a 20-ton brake van with a powerful 'V2' Class engine to haul it. Acceleration was

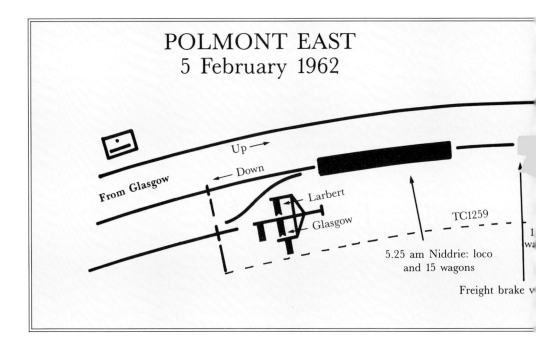

brisk, and 30 mph was reached before half a mile had been covered. It was then that Stanners saw that the directing distant signal for Polmont Junction was cleared for the Larbert line, the right-hand arm, whereas he wanted the left-hand divergence at the junction. Seeing these signals, he braked so as to stop at the Polmont East box and ask what was going on.

Signalman Gentleman had taken the 'Train Entering Section' signal for the express at 7.18, and within 30 seconds his track circuit 1259 had shown 'occupied'. Noticing this at once, he telephoned Bo'ness Junction to query the time that the 'on line' had been sent. Putting the telephone down after this brief enquiry, he looked out of the window and saw to his astonishment that there was a goods train approaching the box. So taken aback was he that he never thought to throw to 'Danger' the outer home signal and thus protect the rear of the train from the express he knew was also approaching. Had he done this, he might have saved the situation in the very nick of time.

Driver Elder, with an ex-LMS 2-6-4 tank engine and four coaches, saw Polmont East's distant signal at 'Caution', but it had been cleared before he passed over the AWS magnet and he received a 'Right Away' bell at 7.19 or a few seconds later. At that stage, the freight train's brake van had just passed beyond the outer home signal. Shortly after passing Polmont East's distant signal, the outer home signal's green light came into view and remained in the driver's view until he was 150 yards away from it. Driver Elder had the train running at about 55 mph as he passed the outer home signal and saw on the line ahead 'a dark mass'. Instantly thrusting his head over the cab-side for a better look, he saw the tail lamp of the train ahead and braked hard, at the same time shouting a warning

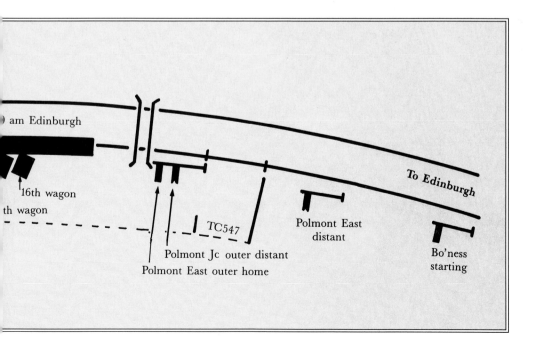

to his fireman and the two other locomen who were 'learning the road' on that cramped footplate. The weight of the passenger train and its engine was only 243 tons and the brake power available to stop it was relatively small at 66 per cent of the tare weight. There were 290 yards in which to stop, and the passenger train was still running at 35 mph at the moment of impact, at a closing speed of 20 mph. Signalman Gentleman sent 'Obstruction Danger', 6 bells, to Bo'ness and Polmont Junction at 7.20 am.

The brake van of the goods train and a four-wheeled van ahead of it were completely wrecked by the big tank engine which drove them forward before its buffers for 255 feet. Within this wreck, guard Jameison had a very rough ride, banged and buffeted in total darkness when a moment before he had been sitting, talking quietly to another guard who was riding with him. Two vans ahead of the four-wheeler were totally wrecked, but thrown out to the left where they hit the cutting side, rebounded and struck the first and second coaches of the passenger train. The vacuum brake pipes having parted both the goods and the express, the two trains came to a stand very rapidly with the undamaged front portion of the goods train 49 yards ahead of the derailed passenger tank engine surrounded by the wreckage of the goods brake and the four-wheeled van. Lying injured but still alive in the mangled remains of the brake van were both guards. These two men and three passengers were the only casualties who needed hospital treatment after this lamentable collision, which had been brought about by lack of discipline, lack of managerial supervision and lack of maintenance of Signal & Telegraph Department equipment.

CHAPTER 23

Settle

1960

THE 'BRITANNIA' CLASS 'PACIFICS' WERE NOT THE BEST DESIGNED locomotives to run on British rails. They had powerful boilers and could run fast, but in some important details their design was poor — forward vision from the cab was very restricted, and the slide bars were another item. There was one 'top' slide bar and two 'bottom' bars side by side held apart by spacing blocks at the extremities to provide space in which the crosshead guide could slide. The length of the bars was 4 ft 11¾ in, and only the top bar of the assembly was fixed to the engine's frames. A bracket 1 ft 11¾ in long was bolted to the main frame and to this was bolted the (all but) 5 feet long top slide bar. The two bottom bars were fixed to the top bar by means of steel bolts, 6⅞ in long and 1⅛ in thick. These bolts had a steel lug under the head and this lug fitted into a corresponding slot in the slide bar to prevent the bolt turning while its nut was being tightened. Each nut was plain — not crenellated — with a cotter pin bearing against it from a hole through the bolt above the nut. The bolts were inserted in their holes from below so that if a nut was to come off, admittedly a very unlikely event, the bolt would fall out of the bar and on to the ground.

When a 'Britannia' started off with a 400 ton train, a typical load for such a machine, with the engine in full gear and with full boiler pressure, the crosshead guide exerted an upwards thrust against the top slide bar of 3.8 tons, and when the engine was coasting at 45 mph there was a downwards thrust on the bottom bar of 0.6 tons. Opposing the constant thrust and release to which the slide bar was subjected was only the short, central bracket which had to hold the entire assembly. In comparison with the massive fixtures which formed and supported the crosshead guides on outside cylindered GWR engines, the 'Britannia' design seemed somewhat understrength, yet it was used with success on the LNER's best engines for many years.

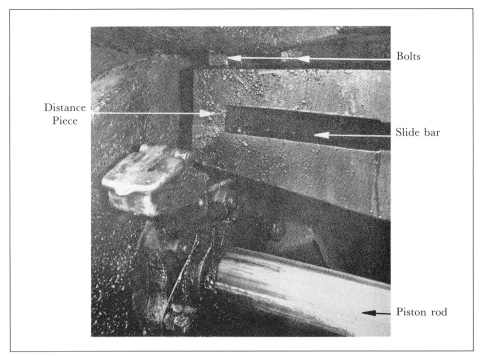

Bolts

Distance Piece

Slide bar

Piston rod

Above *The slide bar fixing arrangement of the 'Britannias' prior to the accident. The 1 ⅛ inch diameter steel bolts are inserted from below through both slide bars and the packing piece and are tightened by a nut with a split pin above it to prevent it turning. The nuts were exceedingly difficult to reach, especially the one on the inner slide bar, and as a result they were not kept properly tight. When the nuts were loose, the bars 'worked', the split pins were sheared, the nuts unscrewed, the bolts dropped out and the bottom slide bars fell off.* (Crown Copyright)

Below *After the accident, the modification. It is obviously a much more thorough job with large nuts below the bottom bar — the bolts inserted from above — and safety cotters hammered through a slot in the bolt so as to bear tightly against the nut.* (Crown Copyright)

'Britannia' Class No 70052 *Firth of Tay* was based at Glasgow Polmadie shed during late 1959 and early 1960, and was employed on expresses between Glasgow and Leeds over the 'Settle & Carlisle' during that time. The engine had been built at Crewe in August 1954 and had received a heavy repair at the works there in September 1959. From then until 21 January 1960 it covered 17,500 miles, roughly 122 miles a day, and as the round trip from Glasgow to Leeds and back was 438 miles, it would appear that No 70052 had taken a lot of time off during those 15 weeks, and indeed this was the case. There had been constant trouble with the slide bar bolts which had frequently worked loose in spite of the supposed restraint imposed by the cotter pins on the non-crenellated nuts and by the internal lugs to prevent bolts from turning. The bolts had been reported loose nine times between 1 September 1959 and 18 January 1960. On one occasion the fitters had found that a front bolt was actually missing, and all this since the engine's thorough overhaul at Crewe works in September. It was particularly difficult for the fitters to tighten the nuts of the front bolts owing to the close proximity above them of the projecting steam chest; a special, thin spanner had to be used to get into the confined space and thin spanners are not best suited for doing nuts up tight.

On 20 January 1960, No 70052 left Glasgow St Enoch, two days after its slide bar nuts had been attended to, on the 9.05 pm express to St Pancras via Leeds. The train consisted of eight coaches, including three sleeping cars, and weighed only 287 tons, a featherweight train on an easy schedule hardly qualifying for the distinction 'express' — but it was non-stop, more or less, and no overnight train ran fast. The footplatemen were from Leeds Holbeck, driver Waites and fireman Chester, both experienced men, Mr Waites being 60 years of age with 18½ years as a driver. The engine steamed well and rode comfortably, and the schedule was not difficult — steam footplatemen could not ask for more. They were working home over a road they knew well — it was going to be 'a piece of cake', except for the weather, that is.

The night was as black as pitch, a gale was raging and snowflakes were whirling through the air. They left the lights of Carlisle Citadel station 2 minutes late, but faced up to the long climb into the desolate hills in good spirits. They passed Appleby at about 50 mph on light steam on the generally falling gradient. Three miles ahead was Ormside box at the foot of the real climb to Ais Gill summit — 16 miles mostly at 1 in 100. Fireman Chester had plenty to occupy him, while Waites peered ahead through the heavy, driving snow as the big engine set its wheels into the 'Long Drag'. Fireman Chester kept working steadily as his mate gradually lengthened the cut-off to keep the 'Britannia' on the 50 mph mark on the steeply rising gradient.

Outside in the bitter wind, the right-hand slide bar was 'working' in an entirely different way. The holes through the top and bottom bars and the packing pieces were worn oval far beyond the limits of tolerance permitted. The bolts through the holes were thin from being stretched after many tightenings, and their lugs had broken off so that there was nothing to prevent the bolts from turning in the holes — and in their nuts.

187

The first nut and bolt fell off at milepost 271 beyond Helm tunnel, and the next dropped out half a mile further on; the inner bottom slide bar fell off two miles beyond that again. No 70052 was hauling its own weight, 148½ tons, and 287 tons of train on a rising gradient of 1 in 100 at 50 mph falling to 35 at the summit, the power being transmitted through the piston rod to the crosshead and then via the connecting rod to the wheels. Now, however, the right-hand crosshead was sliding between the slide bars which were disintegrating. After losing the bottom inner bar, the engine ran on for 8 miles without losing anything more. The engine breasted the rise at Ais Gill, Driver Waites, completely unaware that anything was wrong, eased the engine's effort by shortening the valve travel and closing the regulator somewhat. At once, there was a hard knocking as if a big end was slack; Waites shut off steam altogether, but this made the noise worse, so he opened the regulator slightly once more and kept his speed down with the brake, intending to stop at Garsdale to examine his engine. Just as the engine was about to enter Shotlock tunnel, the outer bottom slide bar fell off, leaving the right-hand piston rod and crosshead moving to and fro without any guidance at all.

Signalman Ashton in Garsdale box received 'Train Entering Section' for the express at 1.10 am, and, as it did not appear after the usual 3 or 4 minutes, he was looking out for it through windows spattered by snow and rattled by gale-force winds. The engine's headlamps appeared over the viaduct at 1.16 am, and the engine stopped 90 yards on the Ais Gill side of the box. After a minute, signalman Ashton could just make out the form of a man with a small electric torch walk around the front of the engine and begin an examination of the right-hand side. This was driver Waites. In pitch darkness, during a howling blizzard on that exposed hillside, he was trying to examine his engine by the light of a little torch. He felt the wheel bosses for excessive heat, he looked at the front and back cylinder covers for damage in case a piston had come adrift, and he examined and felt the connecting and coupling rod bearings, for he was convinced that the knocking came from a faulty bearing. He actually laid his hand on the right-hand crosshead, but he noticed nothing wrong with it, nor did his torch show him that the slide bars were missing.

Mystified, he climbed back into the cab and decided to drive on to Hellifield, some 25 miles further south, where there was a small motive power depot, fitters and lights. As the train started, signalman Ashton opened a window, letting in the gale but hoping the receive some message or explanation from the locomotivemen to explain the delay, some message which the men wished to have sent on ahead. But no shadowy head appeared through the cab-side window and the engine barked past, up the 1 in 337, a distant knock coinciding with the beats from the chimney. The guard was leaning out enquiringly from his van as it passed and Ashton shouted to him that his engine was making a very loud knocking noise. As well it might do, with the right-hand piston driving its crosshead with no guiding slide bars.

So long as steam was driving the piston, the crosshead guide stayed close to or actually pressing against the top bar, dropping away briefly at the end of each stroke before power was re-applied. From the stand at Garsdale to passing Dent signal box, 3¼ miles further on, the average speed was 40.8 mph according to the signal box clocks. From Dent to Dent Head box, the average was 54 mph with an average of 45 up the grade from Dent Head through Blea Moor tunnel to passing Blea Moor signal box. From there the line fell for miles at 1 in 100, and with light steam the train coasted down past Ribblehead station at an average of 52 mph, suggesting that the train had passed that place at 60 mph. Under light steam, the crosshead guide was not so tightly pressed against the top slide bar and the crosshead would have been bending around the end of the piston rod as the connecting rod swept over and over its big end, forcing the crosshead forwards and backwards. The piston rod was also bending where it entered the piston, and for 11½ miles, running at up to 60 mph, the punishment continued.

While *Firth of Tay* was being hurried downhill to reach Hellifield, and doubtless banging away like a berserk steam hammer, a Stanier Class '5' 'mogul' driven by Mr Stewart was coming up the 'Long Drag' on the down line with 550 tons of freight train, regulator full open against the heavy gradient. As the down train passed Settle signal box, the 9.05 Glasgow was passing the up distant signal for that place at about 45 mph. At that moment, the tortured piston rod finally gave way, the constant flexing tore the metal, the cylinder head broke, out came the piston rod and the entire assembly of connecting rod, crosshead and piston rod fell to the track, lanced into the ground and penetrated to a depth of at least 6 feet. The engine passed over its own connecting rod which was dragged out of the ground and then hauled along the sleepers, still flailing but in a trailing position. The 'I'-section connecting rod took on a severe, axial torque — great force was needed to achieve this, and the wonder is that the engine did not do a sort of pole-vault and become derailed as the rod plunged into the track bed. The train was running on an embankment and the ground was relatively soft: had it been a cutting through rock, the outcome would have been very serious as the engine would undoubtedly have been derailed.

Ballast rattled against the cab and sparks were flying as driver Waites, feeling the lurch, slammed his brakes on. The down goods train was then only yards away but in no danger until, 5 seconds before the 'Mogul' passed the crippled 'Britannia', the dragging crosshead caught firmly against a sleeper of the down main line and dragged it sideways — the track was new and well laid, so terrific force must have been required to do this. The 'Mogul' was working very hard on the right-hand curve and its wheels were bearing tight against the right-hand rail which was the one pulled out of gauge by the errant crosshead. The whole weight of the goods engine lurched sideways into the 'kinked' track and burst it wide open. The lateral pressure of the wheels against the rails was such that the spring clips holding the rail to the sleepers were sheared off and the right-hand wheel of the pony truck was bent on its axle, it being 1⅛ in tight to gauge at one point and 1¼ in wide to gauge at the opposite side of the rim. The big goods engine was derailed and lurched to the right, towards the express. It missed the engine but tore out the right-hand side of the first, second and third coaches, killing 75 passengers and injuring eight.

Above *The breakdown crane's outrigger stands on the very spot where the dragging connecting rod and crosshead caught in the sleepers of the opposite track to drag the inner rail wide of gauge just as the 'Black Five' approached from the opposite direction.* (Crown Copyright)

Below *The state of No 70052's connecting rod after it had fallen down, been forced into the ground and then vaulted over by the locomotive. Nearest the camera is the bent piston rod minus its piston. The stub-end of the snapped-off combination lever is attached to the crosshead while the connecting rod, forged to an 'I' section specifically to withstand such strains, is twisted like a stick of old-fashioned barley sugar.* (Crown Copyright)

Fireman Graham on the goods train was looking ahead just before the crash. He saw the approaching train, then saw a line of sparks which seemed to be running towards him. He just had time to yell 'Look out!' to his mate before the crash. There was a terrific bang, the cab filled with steam and the engine lurched about over the sleepers, swaying and bouncing to the accompaniment of the sound of rending steel. As soon as the train stopped, he got down on to the track and went back to find his guard. All this, it must be remembered, was taking place in a gale-force blizzard with several inches of snow on the ground. He found his guard sitting in the snow, his face bleeding from a serious cut, so he took the man's lamp and detonators and ran back towards the signal box to put down protective detonators and to raise the alarm. Fireman Chester went back with Guard Bird to protect the rear of their train. They saw that passengers were climbing out of the train into the blizzard, people dazed and shocked. Hurrying back from their business with the detonators, they put the passengers back into the warmth and shelter of the train. At least No 70052 could provide steam to heat the carriages.

The Settle station signalman sent 'Obstruction Danger', 6 bells, at 1.56 am when fireman Graham burst in with the news, and then called for all emergency services. In spite of the utter remoteness of the spot and the appalling weather conditions, the first ambulance arrived on the scene at 2.05 am, and the first of many doctors at 2.10. All the injured were on their way to Skipton hospital by 2.45, while the uninjured sheltered in the train until 4 am when they were safely ferried by ambulances to Settle station where a relief train was waiting to take them on their way. This left at 5.19 am. Although a section of the down line had actually been demolished, and both tracks damaged, it took the Civil Engineer's Department only 14½ hours to put matters right. Had that goods train been 30 seconds earlier or later, then not one person would have been hurt. As it was, the coincidence of trains was as perfectly timed as malevolent chance could arrange.

CHAPTER 24

Singleton Bank

1961

T HE LONDON MIDLAND REGION (CENTRAL LINES) WEEKLY NOTICE FOR the week Saturday 15 July to Friday 21st July 1961 carried the following announcement on page 22:

16th July

At or between	Lines affected	Remarks
Weeton and Singleton Station	Down and Up BLOCKED	12.01 am to 4.15 am re-sleepering and re-ballasting
Singleton Station and Weeton	UP BLOCKED	4.15 am to 11 am re-sleepering and re-ballasting. Single line working by Pilotman over down line

Weeton and Singleton Station signal boxes were on the ex-Lancashire & York-shire Railway double track line from Preston to Blackpool and to Fleetwood from a junction at Poulton about 2 miles west of Singleton. The line was heavily used, especially in the holiday season, and the boxes were placed close together. Coming from Preston, trains passed Kirkham North Junction, Bradkirk, Weeton, Singleton Bank and Singleton Station, six boxes in four miles.

On Sunday 16 July, Singleton Bank was switched out, so Singleton Station was working with Weeton. The up line (going towards Preston) between Single-ton and Weeton was to be blocked by a ballast cleaning machine, a train of new ballast, a train of new sleepers and a 'Matissa' tamping machine — although not all at the same time — while the down line would be occupied by the 'spoil' train of 39 open wagons to take the dirt sieved out of the up line's ballast by the cleaning machine. After 4.15 am, the Sunday train service began, so the spoil train had to be clear of the down main line and work 'between trains', the revenue-earning service using the down line as a temporary single track. Additional staff were drafted in to work the line, including handsignalmen at Singleton Station and at Weeton to apply the 'G'-clamps and padlocks to the crossovers when they were reversed to take trains to or from the single track; a Pilotman who would ensure that there would be no head-on collisions on the temporary single line; and an Inspector to supervise the entire operation.

The Pilotman was Assistant District Inspector Bush, a human 'train staff' for the night. No train could enter on the single line unless he was either riding with its driver or had, in person, instructed that driver to proceed. Thus, when the Pilotman was at Singleton Station trains could only run from there to Weeton. If there was more than one train to pass through the single line in, say, the up direction, the Pilotman would 'send' the first and subsequent trains through and travel with the driver on the last one so as to be at the other end of the section to meet the next down train and either send it or travel on it back through the section. It was a strenuous job which, when there were a lot of trains running in both directions, required careful planning. This 'crystal-ball gazing' was done by the District Inspector in charge of the whole operation. He phoned up and down the line to see how the trains were running, thought out the Pilotman's moves for him, put to him his suggestions and the two men would discuss each situation face to face in the box or over the telephone.

District Inspector Redmond was in charge. He was a man in his 60s with 40 years' experience as a signalman and Inspector. He seems to have been a very decent man who liked to trust his men to work properly, according to the rules. They would have thanked him for not 'breathing down their necks'. Unfortunately, not all of his men were as experienced as he was. Signalman Whiteside was 46 with 11 years' railway service, Mr Bush had 13 years' service, but signalman Harrison at Singleton Station was 26 years old with only one year on the railway. He had had six weeks' training as a signalman and had held his job at Singleton for only 10 months. Mr Redmond would have been wiser if he had spent some time with Harrison during the 'occupation' to make sure that he was keeping up with the rapidly changing and unusual situations. It was usual for an Inspector to 'make his rounds' and it would not have been resented. As it happened, he stayed in Weeton box for the entire shift. The wages grade men were on 'time and three-quarters' after midnight, they were all mates together, working pleasantly as a gang instead of in the usual, solitary, role. It was the usual, relaxed Sunday engineering job.

What was unusual was that throughout the operation the Rules were constantly being broken. Rule 200(a) was not carried out in that there was no handsignalman with detonators and yellow 'Caution' flag at Weeton's down distant signal. Down trains were travelling on the track being used as the single line between Weeton and Singleton, so it was vital that they stopped at Weeton to

Standard arrangements for single line working 1961

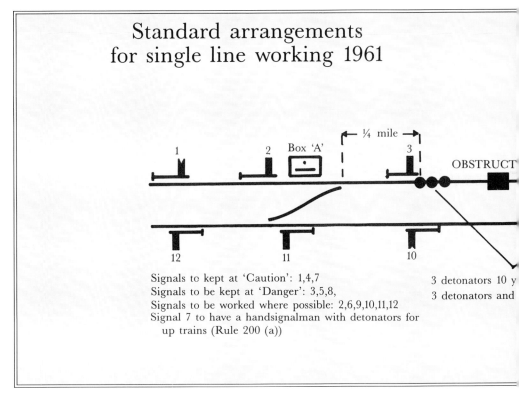

¼ mile

1   2   Box 'A'   3

OBSTRUCT

12   11   10

Signals to kept at 'Caution': 1,4,7
Signals to be kept at 'Danger': 3,5,8,
Signals to be worked where possible: 2,6,9,10,11,12
Signal 7 to have a handsignalman with detonators for
up trains (Rule 200 (a))

3 detonators 10 y
3 detonators and

await the pilotman's instructions. The handsignalman would have 'shot' each down train and showed a 'Caution' hand signal to reinforce the 'Caution' given by the distant signal. Mr Redmond ordered signalman Whiteside at Weeton not to accept a down train from Kirkham North Junction unless the Pilotman was present at Weeton — a wise order, but still the Rule was broken.

At 11.56 pm on the 15th, signalman Whiteside accepted a down goods train from Kirkham North Junction, and at one minute past midnight Inspector Redmond handed the up and down lines over to the Engineers. A statement to this effect was written across the pages of the train register at Weeton and Singleton boxes, countersigned by Redmond at Weeton. At 12.02 am the down goods train was signalled through the blockade to Singleton. It mattered little from a practical of view — the lines were still clear — but it looked odd in 'the book' (the train register) and it was in all honesty, poor railway work. The hand-over ought to have been delayed until the freight had passed.

Behind this goods train were the two work trains. The first was the spoil train to stand on the down line between Weeton and Singleton Station, while the other conveyed the sleepers and the ballast cleaner for the up line. When the first train arrived it was found to be double-headed, the leading engine having nothing to do with the work but merely trying to get home to Fleetwood. What ought then to have happened was that Whiteside should have telephoned Harrison and

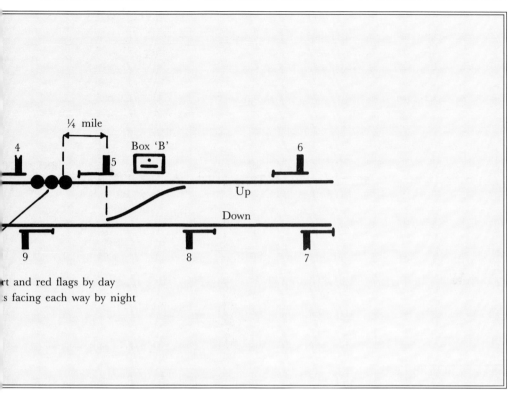

¼ mile

4

5

Box 'B'

6

Up

Down

9

8

7

rt and red flags by day
s facing each way by night

told him that the spoil train was entering the blockade to start work but that
there was an engine coupled ahead which was for Fleetwood and would come
through to the Singleton Station detonators and await events there. The Singleton handsignalman would then have lifted the 'shots' for the engine to proceed.

What in fact happened was that the spoil train was signalled into the blockade as a 'light engine' (breaking Regulation 1) and the signals were lowered.
When the light engine cleared Singleton Station, signalman Harrison sent the
'Train Out of Section' bell (breaking Regulation 6) when in fact the section was
still occupied by the spoil train. Inasmuch as everyone knew what was going
on, none of this mattered too much except to show that the signalmen did not
trouble to work to the rule book and Inspector Redmond's 'light rein' was becoming very light indeed. An incident which might have had serious consequences
occurred when, at 4.15 am, the spoil train arrived back at Weeton box having
come out of the blockade without stopping at the protecting detonators to ask
the signalman's permission (breaking Rule 216(j)). Whilst the train could move
at will between the detonators on the blockaded line, it could not come outside
them — on to 'live' track, so to speak — without permission because the signalman might have had a down train standing at his home signal with the obvious risk of a collision if unauthorized movements emerged from the blockade.
No harm was done but, again, it goes to show how the job was running — 'on

a wing and a prayer', rather than on the solid foundation of the rule book.

At 4.34 am the Engineer handed back to the Traffic Department the down line, and single line working was then instituted. This was effected by the issue to the Weeton and Singleton Station signalmen of a certificate notifying them of the arrangements. Each man wrote boldly across the 'down line' page of his train register: 'Single line working over the down line between Weeton and Singleton Station boxes in force at 4.34 am'. The Pilotman issued the certificate to Whiteside at 5 am, and when an engine for Fleetwood arrived on the down line he rode on it to Singleton Station to hand Mr Monks, who was working the box until 6 am, his certificate.

In typical early Sunday morning fashion, a succession of light engines interspersed with two passenger trains passed over the single line. During the working of the up trains over the down line, the berth track circuit outside the down home signal at Singleton Station was occupied as the up train sped away from Singleton towards Weeton. The occupation of this circuit caused the down line block instrument's needle to flick over to 'Train on Line' which signalman Monks, and from 6 am signalman Harrison, corrected by turning the instrument's handle to bring the needle back to the normal position. During single line working, up trains were signalled on the up line instruments and down trains on the down line instruments, and the danger in what Monks and Harrison were doing with the down line instrument lay in the chance of a confusion arising — they might 'take off' the needle when it was at 'Train on Line' legitimately. Mr Bush, according to Rule 198(c), ought to have arranged for this track circuit to be disconnected and, as this had not been done, the down line instrument should have been regarded as a failure and Regulation 25 invoked.

At 6.34 am, the spoil train came off the single line and went to Poulton Junction to clear the down line for an empty stock train. An up passenger train passed Singleton Station on to the single line at 6.52 and cleared Weeton at 6.57, then at 7.27 the spoil train returned from Poulton and re-entered the single line, clearing Weeton at 8 am. Inspector Redmond and the Permanent Way Inspector, Mr Wilkinson, had been discussing arrangements for the disposal of the various work trains and machines, and it was agreed that the ballast and sleeper train could now be sent to Poulton Junction; the ballast trucks had been unloaded and the truck-loads of new sleepers were now carrying old sleepers. This train came off the up line at Weeton and went on its way over the down line, single track. Behind this was the spoil train. The Engineers wanted to continue to work with this opposite the ballast cleaner, and Inspector Redmond agreed that the spoil train could go into the single line and occupy it for an hour or so until the last of the work was complete. It would then go through to Singleton Station, carrying the pilotman who would then withdraw the single line certificate and thus withdraw the special arrangements on his arrival at that place. Nothing in the Rules prevented this being done, but it was not good practice.

Before leaving Weeton with the spoil train, Mr Bush withdrew the single line certificate and signalman Whiteside wrote across the page of 'the book': 'Single line working withdrawn. Normal working resumed at 8.35 am.' This, of course,

Weeton signal box, signalman Whiteside's post, looking towards Preston. Detonators were placed on the rail nearest the signal box at signalman Whiteside's request to protect the rear of the ballast train which was working further down that line, behind the camera. He ordered the detonators to be lifted once he had obtained 'Line Clear' from signalman Harrison. (Jerry Plane)

was not true. Single line working was not withdrawn until the certificate at Singleton Station had been withdrawn. The spoil train entered the section to Singleton at 8.38, and signalman Whiteside instructed his handsignalman, Mr Semple, to place three detonators on the down line rail to protect the rear of the work train. Whilst admirable in spirit, this was yet another incorrect action. The handsignalman ought to have been working under the direction of the guard of the train, not the signalman (Rule 216), and the practicality of this will soon be seen.

Sunday morning peace reigned over the tracks for 90 minutes as the ballast cleaner loaded spent ballast into the spoil train in the vicinity of Singleton Bank signal box. The train was working for 1½ hours, stationary on the main line without the protection laid down by Rules 175(b) and 216(a), that is to say a handsignalman, working under the guard's instructions, standing ¾ mile to the rear of the train, holding a red flag and having placed three detonators on the rail. Inspectors Bush, Redmond and Wilkinson all believed that this precaution was unnecessary because, as they argued at the Inquiry, the train was protected by the provision of single line working whereby a second train could not enter the single line because the Pilotman was not present at either signal box. Yet Bush had removed the single line certificate from Weeton box and had allowed signalman Whiteside to write the 'withdrawal' statement; Bush or Redmond would, presumably, have countersigned this.

At about 9.30 am a light engine arrived at Singleton Station's up home signal and could go no further because the lines were blocked. At 9.48 the Poulton Junction signalman phoned Harrison to say he had a second light engine, this time to go on to the 'dead road' (the up line) at Singleton/Weeton. At 9.50 Harrison phoned Redmond and asked what to do with these engines. Redmond told

Left *Singleton Bank signal box, the switched-out minor block-post from which Assistant District Inspector Bush made his various telephone calls, presuming that others were listening to him, and close to which the crash occurred.* (Jerry Plane)

Right *Singleton Station box, the post of young signalman Harrison, from whence the fatal 'line clear' was sent.* (Jerry Plane)

him to put the first engine on the down line, give 'Train Out of Section' for it and accept the second engine from Poulton. When that one arrived, he was to tell his handsignalman to pick up the detonators protecting the 'dead road', let the engine on to that road and then put the first engine back on the up line. This work occupied Harrison until 10 am.

Meanwhile, events were moving on. As Harrison replaced his telephone on its rest, Mr Bush picked up the telephone in Singleton Bank box and spoke to Mr Redmond about the imminent cessation of the ballast cleaning work. Redmond replied that when Bush arrived at Singleton Station with the spoil train on the down line he was to withdraw the single line working certificate from that box and re-open the up line as soon as the ballast cleaning machine had been drawn clear by the engine which had just gone in. It must be understood that this telephone circuit was an open one — a 'bus line' in railway parlance — and anyone could hear a conversation simply by picking up his own handset. Redmond and Bush assumed that Harrison was listening in — 'everyone always does,' they said later. Of course, Harrison was busy with his engines.

Having come to this understanding with — as he thought — all concerned, for Whiteside had also been listening in, Mr Bush telephoned Harrison and told him that the ballast cleaner would shortly arrive at his up line detonators and that he, Inspector Bush, would soon be arriving on the down line with the ballast spoil train. Unfortunately, signalman Harrison confused this message and became convinced that the spoil train was also coming back to him along the up line, so convinced in fact that he even mentioned the 'change of plan' to his handsignalman Mr Terras. Signalman Whiteside had been listening in to this conversation and when Mr Bush put his phone down to return to the ballast spoil train, Whiteside continued to speak to Harrison. It was at this point that Harrison's confusion, born of total lack of experience, and Whiteside's patronizing 'old soldier' attitude towards Harrison coalesced to produce a disaster.

According to signalman Whiteside's account, he spoke to Harrison for several

minutes and, thinking that plenty of time had elapsed since Mr Bush had left Singleton Bank signal box and that therefore the ballast spoil train must have passed Singleton Station box, he said to Harrison, 'Are you clear on the down yet?' To which Harrison replied that he was and promptly placed the down line instrument to 'normal' from 'Train on Line'. Signalman Whiteside was particularly keen to clear the down line because an express passenger train was due. Seconds after Harrison had 'dropped his needle', this express train, 8.50 am Colne to Fleetwood, was offered to Whiteside from Bradkirk, which box had recently switched in, and Whiteside accepted it; but before he sent the 'Is Line Clear' code — 4 beats on the bell — to Harrison, he again asked him if the down line was clear. Receiving an affirmative, Whiteside sent the '4 bells', 'got the road' and cleared his down line signals. At that point, the Weeton handsignalman, seeing the signal arms rise, removed the three detonators protecting the ballast train on the down main. He was working for signalman Whiteside, not for the guard of the train, and thus he took this action — which is why the rule book states that the handsignalman in this instance must be under the train guard's orders.

However, this is not quite how signalman Harrison recalled the events. He said that his down line instrument was showing 'Train on Line' when Whiteside rang the '4 bells' code and he, Harrison, telephoned Whiteside to ask him why he had done this. Whiteside replied with a question. 'Why is your needle still at "Train on Line?" Come on Derek, straighten up your needle and give me a "Line Clear"'. This, to me, sounds a very realistic course of events, but of course there is no proof one way or the other. There is no doubt, however, that signalman Harrison felt signalman Whiteside's impatience — Whiteside was years senior to him, Harrison had become convinced that the spoil train was on the up line so, not wishing to appear foolish before a senior signalman, he released his needle and gave a 'Line Clear' without having first received the 'cancelling' signal, 3-5 on the bell, for the ballast spoil train from Whiteside.

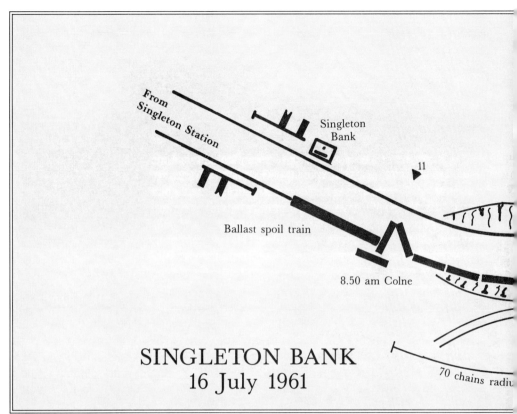

Singleton
Bank

11

Ballast spoil train

8.50 am Colne

SINGLETON BANK
16 July 1961

70 chains radius

Signalman Whiteside obtained 'Line Clear' from signalman Harrison at 10.22 am. Inspector Bush had finished his telephone conversation with Harrison at not later than 10.15, and the distance from Singleton Bank to Singleton Station was barely 1½ miles. The ballast spoil train would have arrived at Singleton Station well within that 7 minutes but for fate. Just as the train was about to

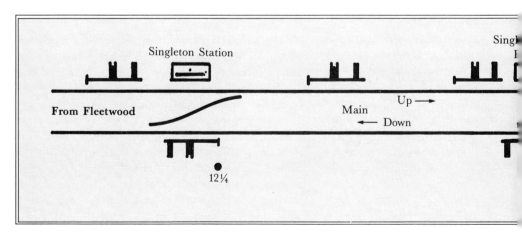

Singleton Station

Singl

From Fleetwood

Main

Up →

← Down

12¼

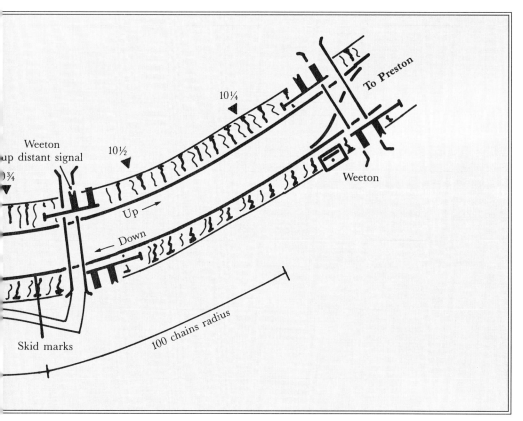

10¼

10½

Weeton
up distant signal

0¾

To Preston

Weeton

Up →

← Down

100 chains radius

Skid marks

leave, one of the permanent way men noticed that the side door on one of the wagons was not properly shut. Some men got down out of the guard's van and walked along the train to see to it. In 2 minutes they were all back in the van waving 'Right Away' when the crash occurred. Mr Bush immediately jumped off the engine and ran to Singleton Bank signal box to warn Whiteside and Har-

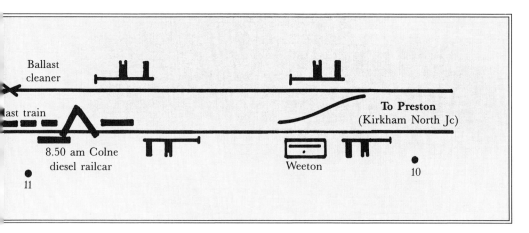

Ballast
cleaner

last train

8.50 am Colne
diesel railcar

To Preston
(Kirkham North Jc)

Weeton

10

11

rison. 'Obstruction Danger' was sent at 10.28 by Whiteside to Bradkirk box, but Harrison could not send the signal to Whiteside because of damage to the lineside poles, bringing down the wires.

From Weeton to Singleton Bank, a distance of just under one mile, the line followed a continuous and ever sharper curve. The line ran in a deep cutting from Weeton westwards for ⅝ mile, the curve tightening until, towards the far end, it passed under a brick arch curving on a radius of 70 chains. Two hundred yards west of the bridge the cutting gave way to embankment. A driver's forward view in the cutting was ever more restricted as the curve tightened between the high walls of earth with the bridge at the west end forming a real 'choke' to visibility.

The 8.50 am Colne express, a six-car diesel unit, passed Weeton box at 60 mph. The ballast spoil train was standing 1,400 yards ahead on the same line and, as fate would have it, with the tail of the train hidden beyond the bridge just beyond the sharpest part of the bend. The first glimpse that the railcar's driver would have had of the ballast spoil train would have been at a range of 457 yards, but he would not have known that he was on the same line as the spoil train until he was 275 yards away from it. Skid marks were found at a point 260 yards from the point of impact. The ballast spoil train, hauled by an ex-LMS 2-8-0, weighed 575 tons and was stationary when it was rammed by the six-car diesel weighing 200 tons including 350 passengers.

Inspector Wilkinson and Sub-Inspector Stables were walking along the track

The 8.50 am Colne to Fleetwood railcar after colliding at 50 mph with the heavy stationary ballast train. (Crown Copyright)

The awful rearing coaches of the Colne express seen from the track. (Crown Copyright)

when the express emerged from the cutting under the bridge. Both men gave the hand 'Danger' signal, but had to jump clear as the train roared past, its brakes hard on, the driver standing up and winding furiously on the circular hand brake wheel. Smoke and dust were flying off the wheels as the brake shoes bit hard. On the ballast train, guard Fenton had just enough time to jump out of the van before it was crushed to pieces by the railcar; up in the big steam engine, the driver had no time to take any action at all to lessen the force of the blow. The driver of the express stayed bravely at his post, trying to brake the train when, having set the brake, he could have left his compartment and run back through the coach. He died instantly and six passengers died with him.

The Inquest jury returned the verdict of 'misadventure...due to the misunderstanding of and the non-compliance with the signalling regulations and rules as laid down by British Railways'. This was a verdict with which the Ministry of Transport's Inspecting Officer, Brigadier Langley, 'entirely agreed'.

CHAPTER 25

Torquay

1962

T ORQUAY STATION LIES ON A STRETCH OF LEVEL TRACK BETWEEN TWO
rising gradients. The signal box was at the south end of the down line
platform close to a road overbridge. Coming from the north, from New-
ton Abbott and Torre the line fell into Torquay on a 1 in 55 gradient, and going
south to Paignton and Kingswear the line rose at the same inclination. The next
signal box southwards from Torquay was Gas House Sidings, 1,500 yards up
the bank. The heavy traffic which once passed over the Great Western line from
Taunton to Kingswear and Plymouth is now a legend; when trains, very often
hauled by unlikely engines, crowded into every station along the line, stood at
remote 'break section' signal boxes and laboured up the steep inclines, the coaches
packed with holidaymakers.

Signalman Pearse came on duty in Torquay signal box at 2 pm on Saturday
25 August 1962 and was at once plunged into the fray. Down trains were running late due to the overcrowding of the line and the poor performance of diesel
and steam engines. The 10.05 am Paddington, consisting of 14 coaches weighing 475 tons and hauled by D833 *Panther*, a 'Warship' Class diesel, arrived in
Torquay at 2.25 pm and left at 2.30, 18 minutes late. Up to that time all delays
to this train had been due to the overcrowded line ahead but now, as the diesel
howled up the 1 in 55, only 50 tons below its maximum load, the driver discovered that it seemed very sluggish and would not accelerate beyond 15 mph.
It dragged its tail clear of the station, signalman Pearse sent it 'on line' to Gas
House Sidings and sent 'Train Out of Section' to Torre.

The Torre signalman at once 'asked the road' for the 7.45 am Paddington,
Pearce 'pegged up line clear' and the train arrived at Torquay behind 4932 *Hatherton Hall* at 2.33, 46 minutes late. The delay was due to the train's diesel engine
having failed at Taunton. The only substitute had been the 'Hall', but the diesel
driver, Mr Willott, and his second man, Mr Greggory, were full of confidence

in their ability as steam enginemen and had taken the 'Hall' without waiting for the assistance of a pilot engine on Wellington bank where 4932 was overloaded by 25 tons. On the climb out of Torquay towards Paignton, the steam engine would be hauling 100 tons more than the permitted maximum, but by the time Willott had reached Torquay he knew he had a good, strong engine on his hands and did not want to cause further delay by asking for a bank engine which was not immediately available.

The disembarking of the Torquay contingent of the passengers took 5 minutes and the train was ready to leave at 2.38. However, the 10.05 Paddington had still not cleared Gas House Sidings box. Given a clear run, a train took 3 minutes between the two signal boxes, but very often a train was held for several minutes at Gas House waiting for the down line platform at Paignton to become vacant. Pearse telephoned the Gas House signalman to ask if the train had arrived and when he was told it had not, Pearse lowered his starting signal for the 7.45 am Paddington to move out of Torquay station and to pull up the hill to the advanced starting signal 334 yards further on. The train moved off at 2.39. Signalman Pearse was following normal, Torquay practice in making this movement, in order to clear the platform for the next train which was even then waiting up at Torre and, hopefully, to give the first train a start — by the time it reached the advanced starter it might have been possible to lower that signal. On the six preceding summer Saturdays, 258 down passenger trains had used Torquay station, and of these 40 had been brought to a stand at the advanced starter, and 65 had had the signal lowered for them as they approached.

As *Hatherton Hall* set off with that wonderful Swindon gun-shot exhaust beat, D833 *Panther* was at a stand on the 1 in 55 rising incline with the tail of its train about 100 yards beyond Torquay's down main advanced starter. The centrifugal governor which brought the low gear torque converter into action was stuck, the engine was driving on top gear, and so had stalled on the steep incline with the coaches straddling the catch-point. The driver, Mr Bowden, knew this and had all the brakes in the train hard on to prevent a run-back and thus a derailment. His second man, Mr Porter, was sent back to inform the guard so that the latter could walk back and protect the rear of the train with detonators while Porter went back to call up an assisting engine.

Now, close to the east side of the line was the Livermead Hotel with a fire escape down the wall on the side nearest to the line. The hotel's gardener, Mr Sandford, had seen the smoke of a lineside fire and had climbed the fire escape in order to find out where the fire was burning. There he had a grandstand view of the railway, and having reached the top he heard 4932 start from the station about 340 yards away. He also saw that the advanced starting signal was at 'Danger' and, not far beyond, was the stationary diesel-hauled train. Obviously the steam engine was going to be stopped at the signal and Mr Sandford, being a good chap and a keen observer of trains, stood at the top of the fire escape to relish the sight of the engine coming up the hill, stopping and then getting away from the signal on the 1 in 55.

On the footplate of 4932 there was a certain tension. Fireman Greggory was

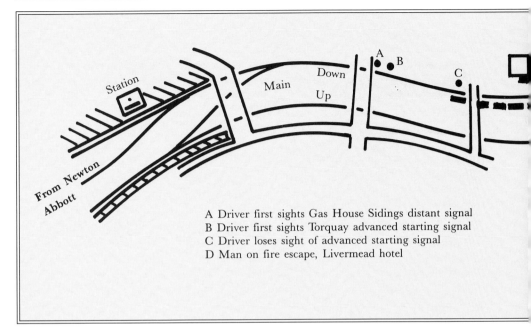

A Driver first sights Gas House Sidings distant signal
B Driver first sights Torquay advanced starting signal
C Driver loses sight of advanced starting signal
D Man on fire escape, Livermead hotel

intent on his fire — with the steep bank ahead — and driver Willott was concentrating on getting the best out of his heavily overloaded engine, feeling how it was doing through his hand on the regulator, through the soles of his boots, listening to the sound the chimney was making and ready for the first sign of wheel spin. They slipped once, and Willott slammed the regulator shut then opened it again carefully; the chimney picked up its bark once more and the engine forged steadily around the sharply curved track, up the 1 in 55, at 20 mph — 100 tons overloaded!

From the station, the line was in a cutting on a right-hand bend, and passed under two bridges out of the cutting on to a bank on a left-hand bend, with the Livermead hotel up ahead on the left and the advanced starter at 'Danger' just beyond. The signal first came into sight of the driver at a range of 186 yards, and right on the spot driver Willott glanced forward and spotted it at the earliest moment. He saw a man's figure at the outer edge of the arm and, as the engine moved around the curve, the figure moved along, just below the horizontal arm until the signal was hidden from the driver's view by the length of the engine's boiler. At this point the signal would have become visible to fireman Greggory, but he was busy with the fire and his mate did not ask him to look out.

The strange sight of the man apparently dangling from the signal arm so attracted driver Willott's attention that, although he stared at it throughout the entire time he had the signal in view, the fact that he was staring at a signal at 'Danger' did not register with him. Much to the amazement of the watching Mr Sandford, the 'Hall' blasted past the signal. Turning to follow its progress, he was aghast to see the passenger train still standing and to see its guard come

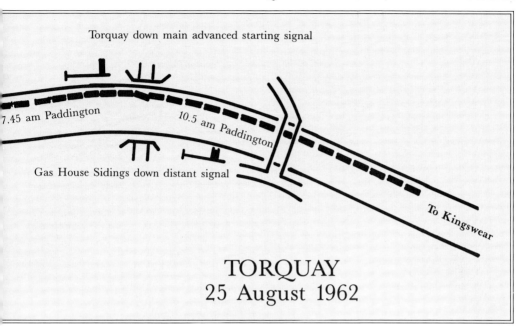

Torquay down main advanced starting signal

7.45 am Paddington

10.5 am Paddington

Gas House Sidings down distant signal

To Kingswear

TORQUAY
25 August 1962

running down the hill waving his arms. Just at this moment, fireman Greggory had finished his 'round'. He looked up, saw the guard and the train about three coach lengths away and shouted 'Whoa!' in the time-honoured way. His driver, who had no forward vision at that point owing to the curvature of the line, braked instantly, and the collision took place at between 5 and 10 mph.

The rear coach of the 10.05 Paddington was forced off its bogies so that the body shot backwards and came to rest on the 'Hall's' buffer beam with the blank door of the corridor connection just touching the engine's smokebox door handle. A doctor who was passing on the road stopped at once and went to the scene. Fire engines and ambulances were on site in 12 minutes and of the 23 injured, seven were taken to hospital. Poor driver Willott was very embarrassed by the affair and made absolutely no excuses for what had happened. It was his first mistake in a career of 27 years on the footplate, 12 as a driver. Owing to the curvature of the line and his position on the engine, Willott could see the Gas House Sidings down distant signal at 'All Right' after he had passed the advanced starting signal. Colonel Robertson, in charge of the Inquiry, was very critical of the signal sitings, but driver Willott was not prepared to find excuses for his lapse except to say, with some reluctance, that he might have been distracted 'by a man from the Livermead Hotel standing up high near the Hotel by the signal', and that the engine then started to slip again and he was distracted by that. Perspective angles had placed Mr Sandford as a 'hanging man' below the signal arm when viewed from the footplate of the 'Hall'.

CHAPTER 26

Knowle & Dorridge

1963

T HE FACT OF HAVING WORKED A SIGNAL BOX FOR 15 YEARS IS NO guarantee that the signalman will be a safer operator than a man who has only worked that box for one year. What is required above all is alertness and a strict adherence to the rules. Familiarity can make a man too flippant in his approach to the job. Knowle & Dorridge signal box was on the

Birmingham Snow Hill to Paddington main line of the old Great Western Railway, a little over 10½ miles south of Snow Hill station. The signal box housed a frame of levers numbered to 74 to work an extensive layout consisting of a quadruple track main line flanked by goods lines, and shunting sidings outside these on both sides of the line. The signal box was situated between the main and relief lines, just off the south end of the station platform. Lapworth signal box was 2½ miles to the south and Bentley Heath Crossing box was 1,194 yards to the north.

Knowle's up main distant signal was below Bentley Heath's up home signal on the same post, and was only 902 yards from Knowle's up main home signal on a falling gradient of 1 in 262. This arrangement gave insufficient braking distance to a train travelling very fast — and the line limit was 90 mph. Indeed, even a loose-coupled goods train might not have been able to stop at Knowle's up home from a braking point at the up distant. For this reason, the signalman in Knowle box gave 'Line Clear' to Bentley Heath for up trains under the provisions of Regulation 4A, which meant that Knowle did not give 'Line Clear' to Bentley Heath until 'Line Clear' had been given to Knowle by Lapworth, and as soon as Knowle had returned 'Line Clear' to Bentley Heath, Knowle's signalman immediately lowered all his up main line signals. If, when Bentley Heath asked 'Is Line Clear?', Knowle could not obtain 'Line Clear' from Lapworth — maybe there was a train in the section — Knowle replied to Bentley Heath with the 'Line Clear to Clearing Point Only', 2-2-2 on the bell. Receiving this code, Bentley Heath did not lower any of his up main signals until the

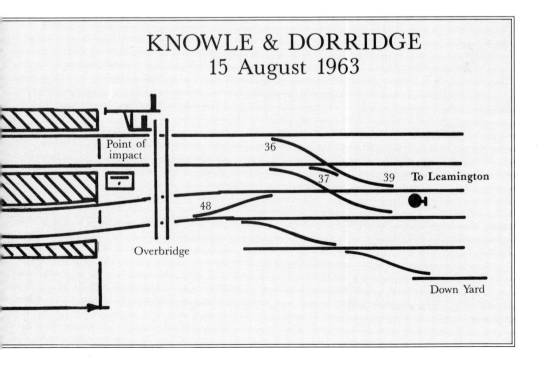

KNOWLE & DORRIDGE
15 August 1963

Point of impact

36

37   39   **To Leamington**

48

Overbridge

Down Yard

train had passed his up main distant signal at 'Caution'. Thus Bentley's distant was co-opted to act for Knowle and plenty of braking distance was afforded to the approaching train.

Signalman Jones was on early turn in Knowle & Dorridge box on 15 August 1963. He had worked the place since 1948, had for years dealt with the heaviest traffic the place would ever see and generally 'knew the job backwards'. However, by 1963 he had dropped into the habit of giving Bentley Heath 'Line Clear' on the up main without first obtaining 'Line Clear' from Lapworth. During the four weeks preceding the accident, he had found the job was getting on top of him to the extent that he had been unable to keep his train register correctly. In the preceding month he had registered three trains which had never run, and had not registered 38 trains which had run, while many trains which were entered did not have the full record of times. At lunchtime on 15 August, the two trains immediately preceding the crash train had not been entered in the register.

At 1 pm he was shunting with the 10.15 am Bordesley to Knowle goods train, worked by a pannier tank and manned by Tyseley men, driver Aldgate and fireman Olson. They had arrived at 10.40 am and had been shunting ever since. At 1.07 pm the train had come out of the Old Yard on the down side of the line whence it had gone to collect some car-flats loaded with Land-Rovers and was standing on the down relief line waiting to cross to the up main line and the New yard, just off the up main at the north end of the station. This was a 'propelling' movement in which the train would be obliged to run 'down' the up main to get to the sidings and which would, in doing so, foul the 440 yard clearing point ahead of the home signal. To make the movement, point lever No 36 and ground signal No 39 had to be pulled to cross the shunt to the up main and, having done this, it was not permissible for Knowle to give 'Line Clear' for an up main line train because the line was fouled within the clearing point. Indeed, Jones ought to have sent 'Blocking Back Inside Home Signal', 2-4 on the bell, to Bentley Heath and pegged his up main block instrument to 'Train on Line' before commencing the movement. In the event, he was unable to say whether he had given 'Line Clear' to Bentley Heath before or after he set the shunting movement in motion, but the point is academic.

At 1.7 pm he gave 'Line Clear' on the up main line to signalman Taylor in Bentley Heath box for the 1 pm Birmingham to Paddington Pullman and then proceeded to foul the up main line with the shunt, completely forgetting about the Pullman. Having 'got the road', signalman Taylor, with 40 years' experience and having worked Bentley Heath box since 1948, closed his crossing gates, lowered his up main signals and then got out the broom to clear up ready for 'going home time'. He did not notice that Knowle's up distant signal was still at 'Caution', and at the subsequent Inquiry stated that he had no obligation to keep a check on it — although I would disagree with that. He usually did watch the distant signal and if it did not 'drop off' he would give his mate Jones a warning buzz on the telephone. This time he remained unaware until the express came through the arch of Widney Manor Lane overbridge 370 yards away at not less than 80 mph. By then it was too late to warn Jones, and in any case Jones could not have lowered his up main signals as he had the shunt moving northwards along the up main as the Pullman came south on the same line slightly less than one mile away and closing the gap at 80 mph.

The Pullman consisted of nine 40-ton wooden coaches dating from 1923 hauled by a 2,700 hp locomotive D1040 *Western Queen*. In the driving cab were the two drivers required on this working, Ernie Morris and Sid Bench, with second man Dave Corkery. All three were Wolverhampton Stafford Road men who had worked the 'Kings' to London a very short while previously. Dave Corkery had in fact finished his day's work — a trip to London and back — and was doing an extra trip because the booked man for the job had gone sick. The coaches weighed 360 tons and the brake force available on them was 386 tons. The weight of the engine was 108 tons and its brakes were able to exert a force of 82 tons on the wheels — 76.6 per cent of the engine's weight — hence the total brake force for the whole train was 465 tons, or almost exactly 100 per cent of the train's weight. The 'Western's chassis consisted of two, solid-drawn tubes of 6½ in external diameter with a wall of thickness of .192 in. These ran the length of the vehicle. Lateral steel plates were welded to the tubes to hold them apart while longitudinal plates of the same thickness, 5/32 in, were welded to the laterals to create a honeycomb structure of great strength. In this frame were mounted the two 1,350 hp Maybach diesel engines. The flesh and blood driving this fairly awesome assembly sat behind a body skin 0.08 in thick support by struts 0.1 in thick.

The driver would have sighted Knowle's up distant at 'Caution' at a range of 230 yards — 5.8 seconds away from it at 80 mph. It may be that he was taken aback by this unusual sight — and he must have been aware of its dangerous implications — for he did not slam his brakes on until he heard the wail of his ATC siren as the engine passed the signal.

The time was then 1.12 pm. Signalman Taylor sent 'Train Entering Section', 2 beats, to signalman Jones and at last Jones woke up to the terrible danger. He ran to the window and held a red flag out for the men on the pannier tank. Fireman Olson saw this, shouted to his mate to stop and the brake was put on at once, the leading car-flat stopping opposite the box. Driver Aldgate had just released the brake when he and Olsen saw the Pullman coming rapidly towards them, smoke and dust rising from the wheels as the driver braked frantically. The guard and shunter, riding in the open verandah of the van which was at the leading end of the train, saw the Pullman a second or two before and all four men managed to jump off, left and right, a few heartbeats before the impact. Two train-spotters were on the platform, enjoying the trains, when this ghastly situation arose, and their evidence to the Inquiry was that the Pullman was running at between 20 and 30 mph at the moment of impact. It was decided later, by experts looking at the damage, that it was nearer 20 than 30.

The flimsy front of the diesel was crushed to the engine-room bulkhead and the hydraulic buffers, taking the blow full face-on, were bent upwards. The brake van and leading car-flat received such a crushing pressure that they shot out

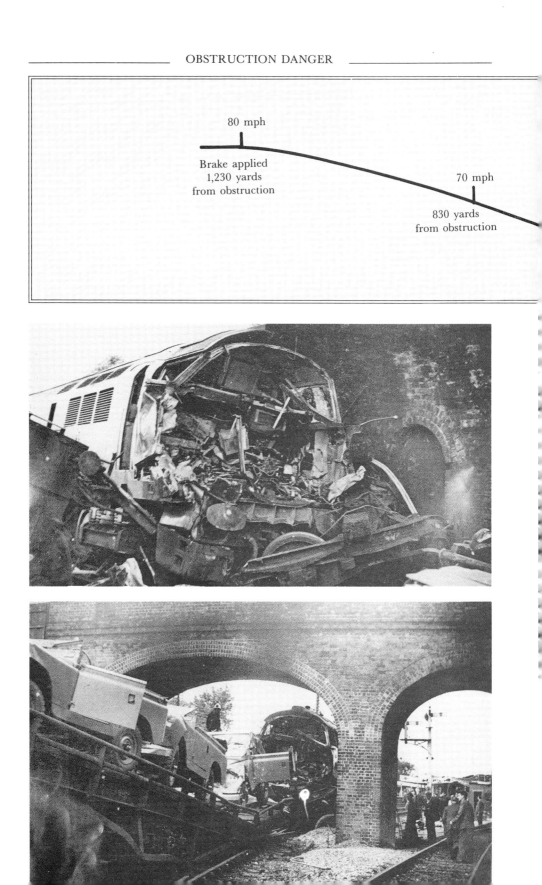

80 mph

Brake applied
1,230 yards
from obstruction

70 mph

830 yards
from obstruction

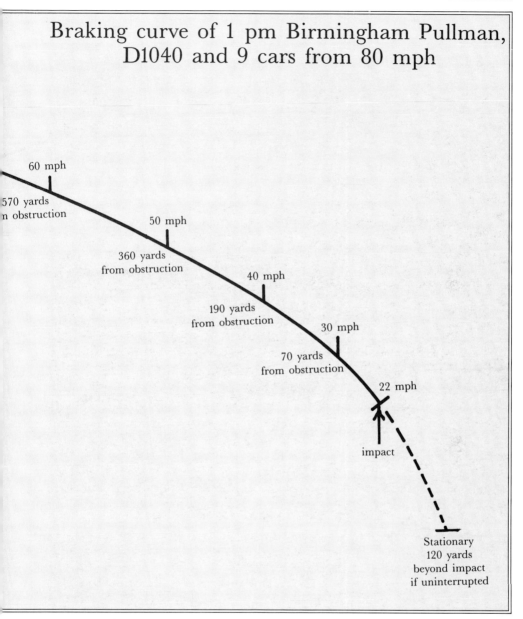

Braking curve of 1 pm Birmingham Pullman, D1040 and 9 cars from 80 mph

60 mph

570 yards
on obstruction

50 mph

360 yards
from obstruction

40 mph

190 yards
from obstruction

30 mph

70 yards
from obstruction

22 mph

impact

Stationary
120 yards
beyond impact
if uninterrupted

Above left *The wreckage of D1040* Western Queen *in which drivers Ernie Morris and Sid Bench died together with their second man, Dave Corkery, who was working an extra trip as a substitute for the booked man who had gone sick that morning.* (Crown Copyright)

Left *Demonstrating once again the terrible forces at work in a collision. This car-flat broke its massive, steel girder spine when caught in the crush between the oncoming* Western Queen *and the weight of the stationary train.* (Crown Copyright)

The fireman of 6987 Shervington Hall *looks back in awe at the broken wreckage, as his engine, blowing off steam, works south from Knowle & Dorridge station with a Birmingham-Leamington local. This train had taken at least 85 minutes to cover the six miles from Acocks Green station, such was the queue of traffic waiting to use the up relief line when the other tracks were blocked by the crash.* (Michael Mensing)

sideways, like soap squeezed in the hand. The next car-flat was directed upwards into the cab of the diesel as its buffers slid up over the inclined buffers of the locomotive. Another car-flat had its back broken, on another the bogie was ripped off. The pannier tank and its train were driven forward 64 yards while all this crushing and breaking was going on until the energies involved had been expended. All three men in the diesel cab were killed. Shortly before this sad day, driver Ernie Morris had featured in a British Railways film called 'Let's go to Birmingham'; the film is still available on video and Ernie can be seen.

The crash was caused by signalman Jones fouling the up main line after he had given 'Line Clear'. He was a very well-respected, long-serving signalman who enjoyed the complete confidence both of his station master and his District Inspector. Neither of these supervisors could say that they had ever found any fault with his booking (keeping of the train register) even though they said that they had regularly checked Jones' book and the inspector had cross-checked it with Lapworth's book. When the Inspecting Officer, Colonel McMullen, carried out his own cross-check of the Bentley Heath, Knowle and Lapworth train registers for the period 16 July to 15 August 1963, he had to go through 4,000 line entries — eleven trains an hour on average throughout 30 days — which is the mark of a very busy signal box. Each line in the book represented one train and each train required 6 bell codes — 24,000 codes to be rung out, all demanding quick thinking, but nothing that many signalmen were not already

The breakdown train came from Tyseley behind 2-6-2T No 4111 — note the 'A' headcode lamps on the front buffer beam. Such trains ran as 'express passenger' and were belled as such — 4 beats — between signal boxes. The steam crane is lifting the shattered remains of a car-flat and in the foreground lies the toppled ex-GWR 'Toad' (freight brake van to the uninitiated) belonging to the shunting train involved in the smash. (Michael Mensing)

doing successfully. The Knowle train register on signalman Jones's shift was found to be lacking 114 individual entries of a bell code time, had contravened regulation 4A on nine occasions, had completely omitted 38 trains, had recorded three trains that did not run and had made 38 other mistakes. Yet neither the District Inspector nor the station master had seen these glaring inaccuracies. Maybe if they had quietly reminded signalman Jones of his responsibilities he would not have become so slack in his working as to cause this triply fatal crash.

CHAPTER 27

Barnham

1963

ELECTRICAL SIGNALLING SYSTEMS ARE NOT ENTIRELY FREE OF MYS-
terious and dangerous malfunctions. Sometimes these malfunctions occur
as a result of the dreaded 'false feed', the 'one in a million' chance. Such
a chance at Barnham, the junction for Bognor Regis, on the Southern Region's
Brighton to Portsmouth line worked on the Southern's famous 'third-rail' system of traction. High voltage alternating current (AC) is taken from the national
grid and fed into sub-stations placed at intervals of about 3½ miles along the
line. In these sub-stations the AC current is transformed and rectified to 650
volts DC (direct current) and is sent into the third rail. This power is picked
up from the third rail by a pick-up shoe on the bogie of the motor coach and
is passed through the controller operated by the driver to the traction motors,
then returns to the national grid via the running rails and the lineside sub-stations.

The running rail is not earthed, not only because it would be very difficult
to provide first class earths at all locations but also because at stations in particular there would be a problem where heavy return currents from accelerating
trains would enter the soil and cause corrosion of underground metal pipes and
cables by the process of electrolysis. Even a two car set in drawing away from
a station can draw 1,000 amps at 650 volts. The sub-stations were well placed
to take this return current but if one station should be missing from the chain
then there would be a a seven-mile section of rail discharging its return currents, and if there should be several trains on one track in that section then,
particularly at the centre of the section, there would be built up in the running
rail a voltage or 'potential' between the running rail and earth. Thus far this
is all very 'iffy' — if a sub-station fails, if there are several trains all drawing
a heavy current — and even then the potential created could do no harm unless
it got into a wire where it was not supposed to be — and all circuits are insulated, are they not? The beauty and the danger of electricity is this, that it will

flow anywhere so long as the most tenuous contact is maintained.

On the morning of 1 August 1963, Signalman Slater was happily working his 75 lever Westinghouse frame in Barnham signal box. His box stood on the down side of the line at the Portsmouth end of the station. A few yards west was the Barnham sub-station and a few yards west of that was the double junction, turning south for Bognor. The station lay immediately to the east of the signal box, an up main platform and a down 'island' platform. Trains from Brighton could be diverted around the rear of the down platform by a set of electrically operated facing points 305 yards east of the signal box. These were worked by a motor when lever No 8 was reversed or placed normal in the frame. By moving this lever, a circuit controller was turned so that the motor was switched on for the 'reverse' (around the back of the platform) or the 'normal' lie of the points. Naturally the circuit controller was insulated and resided within a metal box which, being fixed to the metal girders supporting the frame, was in contact with earth.

Signalman Slater was very busy on that day of high summer. He sent a Bognor to Victoria train away from the island platform via points 8 and 7 and he then brought the 9.18 am Victoria alongside the main line face of the same platform. This train divided at Barnham, the front part going to Bognor and the rear going to Portsmouth. While the uncoupling was taking place he was correct in permitting the 10.17 am from Brighton to approach him from the box

Barnham Junction looking west to Chichester. The route to Bognor curves away on the left while on the right No 33017 waits to leave for Waterloo via Eastleigh with the empty GUVs that formed a newspaper train earlier that morning. (John Vaughan)

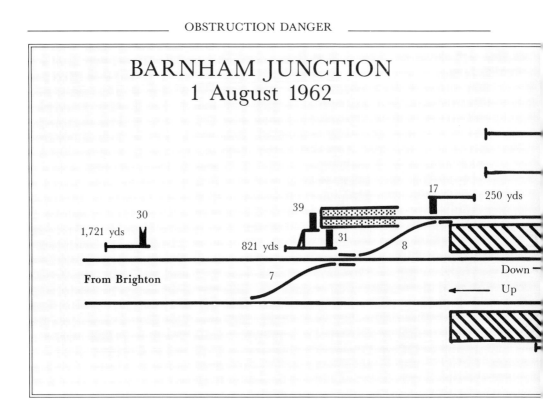

BARNHAM JUNCTION
1 August 1962

30
1,721 yds

39

31

17
250 yds

821 yds

8

From Brighton

7

Down

Up

Barnham Junction in November 1984. A Brighton to Bognor EMU is passing over points No 8 whose predecessors were wrecked when they recieved a false feed and motored underneath the 10.17 am Brighton on 1 August 1962. (John Vaughan)

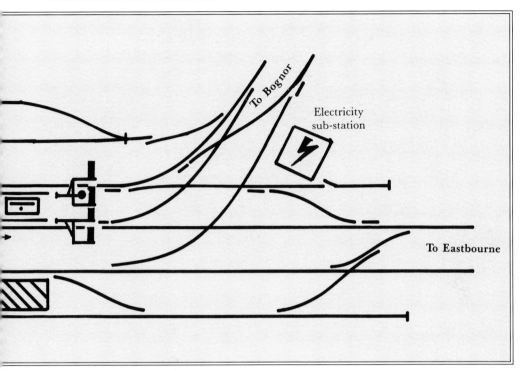

in rear — Ford. As the Bognor portion of the 9.18 Victoria was leaving, at 11 am, the 10.17 Brighton was stopping at the home signal. At that precise moment, the rectifier failed in Barnham sub-station, the circuit breakers tripped and the sub-station was taken out of service automatically. Barnham was now plumb in the centre of a 7¼ mile section in the power supply circuit with Drayton, 3¾ miles away towards Portsmouth, and Ford, 3½ miles east towards Brighton.

As soon as the 9.18 Victoria had cleared the junction points, signalman Slater re-set them for the Portsmouth direction and cleared his signals for the Portsmouth train to leave. In seconds it was whining swiftly away. Slater replaced the starting signal to 'Danger' behind it and promptly cleared his down home signal to permit the waiting 10.17 Brighton to enter the platform. Driver Light put his controller into series and the train, a six car set, drew smoothly forwards. In the space of two minutes, three trains had begun to accelerate in the vicinity of Barnham, drawing in total several thousand amps from the third-rail and putting the return current back into the running rail to create a potential of 60 volts in that area. As the driver approached facing points No 8 with his power still on, he saw the gap between the left-hand switch blade and the stock rail. He had seen the 'main line' signal cleared, yet here were the facing points set 'half and half' while he approached at about 25 mph.

He made an emergency brake application but it was too late to be effective. The leading bogie of his motor coach dropped between the rails and ran on, up the platform ramp, before falling over on to its right side, slewed across both

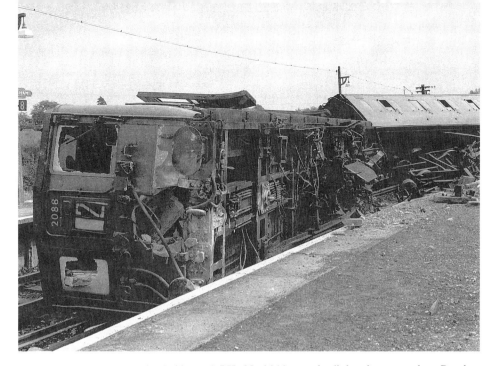

Because of a 'million to one' coincidence, 2-BIL No 2088 was derailed and overturned on Barnham Junction's platform. Slabs of concrete paving were scooped into the driving cab, seriously unjuring the driver who was lucky, looking at the mess, to escape with his life. Two other people were seriously injured and, in total, 32 people had to be taken to hospital in a shuttle service of ambulances. (Associated Press)

main lines. The second coach was also thrown on its right side but the remaining four coaches remained upright and were unharmed. No one was seriously injured. Signalman Slater sent the 'Obstruction Danger' signal to Yapton at 11.03 but not to Bognor or Ford because he was intent on alerting the electrical and traffic controllers at Redhill.

Sub-Inspector Green of the Signal and Telegraph Department was on the platform at the time and ran to examine the facing points.They were gaping under the train and, as he watched, he saw the point motor begin to run, trying to return the points to normal, something it could not do as the wheel of the fifth coach was in the way. When the S&T Department's Inspector Castle arrived, he and Mr Green began a careful check of the wiring, using their volt meter. The electrically operated points No 8 had motored to the reverse position without lever No 8 being moved — there was a false feed somewhere in the system. They checked all the circuits and found nothing until they came to the 'reverse' command wire leading to the errant points. This they found to have voltages of between 5 and 25 volts on it when trains started from the loop line around the back of the down main platform. There should have been no voltage at all, so they went to the locking room below the signal box operating floor and dismantled the No 8 points circuit controller.

A bunch of cables, bound together with cord, passed as a stiff trunk below the circuit controller and between the double row of nutted studs which formed the fixing assembly for the electrical contacts within the box. Lying on top of this cabling trunk was a large, metal washer. One side of the washer was in contact with a nut and stud holding an electrical contact blade, the other side of the washer was touching the body of the circuit controller which, because it was bolted to a metal support of the lever frame, was connected to the running rail — and a potential of up to 60 volts — through the levers and their point rodding. This electrical contact blade, which was carefully insulated from the earthed body of the circuit controller, was none other than the 'reverse' command wire's contact. When the point motor was set for the 'normal' or 'main line' position as it was when the 10.17 Brighton moved away from the home signal, the reverse command wire was connected to the motor and, through the motor, to earth. All that was required was for a sufficiently strong electric current to be fed to the circuit to make the motor turn, and of course this could normally only be done by the signalman reversing his lever No 8. However, if a high enough potential could be created in the running rails, then that voltage would pass to the 'reverse' command wire through the point rodding, lever frame, the body of the circuit controller, and the bridging washer to the otherwise carefully insulated electrical contact blade.

When the wreckage had been cleared from the track, a reconstruction of events took place. The Barnham sub-station was switched out, three trains accelerated from or to the station just as they had done on 1 August and, sure enough, a 60 volt potential was created in the running rail, sufficient to operate the point motor. The circuit controller had last been serviced in April and it was presumed that the washer had lain on the cables, bridging the circuit, all that time, a dormant trap, just waiting for the coincidences of the right traffic situation and the removal of the Barnham sub-station to bring it to life. One gets a nasty feeling wondering where the next washer is, at this moment, lying in wait with the potential of mayhem.

CHAPTER 28

Kingham

1966

U NTHINKING PEOPLE MAKE JOKES AT THE EXPENSE OF THE IRISH, AS
if Irishmen or women have a monopoly on stupidity or, conversely, as
if the British have a monopoly on intelligence. The cause of the Kingham
derailment might seem, to an Irishman, a species of 'Englishman joke', for once
again in this book we have reached what might be considered as the 'light relief'
section. On the day of the crash, 15 July 1966, Kingham, erstwhile 'Junction
for Chipping Norton and Banbury, Bourton-on-the-Water and Cheltenham' was
a ghost station. Both branch lines had been lifted, the bridge carrying the Banbury to Cheltenham Direct Railway over the Oxford to Worcester main line
was derelict, and pink campion and yellow ragwort waved above the empty ballast. The 100-lever signal box still stood, but it was switched out of circuit, its
signals permanently lowered, its remaining points spiked and clamped out of
use pending their removal.

A few yards south of the signal box, on the Oxford side, there had been a
facing point in the up main line so that trains from either Worcester or Cheltenham could run into the branch platform, the rear face of the up main platform.
The tracks had gone, but the actual switch blades of the facing point remained
in place waiting for the engineers to find the time to replace them with plain
track. This facing point in a 90 mph main line had been thoroughly secured
'out of use' since 4 May 1966, not only with a massive 'fishplate' firmly screwed
to the sleeper with two big bolts but also by a 'G'-clamp to nip the switch blade
to the stock rail; this clamp, having been screwed up tight, was also padlocked
and, as if this was not enough, the facing point bolt was still set in its notch
in the stretcher bar and spiked to the sleeper so that it could not be moved. Those
facing points could not have been better or more safely secured.

The line through the station and for some long way to the north and south
is straight, falling at 1 in 402 for up trains, and the Hereford/Worcester to Pad-

dington expresses went through at the full 90 mph when they had had a clear run through Moreton-in-Marsh and had not stopped there to pick up passengers. On 15 July 1966 the 10.25 am Hereford to Paddington express stopped at Moreton and left there 8 minutes late behind a Class '3' diesel of the 'Hymek' type driven by Mr Robbins of Worcester with second man Teague. As they passed through Kingham Station at 76 mph they felt a 'tug' against the engine. Immediately afterwards, as they shot under the road bridge at the south end of the platforms, they felt another, accompanied by a sudden and fierce brake application. Second man Teague put his head out of the cab window and looked back along the train. A moment later he popped back inside to shout to his mate that it looked as if a coach had become derailed. The parting of the vacuum pipe consequent upon this derailment brought the train to a stand by the advanced starting signal, amidst the peaceful fields.

On Kingham station, porter Hemmings was in his room minding his own business as the train roared through. The crescendo of noise diminished a little and then came a second, terrific roaring sound as if a second train was following the first. He put his head around the door and was greeted by the sight of a solitary coach racing along the up platform in a cloud of dust before dropping off the platform to continue its journey, more conventionally, along the rails. It finally came to a stand at the London end, leaning — somewhat wearily perhaps — against the down platform and blocking both roads.

On the train was the Oxford District Inspector, Gordon Jones. When he felt the violent brake application he was at the window at once, looking out to see what was happening but, even after the train had stopped, he could see nothing wrong. He saw the two enginemen on the track, one going towards Oxford to place protective detonators on the down line, and shouted to them, asking what was wrong. They were unsure and shouted back only that 'We've lost the vacuum'. Jones jumped down pretty smartly just as the guard jumped down shouting 'We've lost a coach'. From where they were, several hundred yards south of the station, with the arch of the road bridge intervening, the trainmen could not see the coach lying in the station. Gordon and the guard ran to the rear of the train and saw the broken knuckle of a buckeye coupler hanging down. The inspector at once told the guard to go back with detonators to protect the rear of the train while he, Jones, would go to the signal box, switch it into circuit, put the signals to 'Danger' and send 6 bells — 'Obstruction Danger' — to Moreton-in-Marsh and Bruern Crossing.

By the time Gordon Jones had done all this, after a run of at least half a mile, the emergency services had been alerted and were on their way. The man who dialled 999 was Mr Ahearn — a good Irish name — who ran a garage on the lineside right by the station. He had actually been dialling while the coach was still careering through the station. Travelling ticket collector Forty was lucky to escape with a few bruises. He had been walking towards the rear of the coach when it had become derailed. He had been thrown on his back, owing to severe deceleration forces, had slid swiftly back the way he had come, the length of the corridor, and had been 'pocketed' neatly through the open door of the front

The rear coach of the 10.25 am Hereford to Paddington express was derailed by the loose switch blade and was diverted up the platform ramp to run along the platform for many yards before falling back on to the track where the coping stones have been broken away and the track torn up. (British Rail)

compartment as the coach had tipped over to lean against the platform. 17 people were injured, 11 had to be detained in hospital.

The coach had been derailed on the facing point. The 'G'-clamp was still screwed up tight and padlocked, holding the left-hand switch blade to the left hand stock rail, and the facing point bolt was shoved fully home through its port in the stretcher bar. Only the fishplate had been removed. The facing point looked

The coach came to rest, remarkably undamaged considering the unconventional route it had taken, at the south end of the station. No one was seriously hurt and the loco men on the up platform seem happily blasé about the event. (British Rail)

Looking back the way it had come. The would-be fatal facing point is being examined by Oxford District Inspector Gordon Jones who is standing in the 'four foot' (between the rails). The coach travelled, derailed, along the sleepers until the bogie met the diamond crossing at the centre of the view. The bent rails bear witness to the fact that they deflected the coach up on to the platform. (British Rail)

secure, yet it had derailed the last coach of the train. How could this be? The Oxford District Permanent Way Inspector, Mr Weeks, was called out and he arrived at 1.10 pm. He had last been at Kingham on the 14th when his men, members of the Kingham permanent way gang, had been preparing the facing points for removal — or 'lifting', to use the railway expression. The men had prepared the track by undoing the fishplates at the rail joints, oiling the threads of the nuts and bolts, doing them up tight again, screwing out the fang-bolts holding down the chairs and screwing them in again, all to ensure that the bits and pieces would come apart easily when they came to carry out the relaying job on the 17th. He had left the site on the 14th at 11.45 am and at that time the gang had not put a spanner to the nuts holding down the stretcher bars between the switch blades of the facing point, although they would indeed remove, oil and replace these nuts.

When he walked up to the points at lunch time on the 15th he saw at once that three stretcher bar nuts were missing: the right-hand nut of the facing point bolt stretcher, the left-hand nut of the first point blade stretcher and the right-hand nut from the second stretcher bar. He searched the ballast but could only find one of the missing nuts. This, he decided, came from the left-hand bolt of the the first stretcher; it was dry and rusty and had been removed, not with a spanner, but by being cut with a hammer and cold chisel. None of the nut-less bolts had any oil on them and they were marked as if they too had had their nuts cut away — a job which would require a fair amount of exertion. Whoever the energetic chap had been who had gone to all this trouble, hoping to save them time when the Sunday relaying came round, he had not realized that he had released the right-hand switch blade from any restraint — it could move a full 4 inches to the right if there was any force to cause it to do so. A bruise on the tip of this blade showed where the flange of the wheel had hit it as it had swung to the right due to vibration of the train passing over it. Although the left-hand switch had been fairly spiked and bolted into position, the right-hand rail had been released from the rest of the assembly, and because there was no block of wood between it and the right-hand stock-rail as required by the rule book and by common sense, the blade had duly moved and derailed the coach.

The members of the Kingham permanent way gang denied any knowledge of how the nuts came off their bolts. Patrolman Sollis said that he saw ganger Longshaw half cut through the right-hand nut of the second stretcher — not to remove the nut but merely to break the rust seal and make it easy to turn with a spanner. Mr Sollis was reluctant to say that the nuts had been removed deliberately by the gang or by anyone else, but when asked if he had ever heard

The redundant facing points in the up main line were very carefully clamped and padlocked (bottom left) and also 'spiked' with a fishplate (just above the clamp). Unfortunately someone in the permanent way gang removed the nut securing the left-hand side of the second stretcher bar (immediately below the clamp) and two of the three nuts securing the right-hand side stretcher bars. One right-hand nut was allowed to remain, but its influence was nil owing to the removal of its opposite number. Thus the right-hand switch-blade was free to move — which it did. (British Rail)

of a rusted, tightly screwed on nut removing itself spontaneously from a bolt, he had to admit that he had not. How it was possible for not just one but three rusty, screwed tight nuts to come off their bolts simultaneously was indeed a mystery, he had to agree.

Ganger Longshaw said that he had eased and re-tightened all the stretcher bar nuts with a spanner and had only used a hammer and chisel on the one which was tight, and further he insisted that not he nor, any member of his gang, had heard of the elementary precaution of placing a block of wood between the switch blade and its stock rail! Lengthman Sollis, brother of patrolman Sollis, sub-ganger Field, brother of lengthman Field, all corroborated their ganger's evidence. No one knew how the half split nut came to be discovered in the ballast. The other two nuts were never to be seen again; How they came to disappear will always remain a mystery. Had the third nut not been buried in the ballast, maybe that too would have vanished. In summing up his conclusions, Lt Colonel Ian McNaughton said: 'It is understandable possibly, in view of the close personal and family loyalties existing within the gang...that no individual was prepared to admit the full facts...and though the prime responsibility must rest on ganger Longshaw, I consider that the other members of the gang...must have known what was done and should have realized the danger'.

CHAPTER 29

Blatchford Viaduct

1975

S TILL IN THE VEIN OF 'LIGHT RELIEF', BUT OUT OF CHRONOLOGICAL order, comes the story of the 'Gozunda' that failed. I was on early shift in Witham (Somerset) signal box when, as a result of the failure, early morning up West of England expresses were late passing the box. Enquiries as to the reason for this revealed the whole sad tale of how two men spent a freezing night jammed under the arch of a viaduct. It must have been a horrible experience for them, and of course all the Westbury district signalmen sympathized with them, but we could not help laughing too; uncharitable perhaps, but at least half our hilarity was directed — Luddite fashion — at the fragility of BR's latest toy.

In fact, the 'Gozunda', or Viaduct Inspection Unit, had been in use on British Railways since 1961. It was a rail mounted, articulated arm such as might be seen on an over-sized JCB, with a cage for two men at the outer end. It had a powerful lamp for inspection purposes and a telephone for communication with a third man who was stationed on the rail-mounted vehicle. A diesel engine provided power for the lighting, the hydraulics and for propelling the machine for short distances along the track. Earlier versions had winched themselves along the rails. If the diesel engine failed with the arm 'outboard', there was a hand pump with which to work the hydraulics and, if all else failed, the occupants of the cage were provided with a centrifugally governed winch and cable by which the men could lower themselves to the ground. By stepping into the cage and being launched over the side of a bridge or viaduct, engineers could inspect the underside of arches in a fraction of the time it took by traditional means.

On 30 January 1975, the Chief Civil Engineer was granted an Absolute Possession of the up main line between Hemerdon and Totnes, 16 miles, from 01.50 to 05.20 hours for the purpose of examining the arches of several viaducts. The Engineer did not know how much ground he could cover in one 'possession;

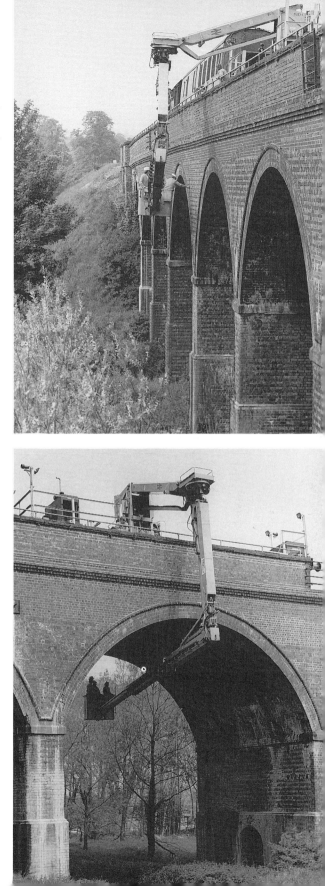

The precariousness of the engineers' perch is well illustrated here as one man leans out with a light hammer to test the soundness of the brickwork of Lavington viaduct. Without even the room to lie down, the little platform would become a kind of torture chamber, jammed all night in the 'wind tunnel' beneath the viaduct arch. (Michael Mensing).

A viaduct inspection unit in use under Lavington viaduct on 15 May 1988. The articulated, swivelling and extending arm is a match for the most inaccessible location, but the lack of comfort shows that it was not intended for all-night vigils 'underneath the arches'. (Michael Mensing)

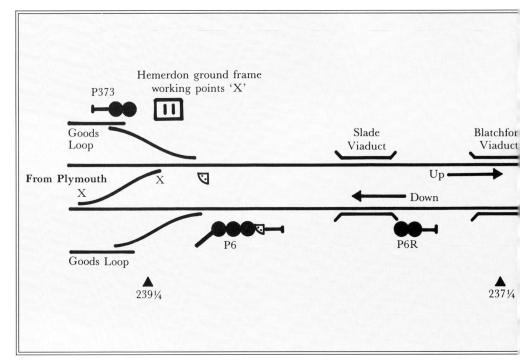

Blatchford viaduct, between Ivybridge and Hemerdon, was originally a Brunellian timber construction opened in 1849, 879 feet long and a maximum of 107 feet above the valley floor. The present structure was completed in 1863 and is seen here as it was in 1898. The unfortunate engineers were marooned under the central arch, nearly 100 feet above the ground, not the most comfortable place to spend a Sunday night in mid-winter. (British Rail)

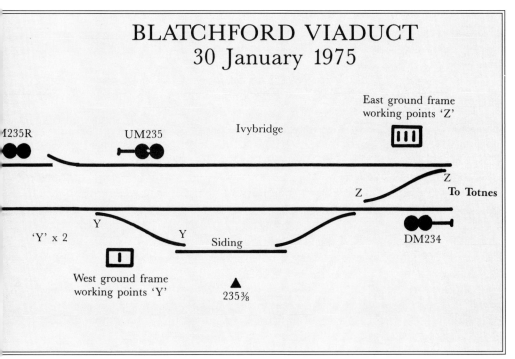

BLATCHFORD VIADUCT
30 January 1975

East ground frame
working points 'Z'

4235R   UM235   Ivybridge

Z

Z   To Totnes

'Y' x 2   Y   Y   Siding   DM234

West ground frame
working points 'Y'   235⅜

because the self-propelled 'Gozunda' was something of an unknown quantity, so he chose midnight and the small hours of a mid-winter night to find out. The 'viaduct inspection unit', a freight brake van and a mess coach, left Plymouth, Tavistock Junction yard, hauled by diesel No 25 219 at 01.35 am with guard Lucas in charge of the train and shopman Millington as mechanic in charge of the unit, although he had no specialized knowledge of its working. Examiner supervisor Wolney was to work from the cage accompanied by the plant hire company's man, Mr Reynolds, who would operate the controls within the cage. The person in charge of the Possession, supervisor Bean, took up the Possession by placing detonators on the up line at Hemerdon and at Totnes and by informing the Plymouth Panel signalman by signal post telephone what he was doing. All this was in accord with the engineering notice book and with the rule book. The Plymouth signalman was careful to remind Mr Bean that he wanted the up line handed back at 05.15 am and the work train set off.

It stopped over the western arch of Blatchford viaduct, roughly 2 miles west of Ivybridge and 2 miles east of Hemerdon, where the line had to cross a deep, narrow valley, ⅜ mile east of the site of the old Cornwood station. The night was pitch dark and bitterly cold as a gale of wind scoured the slopes of Dartmoor. Messrs Wolney and Reynolds got into the cage and Reynolds, by manipulating the levers therein, lifted the pair of them over the parapet, dropped down and finally drove in under the arch of the viaduct where the gale whistled through as if in a wind tunnel. When the examination was complete they asked, by telephone, for the machine to be moved to the next arch. Suspended in the pitch

231

dark, wind torn night, 100 ft above the invisible ground with the sound of gale-tossed trees far below like the sound of a distant sea, the two men successfully visited four arches. At 03.30 am as they were under the fifth arch, the unit's diesel engine failed.

The light went out and the men could neither manipulate their cage nor telephone Millington just a few feet above them on the rails over the arch. The wind was too strong to allow the sound of their shouts to reach the men above and they could not use the 'Rescuematic' (what wonderful names!) winch so carefully and cleverly designed, because they did not know what was below them —they might for example get entangled in trees. The 'Rescuematic' was neither a rescue nor 'matic' in darkness if one was unsure of one's landing. So there they were, stranded 100 feet above the ground under the arch of a viaduct, the gale freezing them and help sitting on top of them just feet away, probably drinking tea in the mess coach.

An hour passed in the windswept darkness. Guard Lucas, wondering how the job was getting on, struggled through the gale to ask shopman Millington how matters were progressing. Only then did he let it be known that he had lost contact with the men in the cage an hour before owing to a complete power failure. Guard Lucas was instantly alarmed at the thought of blocking the up main line after the allotted span and if shouting and whistle blowing could have raised that cage, Lucas and Millington would have done it then. They flashed torches over the parapet into the night — as if the men were out at sea rather than beneath their feet under the arch. The guard blew his pea-whistle, his 'Acme Thunderer', the two men bellowed with all the power of their lungs and even got the engine driver to blow the diesel's horn. Needless to say, the cage remained where it was.

Next they tried a kind of 'Devonshire rope trick'. There was a rope ladder on the train so they tied one end of this to something strong and threw the other end out into space, thinking that the men in the cage might like to leave the relative security of the steel platform for the circus-like atmosphere of the rope, in a gale, in the dark, 100 feet above the ground. In the event, Reynolds and Wolney never had to make the choice. They were too far under the arch to have caught the rope ladder even if it had hung down decorously — as it happened it stood out from the bridge like a flag in the wind. The time was then 5 am the men on the viaduct had exhausted their ideas and themselves with shouting and they took no further action for the moment.

Supervisor Bean called Plymouth signal box from Hemerdon at 04.45 am and again at 5 am to see what progress the train was making, and on each occasion got the same answer — none. On the second occasion the signalman suggested that Mr Bean should go to the site and see what was wrong because the train had been stationary for a very long time. The difficulty then was that the train had been standing for so long that it might at any moment 'up sticks' and head direct for Totnes. If Mr Bean was to go to Cornwood, the train could move off while he was in his car on the road. In that case he would be miles away from Hemerdon at the very time he would be required there to take up the detonators and give the line back to traffic. On the other hand the train might be in trouble and require his presence.

While Mr Bean was wondering what to do, in the darkness by the lineside at Hemerdon, guard Lucas had stopped the 21.50 to Plymouth Friary goods, 6B31, and was riding down to Hemerdon to raise the alarm. On his way he thoughtfully asked his driver to stop so that he could place three detonators on the up main to the rear of the work train because he had very properly decided that it was no longer a train but an obstruction. Guard Lucas arrived at Hemerdon at 05.45 and found Mr Bean still awaiting events. He told him all about the situation at Blatchford and set out at once to walk back the two miles to his train, Leaving Bean to set the rescue in motion.

The supervisor telephoned signalman Wood in Plymouth panel, Wood told the District Engineer and Control, and Control woke the Assistant Area Manager, Mr Hopkins, at 05.55. Doubtless with a groan, the AAM got out of bed. He was not the only sleeper to be disturbed as a result of the contretemps at Blatchford. Shopman Millington had left the site at 05.35 to walk to Cornwood to find a 'national' telephone. He found someone's front door pounded on it till they woke and then asked to use their phone. Trustingly, they allowed him in and he tried to rouse his chief engineer without success. He then rang the Plymouth emergency number he had been given. This was merely the station's main switchboard which at that ungodly hour was closed so that the call went through to the travel centre. The travel clerk took the message and passed it on (later the official decision was taken that 'it was not desirable that the travel clerk be called upon to deal with matters of this nature', so a new emergency number was issued to outdoor staff).

As Mr Millington was walking back to the train from Cornwood, guard Lucas was walking from Hemerdon and AAM Hopkins was getting himself down to Plymouth signal box where he arrived at 06.20. He gathered together a team of three signalmen, including signalman Wood, and at 06.30 they were on their way to Hemerdon crossover, 11 miles away in the back lanes, to institute single line working. At Hemerdon they dropped one man and then proceeded to Ivybridge crossover five miles further on. Supervisor Bean had already withdrawn the key to this crossover's ground frame so the up and down line signals on each side were already at 'Danger' and the 23.45 Paddington to Penzance sleeping car train was waiting to convey the pilotman through the section to 'open up' the single line. The train left at 07.24, about 50 minutes late. While Mr Hopkins was setting up the operation he met the Assistant Divisional Engineer, Mr Fishley, who had come to Ivybridge to walk along the track to the work train. Hopkins was very concerned that the work train might start to move and overrun the Ivybridge crossover. He had already placed protective detonators, but he also told Fishley that the train was not to move from Blatchford viaduct without his, Hopkins', consent. This was a mistake, made under the pressure of work. There was no reason why the train should not come up as far as the detonators. Mr Fishley left for Blatchford at 07.25.

Guard Lucas arrived back at Blatchford from Hemerdon at 06.45 and at 07.20

saw Mr Reynolds walking along the line. He had escaped from the cage using the Rescuematic at 07.10 and had landed in the deep valley. Back on the track with the 'Gozunda', he was able, quite simply, to operate the hand pump equipment to bring the arm and cage in-board, and by 07.45 the train was ready to leave for Totnes. Just as they were about to set off, Mr Fishley arrived with the prohibition on movement. Guard Lucas then asked Mr Fishley to drive him to Hemerdon to obtain the desired permission from Mr Hopkins. They left Blatchford along the track to Cornwood and got into Fishley's car for the relatively short drive to Hemerdon, but came across a road accident and did not get to Hemerdon until 08.20.

Armed with the necessary permission — or unnecessary permission perhaps — Lucas and Fishley took the same circuitous route back to Blatchford to avoid the road crash so that the viaduct inspection train did not set off for the detonators at Ivybridge until 08.55. There it was held until 09.11 to allow the 08.20 Plymouth to Leeds express to come off the single line and precede it eastwards. After the Leeds, single line working was withdrawn and the work train made its way to the sidings at Totnes. With that, those remaining out on the track relaxed and forgot to tell Plymouth Panel signalman that the up line was now clear and free for traffic. As the down line was not any longer a single track, the signalman had no choice but to hold the up trains whilst desperately trying to contact the one person — whose blushes I shall spare — who could give the word and free the up line. At last, at 09.31, by telephone, the word was given and the passengers on the 06.35 Penzance and 09.10 Plymouth expresses breathed a sigh of relief as their trains moved forward.

CHAPTER 30

Ealing Broadway

1973

T HE 'WESTERN' CLASS DIESELS CARRIED A 110 VOLT BATTERY WITH which to operate the pre-heater and other auxiliaries. The battery consisted of 16 units in series, housed eight-a-side in a cupboard slung below the main frames between the power bogies. Each cupboard was closed by a double-skinned metal door, 44½ x 22½ in, with an inner lining of wood and weighing in all 80 lbs. The door could be lowered to the horizontal and was then held in position by hinged metal struts so that it could be used as a work bench by the battery attendant, hence the wooden lining. Each cupboard door was kept shut by a pair of carriage door locks of the kind where a square-ended key is inserted in a square hole and turned to pivot the locking blade into its slot.

Experience with the early 'Warship' diesels showed that workmen sometimes forgot to turn the locks after the door had been lifted into position — it was heavy enough to remain closed when the engine was stationary or slow moving, but at speed would fall open and strike lineside objects in passing. To guard against this, the 'Warship' class was fitted with a 'pear-drop' catch on each cupboard door. This consisted of a pear shaped piece of metal which fell by gravity into a slot in the door frame when the door was slammed shut, the shape allowing the door to be pulled open and slammed, the catch rising and falling. It was 'cheap and nasty' solution to the problem which would have been better served by a spring-loaded ball. Sometimes the 'pear-drop' refused to lift when the door had to be opened and sometimes it refused to fall when the door was shut, so when the next generation of diesels appeared — the 'Westerns' — they too were fitted with the self-same catch. At Laira depot, someone made an unofficial modification to the catch. A 5/16 in diameter set screw was fitted to the catch in such a way that, by turning the screw with the finger and thumb, the catch could be raised and locked or, releasing the screw, drop the catch into its slot. The arrangement made the 'pear-drop' controllable. It also made it possible to lock it up, out of action.

Diesel no 1007 *Western Talisman* was built at Swindon and entered service at Laira on 1 August 1962. It weighed 109 tons in working order and had an official maximum speed of 90 mph. Each of its six-wheeled bogies was driven by a 1,350 hp Maybach diesel engine through a Voith-North British hydraulic torque converter. It was indeed a powerful beast, but like all the rest of its ilk *Western Talisman* was prone to sudden crippling failures. From 8 to 12 December 1973, D1007 was in Laira shops for its '250-hour service'. On the 12th it worked the 05.45 Plymouth to Paddington express, and went down with the 17.45 Paddington to Westbury, a distance of about 360 miles including 'light' running. By that time it required the attention of fitters for the loss of coolant , transmission oil leaks and a reversing fault. Westbury's fitters could not handle the job, so the engine ran 'light' to Plymouth, about 150 miles.

At Laira on the 13th it was decided that nothing short of an engine change at 'B' end would put matters right; a rapid lift was done and on the 14th the engine worked the 19.00 to Bristol where it arrived with a fault in its AWS gear. Next day it worked home with the 07.15 to Exeter and the 10.40 to Plymouth, where it was taken out of traffic once more with AWS and pre-heater faults. This kept the expensive unit out of traffic until the 05.45 Plymouth on the 17th. At Reading, *Western Talisman* lost its 'A' engine and an assisting locomotive had to be attached to the front to work the train to Paddington. From there the engine worked 'light' to Old Oak Common on its 'B' engine. The locomotive was berthed in 'the Factory' for heavy repairs to the 'A' engine's injectors and fuel supply.

While the fitters were working in the engine room, the batteries were given a routine booster charge. The battery door cupboard was unlocked, the 'pear-drop' raised and secured out of the way and the door lowered. The battery attendant attached the charging cables and went on his way. A supervisor came to speak to the fitters and to do so he placed a ladder against the locomotive's side, under an engine room window and to one side of the lowered battery cupboard door. One of the fitters came out through that window to go to the stores and returned the same way. A pair of labourers came along to give the body skin a wipe over with rags. Two days later, on the 19th, the fitters pronounced their work complete and wished to give the engine a spin outside. Someone took away the ladder, someone else took away the charging leads — which had been attached for the whole two days — and someone else threw the battery door up into position. No one recalled who had done what.

After some fine adjustments, the 'A' engine was passed as fit for traffic and the locomotive was restored to work the empty coaches to Paddington for the 16.48 Worcester, and then to take its own train, the 17.18 Oxford. The latter train consisted of 11 BR Standard Mk 1 coaches with a total seating capacity of 622. The train left Paddington with every seat taken and 25 passengers standing, many of them railway technicians, clerks and officers from Paddington, Waterloo and BRB headquarters. The engine was driven by Mr Owen of Old Oak, a man who started his driving career on steam engines in 1959. The diesel engine was on top form and with a gross trailing load of around 420 tons it had accelerated to 65mph at Ealing Broadway station, 5¾ miles from Paddington.

The engines under the thin sheeting were howling confidently, still accelerating, with a green light ahead at Longfield Avenue Junction where there was a facing connection from down main to down relief line. As the engine passed the western end of Ealing's platform, driver Owen felt a lurch which he put down to bad track and made a mental note to report it when he stopped at Reading. He got the bell off the AWS magnet as he approached the Longfield Avenue signal and immediately afterwards there was a terrific thumping at the rear of the locomotive before the whole 109 ton machine seemed to leap into the air before crashing on to its right-hand side to go screeching along the rails, decelerating very rapidly from about 67 mph.

Neither driver Owen nor his second man Mr Woolnough was injured, and once they had regained their wits after the awful shock of over turning they immediately went into action. Woolnough operated the fire precaution handle for the engine room and then went out through the near side window, which was then above his head, to get to a signal post telephone and warn Old Oak signal panel. Driver Owen gave him a lift to climb through the window and then scrambled up and stuck his own head and shoulders out to take a look around.

Western Talisman's luck ran out at Ealing Broadway on 20 December 1973 after someone forgot to close a tiny safety catch on the battery cupboard door. The result was this carnage. The coaches have concertina'd in the classic manner, one crushing the end of the next, their bogies being torn off as the vehicles were derailed at speed. (Associated Press)

His train was scattered all over four tracks, a startling and shocking sight on top of the shock he had just received. Dropping back into the cab, he found a tin of detonators, threw them out the window and scrambled after them, intent on placing some protection on the up main and relief lines further west.

The leading coach was still upright although derailed 'all wheels'. The second coach was at right angles across the track and had crushed the rear end of the leading coach. The third, fourth and fifth coaches had impacted into a tight, zigzagged mass, their ends crushed, leaning against the cutting side. The heavy, cast-steel 'Commonwealth' bogie from the rear of the third coach had been torn off and forced through the side of the fourth coach, killing and injuring several passengers. Most of the 10 dead and 8 seriously injured were here; 86 others were hurt. The rear five coaches were more or less intact. In the third coach, Mr Pearson, an assistant in the Passenger Manager's Officer at Paddington, crawled through the sliding ventilator above the main window and, seeing the carnage, hurried away up the cutting, through a back garden to the main road where he dashed into an office, commandeered their telephone and set up a liaison post, first phoning his own office to raise the alarm. He did good work here for about 90 minutes.

Mr Pope, a signal engineer at British Rail Board headquarters, who had been a member of Western Region Signal & Telecommunications Department and had assisted in the installation of Old Oak signalling modernization, was riding with a friend in the third coach. He had heard a lot of banging before the coach swung violently to the right. He was pressed against the window by g-forces but his friend, sitting diagonally opposite him, was thrown from his seat and through the window by the same force. The coach stopped as he went through the glass, and he landed on the track relatively unhurt. Mr Pope found himself hanging out of the broken window with a badly cut face. He climbed out, saw that his friend was all right and went at once to a signal post telephone to report the crash to Old Oak panel. In the fifth coach, Mr Cattermole was travelling home from his office at British Rail Board headquarters. He heard a loud, metallic crash, ten seconds later he realized that his coach was derailed and immediately after that his compartment was crushed and the side of the coach torn away from the frame. With the same presence of mind shown by the other railway men on the train, he squeezed out through the gap in the coach body and ran to a signal post telephone. There he found Mr Pope, his face covered in blood, already in contact with the panel signal box.

Travelling on the train which had stopped at the red signal next in rear of the crash was Chief Technician Turner. He got down from the train and walked forwards to the site of the crash, noticing with some alarm that the coaches had gouged deeply into the earth at the foot of the cutting side. They knew that buried along that length were signal control circuits and a 660 volt power cable. He hurried to a signal post telephone, warned the panelman not to place any reliance on his panel indications between Ealing and Hanwell and told him how to have the 660 volt cable isolated. Going back to the motor which worked the facing points, Mr Turner saw that although the machine was badly damaged it was and had been correctly set and bolted for the train to run down the main line. The rodding from the motor to the switch blades had been dealt such a blow that the rod had bent and dragged the points open by an inch — all that was necessary to permit a wheel flange to pass on the wrong side of the switch rail. The rear bogie of the diesel had been allowed to drop off the rails and had dragged the train with it until the operation of the automatic brake had brought the train to a stand. Searching in the jumble of ballast and debris from the crash he found a very heavy-looking blue panel a few feet west of the points. He did not know what it was, but felt that it was important and told a policeman to stand guard over it.

Traction inspector Holder arrived at the site at 18.35. He saw the policeman guarding the battered blue thing but did not recognize it for what it was even though he turned it over and studied it. Only when he had examined the engine and had seen that the battery box cupboard door was missing did he realize what the object was. He went back and re-examined the door. One main lock was missing due to crash damage, the other was in place in the unlocked position while the 'pear drop' catch was in the raised position with the set-screw tightened to prevent it falling. He walked back along the track to Ealing station and found a heavy coping stone in the ramp at the west end of the platform had been displaced. There was no damage to the ramp at the east end of the platform, so it was obvious that the door had dropped open as the engine was passing through the station. The door would have had clearance in the recess beneath the platform edge until it met the coping stone as the ramp sloped down to track level. In dislodging this heavy weight, the door was forced downwards, breaking the light stays which held it horizontal, and it then hung perpendicular all 80 lbs of it, skimming the ballast and scattering stones like shrapnel until it collided with the point rodding at right angles to its path, bending the rods and opening the points. Had it fallen open just a few seconds earlier it would have met the rising, eastern, platform ramp and thus been thrown shut — but then it could have fallen open again when the train was running at 90 mph.

Although the weight of circumstantial evidence pointed to the points being opened as already described, the railways authorities wanted to be quite sure that there was no other, more deep-seated, technical reason for it. To establish beyond all doubt that the rodding had been struck by the battery cupboard door, some flakes of paint found stuck to the rodding were microscopically examined. The fragments were found to consist of paint in nine layers, a veritable history of the livery of the 'Westerns', 'desert sand', green, maroon and blue. What was never discovered was who was responsible for turning the engine out of the factory without securing the door.

CHAPTER 31

Chinley

1986

THE DOUBLE TRACK SHEFFIELD-MANCHESTER MAIN LINE OF THE OLD Midland Railway fell at 1 in 100/150 for three miles from the summit of the line inside Cowburn tunnel down to Chinley East Junction. There it became quadruple track for the four miles to New Mills Junction, falling at 1 in 90, passing on the way Chinley North Junction and Chinley station with its six platforms. Coming up from the south, over a magnificent viaduct, was the main line from St. Pancras and Derby, joining the Sheffield-Manchester line, facing Manchester, at Chinley North Junction. Forking eastwards from the Derby line, a double track chord line curved away to Chinley East Junction to face Sheffield. By March 1986, the six-platform Chinley station, with its fine, local stone buildings, had been reduced to a rubble-strewn halt, the quadruple tracks had been reduced to double and the main line to Derby and London had become a single track goods line to quarries at Peak Forest. Of all the signal boxes which formerly controlled the area only one remained — Chinley North Junction — where a 'one control switch' panel was used to control the pitiful remains of a once great railway installation.

The panel or console carried a diagram of the tracks and the signals controlled. Along the bottom of the console were twelve 'route switches', one for each of the possible routes over the layout, and above these was a row of eight point switches with three positions: when vertical they were set for 'automatic' working and in fact played no part in the proceedings; turned to 'R' or 'N' they caused the point they controlled to switch to the 'reverse' or 'normal' setting. These points switches were for use when the route did not answer to the route switch. If all failed then the signalman took a hand pump and a key from the signal box and went to the point motor. Having unlocked its cover, he turned the change-over handle from 'auto' to 'manual', attached the hand pump and pumped the hydraulic motor until the points were set as he required. The con-

Above *The blend of old and new on Chinley panel — LMS colour style and gradient charts with modern block instruments and point operation. Each of the possible routes on the panel is controlled by one switch, black or yellow, set into the horizontal part of the console. Should any point in a route not answer the route switch, the signalman can call it by operating its individual switch set at the top of the vertical section of the console. The block instruments are set into the console.* (Author)

Below *The central section of the small signalling console in Chinley box. The lines to and from Peak Forest are at the top, the main line from Manchester to Sheffield is at the bottom. Signal CY 157 is at the bottom left and the forgotten crossover, points 350, on the far right. The style of the actual diagram is very similar to that employed by the LMS in its signal box diagrams and, continuing the old-fashioned motif, the diagram is not equipped with a method of indicating which route has been set. A sad, perhaps fatal, flaw in the design.* (Author)

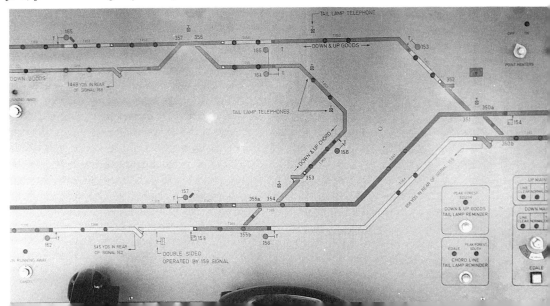

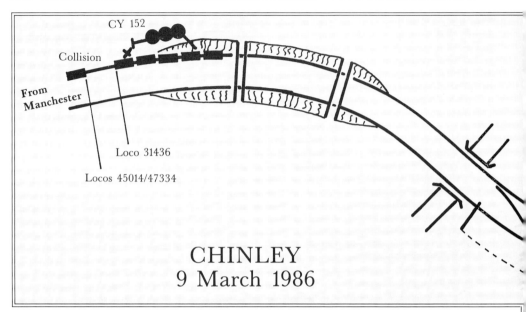

CY 152

Collision

From Manchester

Loco 31436

Locos 45014/47334

CHINLEY
9 March 1986

sole showed the aspect of each signal and showed the position of a train by a line of red lights which moved along the diagram as the train moved over the tracks. What the console did not show, as all larger panels did, was a prior warning, by a row of white lights, of the route which had been set up for the approaching train.

In charge of the signal box on the 18.00 to 06.00 shift on Sunday 9 March 1986 was a 22-year-old relief signalman, Mr Holland. he had joined the railway in June 1980, aged 16½, and had taken a seven-week course in signalling at the Manchester (Victoria) signalling school. There he had learnt the rules and regulations for traditional block working, had learnt the use of the traditional lever frame and instruments and had been generally taught the nineteenth-century system, although there were three 'panel' signal boxes in the Manchester area. He passed his written examination on the rules with an 89% pass mark and took a glowing report from the Area Movements Inspector (the District Inspector), Mr Keighley, who wrote, 'excellent, interested, thorough, keen and very intelligent'. On 24 May 1982, Holland was passed as competent to work the little 'A' class signal box at Edale after a period of learning. This was a simple place to start to learn about the realities of railway work — a good start.

Six months later he learnt and was passed as competent for the next box east of Edale — Earles Sidings, a class 'B' job. While he worked there he received a commendation for his actions in trying to avert an accident after wagons had run away from the sidings. In the next three years he became a relief signalman and was passed as competent to work ten mechanical signal boxes in the Chinley/Peak Forest area, but not the panel in Chinley North Junction. In November 1984, he spent a few days learning this job and was then signed as competent to work it. He was obviously very confident and enthusiastic, but anyone can

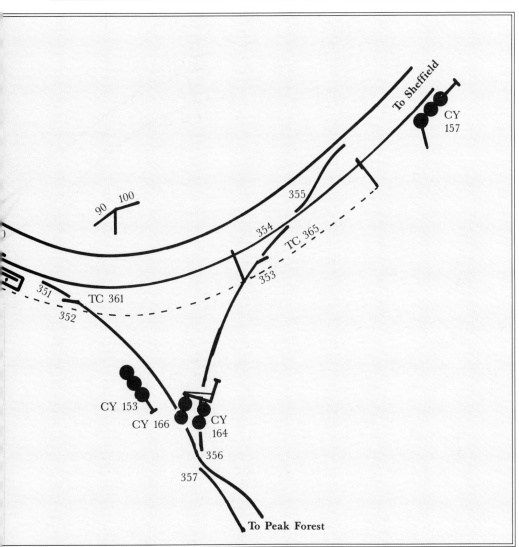

turn a switch or pull a lever. The question was whether 'a few days' was sufficient to become thoroughly familiar with the working of the complicated electrical circuits and modes of operation.

Sunday 9 March should have been his day off duty. He spent Saturday evening with his fiancée and was having a lie-in at home on Sunday morning. At
noon he was asked by telephone to work Chinley panel that evening, starting
at 18.00, and, being a keen lad for railway work and also wishing to earn a crust
for when he got married the following year, he gladly agreed and reported for
duty in the box at 17.43. The traffic was busy, but he had the schedule at his
fingertips and handled it well.

At 18.30, however, the mains electricity power supply to the signal box failed, the lights in the box and in nearby houses went out and all the track circuit lights on the console went to red — 'occupied'. A few seconds later the diesel engine powering the emergency generator roared into life, and the console was restored to normal working except that track circuit 365 at East Junction continued to show 'occupied' locking points 354 and 355. Points 354 were set for the chord line at the moment of failure, so they remained locked in this position while 355 were locked 'normal', for the straight run. Signalman Holland reported the failure to Control at 18.31 and asked for the Signal & Telecommunications Department technician to attend.

At that time, diesel locomotive No 47145 was standing at signal CY 152, waiting to turn around on the triangular junction. With East Junction points out of action and no prospect of them being brought into use for some time, Holland told the driver of 47145 that he would be sent across to the Buxton line — Up and Down Goods — and from the South Junction he could go to the East Chord to clear the lines for other traffic. The engine received the aspect from CY 152/2 and crossed to the Buxton line through points 350 and 351, both of which were reversed. After the engine had cleared to the goods line, Holland saw that track circuits covering points 350 and 352 were still showing 'occupied'. He telephoned the signalman at New Mills and told him that, until the track circuits were put right, they would have to give up the 'Track Circuit' block working and work by the old 'Absolute Block' system.

Holland gave 'Train Out of Section' for 47145 at 18.36 and at 18.37 New Mills asked 'Is Line Clear?' for two engines coupled for Buxton. Holland 'gave the road', the engines eventually passed the signal box at 18.43 via points 350 and 351 and signalman Holland sent 'Train Out of Section' for them at 18.43. At once he was asked 'Is Line Clear?' by New Mills for the Manchester-Cleethorpes train, IE74; Holland gave 'Line Clear' and set points 350 'normal'. The IE74 was sent 'on line' 2 minutes later, Holland 'got the road' from Earles Sidings — Edale box being switched out — and at the same time the Earles Sidings signalman 'asked the road' for the 18.33 Sheffield to Manchester, IM42. Signalman Holland accepted the train and, by phone, told his mate at Earles that it would be delayed at Signal CY 157 because of the failure of track circuit 365.

The Manchester to Cleethorpes train passed Chinley North Junction at 18.55, Holland sent it 'on line' to Earles Sidings and noticed that track circuits 350 and 352 had cleared correctly behind it. He telephoned the signalman at New Mills to tell him that IE74 had passed and that they could revert to normal, track circuit block, working. The New Mills man then told him that there was another pair of engines coupled, 45014 and 47334, about to leave New Mills for Chinley and Peak Forest. Holland asked the New Mills signalman to warn the driver, Mr Plant, that when he arrived at CY 152 and went to the signal post telephone to carry out rule 55 he might not receive a reply because he, signalman Holland, would be out at East Junction, hand pumping points 354 to normal for IM42 to pass. Driver Plant was therefore to stay behind the signal until he received the correct aspect. Signalman Holland then informed the Great

Rocks and the Earles Sidings signalmen that he was leaving the box for a while, got in his car and drove the half mile to East Junction. Up to that time he had acted very correctly.

At points 354 he unlocked the lid, opened it, set the handle from 'auto' to 'manual' and pumped the blades into the 'normal' position — straight down the main. He then re-set the handle to 'auto', locked the lid and drove back to the signal box, arriving at 19.04 at just about the same time as the two engines arrived at CY 152. He telephoned Earles Sidings to say he was back and to ask what time the IE74 cleared and what time IM42 passed Earles towards Chinley and was told '18.59' in both cases. It then occurred to signalman Holland that he could run the two engines across to the Buxton line before IM42 arrived — especially as that train would have to stop at CY 157 due to the track circuit failure. He turned route switch 152/2 which reversed points 350, while 351 was already reversed from the last set of engines which went to Buxton.

As he made this flick of the switch, he realized that signal CY 152 would not give a 'proceed' aspect because the points at East Junction were set for the down main line — a conflicting movement. He at once replaced the route switch, but points 350 stayed reversed and would remain so until he 'called' another route which would require them to be set to 'normal'. This was how the panel was designed. This does not seem to be desirable — when a manual point lever is set to 'normal', the points to which it is attached also go to 'normal'. Point 351 was reversed, making a conflicting movement with points 354 which Holland had hand pumped 'normal' — a matter of necessity, something he was entitled to do, but an action outside the protection of any safety devices other than his own alertness.

There does seem to have been something of a 'rush' going on. At 19.06 or 19.07, IM42 arrived at signal CY 157 and very promptly driver Everett got down from his cab and carried out rule 55 from the signal post telephone. He had four Mk 1 coaches and diesel No 31436, the latter not being fitted with a search-light. On the telephone, signalman Holland told the driver of the track circuit failure, told him it was in order to pass the aspect at 'Danger', asked him to make sure points 354 were correct before he passed over them and 'then you should be OK'. Signalman Holland watched his diagram light up with a line of red lights as the train moved over points 354 on to track circuit 361. Only as the engine was close to his signal box, 1,100 yards after it had passed signal CY 157, did he remember that points 351 and 350 were reversed. He grabbed his electric hand lamp, switched it on to a red light and held it from the window. Driver Everett did not see the danger signal, Holland heard the crunch as the engine ran through points 351 and watched helplessly as the train turned from the down to the up main line and accelerated down the hill.

Standing 660 yards along the up main line were the two locomotives, 45014 leading, 47334 behind, weighing in total 247¼ tons. For driver Everett, the line curved to the left through a broad cutting with two arched bridges between him and the engines. He would not have seen their lights until he was about 250 yards away, but one can only wonder why it was he drove along the wrong line

A Class '47' approaches facing crossover 350 leading from down to up main. This was the set of points which was reversed and then forgotten by the signalman, forming the basic cause of the crash. (Author)

for over 440 yards without slackening speed. The guard of the train said he never felt the train make the transition through the crossover from the down to the up line, so perhaps the driver was also taken completely by surprise. Steam engine drivers had made the same mistake at Thorpe-le-Soken and at Norwich, but driver Everett, sitting right at the front of his engine, had a far better view of

A Class '31' on an up Manchester to Sheffield express passing Chinley box. The fatal crossover runs from the '70' speed restriction sign in the down main to a point covered by the third coach of the train. (Author)

the line ahead. Certainly it is not the sort of thing drivers on double track main lines expect, and when driver Plant, sitting in 45014, first saw the lights of the Class '31' approaching, he said to his mate, second man Millward, 'Here it comes. This is what we've been waiting for'. He meant that they had been waiting for the main line train to pass so that they could be crossed over the up main to the Buxton line. The words were no sooner out of his mouth than he realized that the engine was approaching on their line — and approaching quite fast.

Both men could have jumped for their lives. Instead, driver Plant yelled for his mate to lie on the floor as he, Plant rapidly placed the engines in reverse and opened the throttles. Mr Millward, lying on the floor, felt the wheels turn an instant before the passenger train struck home. The cab of the Class '45' was undamaged as the engines were batted away down the 1 in 90 gradient, but the cab of the Class '31' was crushed to the engine room bulkhead killing driver Everett at his seat. 45014 and 47334 stopped 110 yards down the hill, the cab of the '45' full of smoke and both doors jammed. The driver's door window was broken, so the men both climbed out through that and while Plant ran forwards to the passenger train, Millward used the fire extinguisher from the cab to put out a fire in the battery cupboards and then ran across to signal CY 151 to report to the signalman.

'You have sent him down on top of us,' said Millward.

'Has he hit you?' came the agitated reply.

The passenger train weighed 246 tons and at the moment of impact its guard, Mr Keyworth, was thrown off his seat on to the floor of the brake van. Picking himself up straight away, he had the presence of mind to don a high visibility vest before grabbing his electric hand lamp and getting down on to the track. Running forward to the engine, he shone his torch on the ghastly mess which had been a cab and called his mate's name. There was no reply and he realized that Everett must be dead. Thoroughly shocked and upset, he dashed back to the signal box and burst in. 'You've killed my mate,' he shouted.

This was the final, terrible end to a sequence of events which began with the failure of track circuit 365. The S&T department technician traced the fault to a fuse. He took it out, wiped its contacts and replaced it. The track circuit worked perfectly.

Signalman Holland did a conscientious job to the best of his ability, but he had insufficient training and experience — he had only spent a few days, less than a week, 'learning' Chinley panel when all systems were working well. He ought to have had a better understanding of the panel's workings, but the Manchester signalling school had paid little attention to such matters and in its practical training facilities it was entirely devoted to mechanical signalling. *After* the event he was given a lecture on the way in which the locking relays and the track circuits, route switches and point motors inter-reacted, all of which was fresh knowledge to him. What a pity these lessons could not have been taught at the signalling school, what a pity the panel was lacking the 'white lights' warning of the direction in which the train was routed; had these things been done, then perhaps poor driver Everett would not have been killed.

The remarkable thing is that throughout the history of railways there has never been much formal training for signalmen and — until recently — none at all for drivers. The recruits usually learned the job as they went along and, years ago, they spent so many years rising through the grades that they had a fair knowledge of the difficulties and how to deal with them by the time they reached such responsible positions as that held by signalman Holland. Those men who live near a signalling school can take advantage of that facility, but what cannot be taught is experience, how to react in a crisis. In these days of all-electric signalling, when signalling is made as inexpensive as possible with as few men and signals as possible, the need for training and experience is even more vital. Training not just in the normal routine and the rules but also in the situations that may arise.

At one time, the Great Western Railway used to issue a foolscap sheet of 'cautionary tales', to all signalmen describing a crash or derailment somewhere in the GWR, showing how it came to happen and what rules had been ignored to cause it. That practice could be revived. Railwaymen of all grades should be very well aware of the nature of their job and how even a sloppily delivered message — or no message at all — can result in a serious crash of trains. There is no room for complacency in a panel signal box or on the 'footplate'. The former controls scores of miles of track, the latter travels along the track at up to 125 mph — trusting to the signalling. Perhaps every railwayman should be issued with his own copy of *Obstruction Danger* when he is first issued with his rule book...

Appendix 1

Railway companies with less than 90 per cent of their double track mileage worked by the Absolute Block system on 31st December 1889-1893

	1889	1891	1892	1893	
Manchester South Junction &					
Altrincham	89	100	100	100	
Maryport & Carlisle	4	100	100	100	
Taff Vale	19	20½	22	100	
Dublin, Wicklow & Waterford	21	22	100	100	
Great Northern (Ireland)	14	68	100	100	
Great Southern & Western	24	49½	100	100	
Midland Great Western	55	100	100	100	
Severn & Wye and Severn Bridge	—	—	67	67	(100% in 1894)
Waterford, Wexford & Limerick	31	31	31	31	(100% in 1895)

Continued overleaf

Railway companies with less than 90 per cent of their points and signals worked from interlocking frames on 31st December 1889-1895

	1889	1890	1891	1892	1893	1894	1895
Belfast & County Down	89	89	76	95	97	97	97
Brecon & Merthyr	73	73	73	83	100	100	100
Cambrian	45	53	68	82	89	93	97
Colne Valley	36	36	79	79	79	100	100
Cork, Bandon & South Coast	46	47½	52	62½	82	97	97
Cork, Blackrock & Passage	43	40	40	40	100	100	100
Cork & Macroom Direct	100	100	100	100	100	86	86
Dublin, Wicklow & Wexford	67	68	70	92	100	100	100
Festiniog	68	62	87	87	87	90	90
Furness	85	87	92	94	92	96	96
Greenock & Wemyss Bay	53	53	65	84	(taken over)		
Great North of Scotland	51	61	62	68	70½	86½	89
Great North (Ireland)	26	26	26	96	96	96	99
Great Southern & Western	61	75	82	96	98	100	98½
Hammersmith & City	89	87	100	100	100	100	100
Isle of Wight	76	76	76	81½	81½	81½	81½
Isle of Wight Central	81½	61½	76	78	78	71	84
Londonderry & Lough Swilly	31	75	82	96	98	100	99½
London, Tilbury & Southend	89	91	91	100	100	100	100
Manchester & Milford	13	13	13	13	13	13	100
Maryport & Carlisle	88	93	100	100	100	100	100
Midland Great Western	81	90	94½	97	98½	99	99
Neath & Brecon	60	60	91	61	66	94	99
North British	78	81	82	88	96½	99½	100
North & South Western Junction	85	89	89	100	100	97	97
Pembroke & Tenby	nil	nil	nil	nil	78	100	100
Portpatrick & Wigtownshire	66	75	86	95	95	95	95
South Eastern	70	72	73	82	94½	100	100
Waterford & Central Ireland	21	21	21	21	21	97½	100
Waterford, Wexford & Limerick	39	39	39	65	65	91	98
Waterford & Tramore	nil	nil	nil	nil	nil	nil	nil
West Clare	57	57	57	57	100	100	100

Appendix 2

Manned and un-manned level crossings

MULTIPLE ASPECT COLOUR-LIGHT SIGNALLING REDUCED HIXON signal box to the status of a level crossing ground frame on 23-24 February 1966. The attendant signalmen then became crossing keepers whilst retaining their former rates of pay. Under the new system, the crossing keeper could not close his gates across the rails to permit a road vehicle to cross the line until he had received an electrical release from Colwich signal box which enabled him to place at 'Danger' and 'Caution' respectively the home and distant signals on the up and down lines approaching the crossing. This system, in effect identical to the earlier system, remained in force for 14 months and continued the long-standing record of perfect safety at Hixon. Automatic half barriers were installed and brought into use in April 1967, but there was now no interlocking between the barriers and the signalling and one can only guess at the misgivings felt by the erstwhile Hixon signalman/crossing keepers as they were sent away, redundant. Eight months later, the terrible crash took place. As a result of this, a moratorium was placed on the hitherto rapid increase in the use of this type of crossing until the recommendations of the formal investigation into the crash were published.

These recommendations included a more urgent wording on the roadside warning notices concerning heavy slow-moving vehicles with a definition of what constituted 'heavy' and 'slow moving'. The principle of 'brisk operation' still applied because safety at these crossings depended on the users realizing that they were in imminent danger of death if they went on to the crossing after the warning lights began to flash. An amber flashing light was added, to be exhibited for 3 seconds before the red flashing lights commenced. Ten seconds later, the barriers fell and 14 seconds after that the fastest train would pass. If another train was closely approaching from the opposite direction, the red lights continued to flash and a flashing illuminated sign warned road users of its imminent approach. This replaced the plain metal warning sign on the roadside. Since 1983, the use of the flashing warning 'Another Train Coming' has been discontinued in favour of the original notice on a metal plate stating 'If lights continue to flash another train is coming'.

The most telling result of the inquiry into the Hixon crash was the moratorium on further automatic half barrier crossing installations — almost all the AHB crossings in use today were installed 'pre-Hixon'. Some have been removed by the closure of the railway line, others have been abolished by the building of a bridge or by the substitution of a manned, full barrier installation supervised by closed circuit television if the location is remote from the operator. This last remedy, the manned full barrier, had been in use since 1961 but had found little favour with the 'powers that be' because it was expensive to install and maintain, but after Hixon, and even more so after 1973 when some lines were prepared for 125 mph trains, the system came much more into prominence and in 1982 there were 450 manned full barriers. It was largely due to the introduction of the HST — 125 mph trains — that the AHB crossing fell out of favour with the planners.

No matter how careful are the safety precautions, there will always be the odd occasion when a mistake is made with the result that someone is hurt or killed. However, I think it is better to place safety in the hands of an experienced, caring human working with the protection afforded him by clever engineers, than to leave it to a — generally — inexperienced, impatient road user and a set of flashing lights. In 1962 there were 4,386 manned and gated level crossings in Britain. Below, courtesy of the Ministry of Transport, I give their safety record:

	1960	1961	1962
Persons killed	10	11	6
Persons injured	22	16	15

The fatality figures for 1960-61 represent, approximately, one death for every 438 level crossings, whilst that for 1962 is, approximately, one death per 876 crossings. The latest figures from the Ministry of Transport available to me through Her Majesty's Stationery Office relate to 1984 and are given below:

Manned gated crossing	(657)
Total accidents	29
Persons killed	Nil
Persons injured	3

Manned full barriers	(394)
Total accidents	2
Persons killed	Nil
Persons injured	4

Automatic half barriers   (280)
Total accidents   6
Persons killed   3
Persons injured   3

Of the 29 accidents in the manned crossings, 3 were road/rail collisions due to faulty equipment and the other 26 were due to human error. Of these 26, most were unconnected with trains but due to sheer bad driving by motorists who crashed into each other.

Index